THE PROBLEMS OF PHILOSOPHY

Each volume in this series is devoted to the exploration of a single philosophical problem or group of problems. The books are large enough to allow adequate space to all major viewpoints. Selections are from contemporary as well as from classical philosophers, and whenever the issues under discussion involve ideas of other disciplines, extracts from scholars in these fields have also been included. Thus, several of the volumes will contain selections from physicists, mathematicians, psychologists, theologians, historians, and others. Each volume is edited by a specialist who has written a detailed introduction and supplied an annotated bibliography. If there is a sufficient public response, it is our aim to revise the volumes periodically and bring the bibliographies up to date.

We hope that these books will prove useful to readers of very different backgrounds. Teachers of philosophy who wish to discuss a given topic in depth have been handicapped by the absence of anthologies of this kind and by the inaccessibility of much of the material now made easily available. Scholars in related fields who wish to acquaint themselves with what philosophers have said on a given topic should also find these volumes very helpful. Above all, it is hoped that this series will be of value to the constantly growing "lay public" interested in serious subjects. The reader who wants to understand the rival philosophical positions can learn far more from studying the philosophers themselves than from the colorless and frequently inaccurate summaries contained in general histories of philosophy. The aim throughout has been to present only material distinguished for its clarity and intelligibility. If there is any presupposition shared by all the editors, it is the conviction that in order to be profound it is not necessary to be obscure.

PAUL EDWARDS, *General Editor*

PROBLEMS OF PHILOSOPHY SERIES
PAUL EDWARDS, GENERAL EDITOR

Perception and the External World

READINGS SELECTED, EDITED
AND FURNISHED WITH
AN INTRODUCTORY ESSAY BY

R. J. Hirst

THE MACMILLAN COMPANY, NEW YORK, NEW YORK
COLLIER-MACMILLAN LIMITED, LONDON

Third printing 1970

The Macmillan Company
866 Third Avenue, New York, N.Y. 10022
Collier-Macmillan Canada Ltd., Toronto, Canada
Library of Congress catalog card number: 65–14335
Printed in the United States of America

Grateful acknowledgment is hereby made to the following for permission to use material reprinted in this volume:

Open Court Publishing Co., Wilmette, Illinois, for material from *The Revolt Against Dualism,* by A.O. Lovejoy (1929).

The author, and The Royal Institute of Philosophy, London, for material from "The Neurological Approach to the Problem of Perception," by Lord Brain, *Philosophy,* XXI (1946).

The author, and Oxford University Press, London, for material from *The Nature of Experience,* by Lord Brain, viz. pages 11–22 of the 1959 Riddell Memorial Lectures delivered at the University, Newcastle upon Tyne.

Routledge & Kegan Paul Ltd., London, for material from *Principles of Gestalt Psychology,* by K. Koffka (1935).

George Allen & Unwin Ltd., London, and The Macmillan Company, New York, for material from *Some Main Problems of Philosophy,* by G.E. Moore

(1953); from *The Ways of Knowing*, by W.P. Montague (1925); from *Philosophical Papers*, by G.E. Moore (1959).

Methuen & Co., Ltd., London, for material from *Perception*, by H.H. Price (1932).

George Allen & Unwin Ltd., London, for material from *Our Knowledge of the External World*, by Bertrand Russell (1922).

Macmillan & Co., Ltd., London, for material from *The Foundations of Empirical Knowledge*, by A.J. Ayer (1940).

The Clarendon Press, Oxford, for material from *Sense and Sensibilia*, by J.L. Austin (1962).

Hutchinson & Co. (Publishers) Ltd., London, and Barnes & Noble, Inc., New York, for material from *The Concept of Mind*, by Gilbert Ryle (1949).

Mrs. Margaret McGilvary Zimmerman, and the editor of *The Journal of Philosophy*, Vol. XXX (1933), for material from "Perceptual and Memory Perspectives," by E.B. McGilvary.

George Allen & Unwin Ltd., London, and Dover Publications, Inc., New York, for material from *The Analysis of Matter*, by Bertrand Russell (1927).

The author, and the director of *Revue Internationale de Philosophie*, Brussels, Vol. I, No. 3 (1939), for material from "A Statement of Critical Realism," by Roy Wood Sellars.

The author, and The Aristotelian Society, London, for material from "Phenomenalism," by A.J. Ayer, *Proceedings of the Aristotelian Society, 1946–47.*

CONTENTS

P A R T   I I I

Types of Realism

P A R T   I V

Radical Theories

INTRODUCTION

The Subject of This Book

The term "perception" may be used generally for mental apprehension, but in philosophy it is now normally restricted to sense-perception, i.e. to the discovery, by means of the senses, of the existence and properties of the external world. Philosophers have been concerned with the analysis of perception, i.e. the study of its nature and of the processes involved in it, and with its epistemology, i.e. with how far, if at all, it can be regarded as a true source of knowledge about the world. Both of these themes are illustrated in these selections, and an attempt has been made to exemplify the main problems and some of the more influential attempts at a solution.

Surprise may be felt at the range of these problems and at the controversy that surrounds them, for, to uninstructed common sense, perception seems a simple effortless process, something we all do constantly, something even children and animals can do. We simply open our eyes and see the world in all its variety and colour, while complementary and confirmatory information floods in to us by hearing, touch, and other senses. True, perceiving sometimes goes wrong: we fail to notice the red light, or to hear the bell, or we find the tie is quite a different colour when we get outside the shop. But these often have quite a simple explanation—inattention, deafness, or fluorescent lighting—and we have no doubt that with sufficient care, and with the co-operation and corroboration of others, we can establish the true nature of the objects or scene we wish to observe.

This common-sense notion about perception is often referred to as Naïve or Natural Realism. It may be formulated in slightly different ways, but the essential point about it is the belief or implicit assumption that in normal circumstances, and certainly if we take due precautions, we see the world as it is: the coloured shapes we see, the smooth cool surface we feel, the tang we taste are all actually and literally character-

1

istics of objects present to us; sounds and smells perhaps are emitted *from* rather than present *in* things, but they are none the less objective features of reality. None of these characteristics and none of the objects which possess them are in any way subjective or private to the percipient in the way that dreams are. They are all external to us, are "public" or neutral between observers, are independent of our perceiving, and persist in exactly the same way unperceived, e.g., the furniture continues to exist with its own shape and colour even when the room is empty and there is no one to see it.

The great majority of philosophical (and scientific) writing on perception has sought to show, or has assumed, the falsity of this Naïve Realism. Even when defending common sense, some writers, e.g. Moore, have in fact proposed analyses inconsistent with it, though in recent years there has been a reaction and some philosophers, particularly at Oxford, have sought to support the plain man against the wiles of their colleagues. Usually, however, it has been held that the facts of illusion, hallucination, and perceptual relativity, of the causation of perception and the psychological processes involved in it, all force us to a quite different conclusion: namely that in perception we are never directly or immediately aware of external physical objects, for strictly our immediate awareness is limited to series of what, following the majority of the selections, we shall call *sense-data* (singular *sense-datum*); examples of these are sounds, tastes, smells, feelings of pressure or warmth, and, above all, the coloured expanses of varying shapes and depths which make up the field of vision. Though we attribute these to external objects, they are strictly private and subjective data, numerically distinct for each person even if similar in character; and if they are the sum total of our immediate knowledge, no public external world is directly observed as had been originally thought. Once this is recognized, a host of doubts and disagreements arise. Can we infer the existence of the external world as the common cause of sense-data, or might it not exist except as a pattern of everybody's different sense-data?

Though elucidation and justification of this must come

later, it is now possible to indicate the main classification of passages in this book and explain the terms used. This claim, that there is a far-reaching distinction between the common external world and the sense-data which alone we immediately experience, is often referred to as Epistemological Dualism, or in this context simply as Dualism. Selection 1 briefly reviews the main grounds of this Dualism; Ss. (i.e. selections) 2–5 present supporting evidence from prominent scientists; Ss.6–9 give the main non-scientific arguments and introduce the most influential form of Dualism, the Sense-datum Theory (so-called because it introduced the term); while Ss.12–13 indicate the main lines of advance from there. Recent counter-attacks on behalf of common sense are represented by Ss.10–11. The remaining selections are primarily concerned with the relation of sense-data to the external world. The term Realism is a general name for the view that material or physical objects exist external to us and independent of our sense-experiences. It thus includes Naïve Realism or any slightly more sophisticated theory, such as McGilvary's "Perspective Realism," (S.16) which claims that we directly perceive the external world as it is. The predominant dualist versions of Realism claim that sense-data are caused by external objects which to some extent resemble them. The traditional version of this was Representative Realism (sometimes called the Representative Theory) advocated by Descartes or Locke (S.14), but it presented several well-known defects, notably that if our direct experience is only of private data, the nature and even the existence of the external world behind them must always be unknown and conjectural. Later Realists tried to overcome these defects in various ways (see Ss.17–19), but a more radical approach has been to deny the existence of these alleged yet unobservable material causes of our perceptions: what we call the external world must only be a pattern of our sense-data, actual and possible (Ss.20–23).

The remainder of this introduction considers these arguments and theories in greater detail, but first a terminological note. Several terms besides "Sense-data" are used for the immediate data of experience, viz. *ideas, (sense-) impressions, sensations,* and *percepts.* These often carry slightly different suggestions: "ideas" as used by Locke and Berkeley implied no distinction of kind between the data of perception and the images of thought or memory (cp. S.20 p. 254); sensations were usually associated with psychological theory, as being the supposed immediate effects of stimulation of the sense organs from which the percipient infers the presence of physical objects (cp. S.5 p. 87); "percept" often suggests that the immediate data are ostensible objects, an "apparent tomato" rather than a "red colour patch" (though Russell, in S.17, does not seem to intend this). Since "sense-datum" was deliberately introduced as a neutral term free from all such implications, it is a convenient one to use even when not discussing the actual Sense-datum Theory.

The Argument from Illusion

The traditional main ground for Epistemological Dualism is the Argument from Illusion, but in fact this "argument" is more than one argument and covers more than illusions. The relevant phenomena may be distinguished as:

(1) ILLUSIONS PROPER, where the percipient is deceived about the identity, position, and properties of the objects present to his senses. Examples are given in Ss.5–9; they include mirages, mirror effects, and optical illusions, e.g. when equal lines are made to look of unequal length. Diseases or drugs may produce them, e.g., the double vision of alcoholism, and perception of motion introduces others, as when one's stationary train seems to move if an adjacent one starts.

(2) THE RELATIVITY OF PERCEPTION: a round plate may look elliptical when seen from an angle or a square table look diamond-shaped; the same water may feel cool to one person and warm to another; the same wine may taste sweet or dry according to what one has just been eating; hills may look blue at a distance and green close to; a red cloth may look black to a colour-blind man. These are not necessarily illusions since deception may be absent; the essential thing is that the apparent properties of the object vary relatively to the position

of the percipient, to the distance and media between him and it, to the light, to the state of his health, body or sense organs, etc.

(3) HALLUCINATIONS. (*see* S.3) In pure hallucinations—e.g. the pink elephant a drunkard sees, the apparitions of delirium, Macbeth's dagger, or phantom limbs—some physical object (or person) is "perceived" when neither it nor anything resembling it is present. Contrast illusions where the mistake is about the properties, position, or identity of some object actually in view. Some, perhaps most, hallucinations (and dreams also) are "triggered," i.e. are set off by some perceived feature of a very different character; e.g. a beam of light is taken to be a person. Many are "integrated," i.e. fit in well with the real background, cast shadows, vary in size and perspective as they move.

Four kinds of argument are developed concerning these.

(1) THE SCEPTICAL ARGUMENT. However sure we are about our perceiving, it is always possible that we may be being deceived by one of the many kinds of illusion or hallucination, because it is characteristic of such states that one cannot tell that one is suffering from them. This possibility of error means that perceiving is never absolutely certain, and hence for indubitable knowledge one must rely not on the senses but on some other faculty, e.g. intellectual intuition. This traditional argument is not one for epistemological dualism, but requires mention here for its historical importance. It cuts little ice nowadays, partly because there is equal difficulty in being sure that an apparent intuition is genuine, and partly because it is misleading: the sceptic seems to be suggesting that even well-tested perceptions are uncertain in the normal usage of the word, e.g. in the way that the result of a horse-race is uncertain, whereas he is in fact using an inappropriately high standard which would allow certainty only to logically necessary truths (i.e. those which it is self-contradictory to deny).

(2) THE ARGUMENT FROM DIFFERENTIAL CERTAINTY. This also starts with the premise that there is always the possibility of error in any case of perceiving, though it can avoid the

exaggeration of (1) by taking isolated, untested or uncor-
roborated cases, where there is a fair practical possibility of
error. It goes on: we cannot be sure that we are aware of
any particular material object, e.g. a tomato; the object seen
may in fact be something quite different—a wax imitation
perhaps—or be a reflected patch of light or a hallucination,
i.e. not a material object at all. Yet whatever the illusion may
be, there can be no doubt that when we seem to see a tomato
we are directly aware of a red, round, bulgy patch of colour,
i.e. a sense-datum. For this way of introducing sense-data see
Ss. 7 and 9; Russell's distinction of hard and soft data (S.8)
is really making the same point. With this argument goes an
elucidation of the notion of direct or immediate awareness,
i.e. awareness without inference or intermediate stages. Often
this awareness is called sensing; sense-data are also said to be
"given," which is another way of expressing their immediacy
and certainty.

(3) THE ARGUMENT CONCERNING THE CONTENT OF ILLU-
SIONS. Whereas (1) and (2) are concerned with cases of error,
i.e. illusions and hallucinations, this argument is regularly extended also to cases of perceptual relativity (cp. Ss.6 and 1),
since it does not depend on there being deception. In all these
situations there is awareness of something which does not coincide with the object or object-properties which are in fact
present—e.g. the apparitions of hallucinations, the elliptical
appearance we see when we look at a round plate, the black
shape the colour-blind man sees when looking at a red box, the
oasis of a mirage, or the second bottle in double vision. None
of these can be identified with real objects or properties: they
must therefore be sense-data only, i.e. private, mental objects
of awareness quite distinct from external material objects.

(4) THE CONTINUITY ARGUMENT goes a stage further: If
one were to change from seeing a private and transitory sense-
datum to seeing a public enduring physical object ("public" =
observable by several persons at one time), one would expect
a sudden change in the character of one's sensory experience.
But no such jump occurs; there is normally an unbroken
continuity between situations where we cannot actually be

seeing the object, but are aware only of sense-data, and those where we think we see the material object. As we move from where the plate looks elliptical to where it looks round, or as the drunkard looks first at the pink rat and then at the real bed on which it sits, there is a smooth transition. Consequently in both kinds of case—illusory and seemingly genuine perceptions—we must be directly aware of the same kind of entity, namely sense-data.

Objections to the Arguments from Illusion

Several attempts have been made recently to show that these arguments do not justify the conclusion that our immediate awareness is of sense-data only.

Against the argument from differential certainty it is claimed:

(1) It misrepresents the nature of perceptual experience: introspective examination suggests that our awareness is of putative (ostensible) objects not of colour patches—one sees a tomato or something looking like one. Awareness of colour patches, as such, is a different kind of observation from normal perceiving, not an element within it. One may more readily be said to be directly aware of sounds or smells as such, but even then one is aware of them as public and external, not as private data. Ryle and others go further and say that the whole notion of awareness of (i.e. observation of) sensations or sense-data is mistaken and if pressed involves an infinite regress (*see* S.11).

(2) When it is claimed to be certain that one is sensing the red, round sense-datum it is supposed that the latter exists as a red, round entity of some kind. But there is no absolute certainty of this (indeed J. L. Austin claims that it may be less certain than statements like "This is a pig"). Strictly one can only say that something *looking* red and round exists; it may in fact *be* orange and oval, and only look red and round in this light and from this angle. The argument seems to reify (i.e. treat as existent things) looks, feels, or sounds, which are strictly looks, etc. *of* objects (*see*

S.11). Furthermore, in the so-called adverbial analysis of sensing, C. J. Ducasse and others have claimed that the red content
or datum is not distinguishable from the sensing of it and
has no separate existence. Though not very convincing so far
as sight is concerned (it is more plausible for feels and
tastes), this further undermines the claims to certainty.

(3) The argument is too ready to deny that we see
physical objects in cases of illusion and distortion. When we
look at the putative tomato, even if it is a piece of wax or a
reflection of a tomato or an image on a screen, we are still
seeing a material object, namely wax, or the tomato "in,"
i.e. *via* the mirror, or a screen illuminated in a certain way.
There is no need to suppose that we are aware of something
else, i.e. a sense-datum. This point is vigorously elaborated
in S.10.

Criticism of the argument concerning the content of illusions depends on the type of situation. In "Perspective Realism" (S.16) McGilvary makes a sustained attempt to explain
the relativity of perception without introducing sense-data,
and generally objection (3) above applies to cases of illusions
and relativity; one is simply aware of an external object
appearing different from what it really is, e.g. a round dish
looking elliptical. The argument from illusion oddly assumes
that things cannot look other than they are. This assumption
is linked with the notion of immediacy: it is gratuitously
supposed that in seeing a dish looking elliptical one is immediately aware of an elliptical existent, but this is to beg
the question by equating immediacy with incorrigibility so
that what looks elliptical is said to be elliptical. The same
answer is made a little less cogently with respect to double
vision (that one is seeing one bottle looking double) and
mirages (we see a real oasis looking nearer than it is). Furthermore if it is accepted that the objects of awareness in
illusions and relativity are ordinary physical objects, the
continuity argument falls to the ground in these cases.

For some people this general answer is immediately convincing and it seems incredible that the argument from illu-

sion was ever taken seriously. But others protest that it is
inadequate and neglects the immediacy of perception; in the
various situations mentioned they seem clearly and directly
to be aware of an elliptical shape, cool liquid, a blue
expanse of mountain, two bottles (in double vision), or, if
colour-blind, a black expanse of cloth. So to be told that one
is aware only of a round plate, warm water, green mountain,
one bottle, or red cloth, etc., is to them unconvincing and
fails to do justice to the facts of experience. This feeling for
the immediacy of sensory awareness, and the belief that it is
such a direct confrontation that its apparent object must
exist as perceived, lie at the bottom of the Sense-datum
Theory. The alternative account is to dismiss as illusory this
apparently direct and mistake-proof confrontation in perception: perceiving is affected in its accuracy by position,
distance, intervening media, the state of the sense organs,
and many other factors which may prevent one's seeing the
object properly.

A different approach is needed for hallucinations. Austin
(S.10) points out that the argument there relies on certain du-
bious assumptions, viz. that if two things (i.e. a genuine perception and a hallucination) are not generically the same they
cannot look alike, and that they cannot be distinguished if in
fact we fail to distinguish them. This criticism certainly undermines the argument from illusion as a demonstration; for it
to be that, these assumptions would have to be accepted as
universally true. But it can be replied that an explanation is
still required for the general similarity between hallucinations
and genuine perceptions. A common explanation of hallucinations is that they are mental images of unusual vividness
which are mistaken for real things. But it is doubtful whether
this will stand up to the continuity argument; hallucinatory
objects may be integrated with a perceived background, e.g.
the apparition may walk across the room and cause shadows,
and as the hallucinatory images are private so must be the
data of the background. Because of the importance of this
issue, a detailed account of hallucinations is given in S.3.

The Scientific Arguments

Even if the above answers to the argument from illusion seem convincing, they are not final; for one may legitimately ask *how* illusions and hallucinations occur, and the scientific explanations then offered lead to stronger arguments for Epistemological Dualism. The round dish looks elliptical because the angle of sight changes the pattern of light rays striking the eye; in mirror effects, mirages, and when the stick half-immersed in water looks bent, reflection and refraction have altered the path of the light rays; distant objects may appear the "wrong" colour because dust scatters the rays or absorbs some frequencies rather than others; in colour-blindness lack of certain retinal pigments alters the eye's response to light; while some optical illusions rely on misleading psychological cues. In short these phenomena point to the causal and psychological processes underlying perception, and we must now consider the dualist arguments based on these.

The main causal argument (*see* Ss.1 and 2) points to the abundant evidence of a causal chain from external object to percipient's brain in perception, e.g. in sight the chain process is: light waves travel from the object, strike the retina of the eye and produce chemical changes in it: these in turn cause impulses to travel along the optic nerve to an area of the brain where they set up activity which spreads also to certain association areas; this done the person sees the object. This causal process is a necessary condition of perception of the external object, for if it is interrupted, e.g. by damage to the eye, no perception occurs. On the other hand it is theoretically possible that if the same kind of brain activity were to be caused in some other way, an experience indistinguishable from perception would occur without any external object. This apparently happens naturally in some illusions and in hallucinations, including phantom limbs, while electrical stimulation of the appropriate areas of the brain may cause sensations of colour, smell, touch, etc. Again, after-images (cp. S.4 p. 71) are really after-sensations due to the stimulation or fatigue of the sense organ continuing after the original perception. Hence it is argued:

(1) Perception cannot be the direct contact or immediate confrontation with an external object it seems to be, since it requires this causal chain from object to the percipient's brain and is prevented if that is interrupted. Directness or immediacy, in this context, must mean no intermediary, no possibility of interruption, as well as no inference.

(2) Perceptual awareness and its immediate objects (sense-data) are "generated," brought into being, by the causal process, presumably by its last stage, brain activity—in other words in so far as perception is direct it is awareness of some content or object quite distinct from the external object.

Supporting points are:

(A) The *time lag,* which occurs in all perception and is marked in some (e.g. hearing distant gun fire, seeing a star), means that the immediate object of perception cannot be identified with the external object, particularly as the latter may have disappeared or moved by the time the perceptual experience occurs.

(B) The *simplicity and uniformity of nervous processes* (see p. 42) shows that they cannot transmit the variety of colour and sound and other secondary qualities which we are conscious of in perception. These qualities must therefore characterize sense-data only, and may in fact be due to something quite different in the object. This is reinforced by the considerations advanced on pp. (44-45) and by the general contrast between the world as described in modern physics and the world as we see it, though that contrast may simply be because physics is describing microstructure.

(C) *Causal conditioning* occurs in many cases of relativity and illusion: the nature of the immediate object in perception is affected by factors quite external to the object (e.g. position or health of the percipient, the state of his sense organs, the media between him and the object) and so it cannot be identified with object properties.

Psychological processes. The nature of what we are aware of in perception depends also on various psychological factors. Examples are:

(1) Perception is regularly enriched by imagery or thought, a characteristic normally only revealed when it goes wrong, e.g. when we "see" what we expect to see rather than what is present, or hear the expected visitor when no one is there. Many psychological experiments have been concerned with this, e.g. vague or ambiguous stimuli (pictures or sounds) are presented to different groups of people who see or hear them as definite objects or words, and the direction in which they are thus unconsciously supplemented or altered can be shown to be governed by suggestion, by the emotional or physical state of the person, or by his interests. Another kind of case is the divergence between different eye-witnesses' accounts of an incident, which may all differ from a film record; again, blind spots or other visual defects are often not apparent to the subject who unconsciously fills in the gap (this happens to us all if we look with only one eye, for there is a blind spot where the optic nerve leaves the retina). Extreme cases are the integrated hallucinations already mentioned, and in general this supplementation is difficult to explain unless our perceptual awareness is of sense-data similar to private mental imagery.

(2) Our perception is clearly affected by learning and past experience. One can learn to identify objects seen or photographed from unusual angles, to distinguish different birds' songs, different instruments in an orchestral piece, or different types of tea. Driving a car involves judgements, or rather perceptions, of distance, relative speeds, etc., which are acquired by experience. Psychological investigation has shown the role of learning to be far greater than this. Perception of spatial relations generally depends to a large extent on learning (normally unconsciously and in childhood) to harmonize sight and touch and to use various "cues." Amongst the cues used for perception of distance and of solidity are shadows, aerial and linear perspective, parallax (or relative movement), and the interposition of objects. All this

suggests that perceiving is not a direct awareness of external objects; the content or immediate object of one's awareness is the product of complex processes in the person and so is private to him. This is supported by the "reversals" where a drawing stays constant but is perceived differently at different times, so that now one pattern or shape stands out as the figure, now another. Examples are the goblet which may appear also as two faces in profile, the staircase which seems seen now from above now from below, or Fig. 2 p. 86. This is claimed to be due to organizational processes in perceiving.

(3) The "phi-phenomenon," i.e. the impression of movement between adjacent stationary stimuli which are activated in succession. This underlies the consciousness of movement on a cinema or television screen, and is used in illuminated advertisements where if series of lights are successively switched on for a brief time one is perceptually conscious of a moving figure or even of words moving along. Successive illumination may also make moving objects appear stationary: thus when illuminated by the flashing light of a stroboscope, a moving crank in a machine may, if the flashing is properly adjusted, be seen as stationary and examined for defects; if there is a slight maladjustment of the flashing it may seem to rotate slowly backwards like the wheels of coaches in Western films. These facts may be used in the argument from illusion and point to a clear distinction between the sense-datum and the object properties.

These causal and psychological arguments seem among the strongest supports for Epistemological Dualism. Many philosophers are suspicious of them, however, because they seem to imply Representative Realism (p. 16), a theory so false, they think, as to vitiate anything that entails it. Thus the Sense-datum Theory, though dualist, avoids them, preferring to base its case on the analysis of experience and of illusion. Philosophical defenders of Direct or Naïve Realism have had little success in refuting these arguments. Austin, for example, does not discuss them, despite his strong attack on the argument from illusion, and a common line (illustrated in S.7) is to claim that they are irrelevant to the philosophical task of understanding perceiving itself. But how can one understand perceiving without understanding its causation? And, as is argued in S.2, even the Sense-datum Theory cannot be isolated from physiological considerations.

Sensing and Perceiving

If dualism is accepted two main problems arise: (I) the relation between sensing (the direct awareness of sense-data) and perception (i.e. discovering the nature and properties of external objects); (II) the relation between sense-data and external objects. Our main concern in this book is with the second of these, but for completeness a little may be said now on the first. This may be conceived as the problem of the analysis of perceptual consciousness, i.e. of the state of mind or consciousness which occurs in perceiving and in subjectively indistinguishable conditions such as hallucinations. The traditional account is that it consists in the interpretation of sense-data, i.e. when seeing a tomato you are aware of a red, bulgy sense-datum which you interpret as a tomato. In earlier versions synthesis was the characteristic feature of the interpretation, for it was assumed that sense-data were atomic either as point-sensations or at least as the smallest areas of uniform colour in the visual field. There would thus be many sense-data of sight, plus those of other senses, in the perception of any one object. But modern psychology has abandoned the notion of point-sensations and modern sense-datum theory is prepared to treat as one sense-datum the whole of the visible surface of the apparent object. Consequently interpretation is now thought of more as inferring the object from the presented data. This type of view is criticized in S.5 though it still has its adherents. The main difficulty in it is that we are not aware of judgement or interpretation in normal perception; to which the reply usually is that it has become automatic and subconscious through familiarity—though this would suggest that the corresponding conscious inferences were common in early childhood, something for which there is no evidence.

The diametrically opposed view, which one may call the Percept Theory, is simply that perceptual consciousness is not analyzable and is always of percepts or ostensible physical objects; our consciousness is, for example, of a seeming tomato and cannot be split into awareness of colours, shapes, etc. plus interpretation. In certain circumstances we may be conscious of the coloured shapes, but that is a special and different kind of perception that a painter might use, not a core within all perceiving. There is a range of intermediate views between these two approaches. S.13 gives a well-known philosophical one: perceptual consciousness is taking for granted that the sense-datum belongs to a material object; it is a state of mind which is less explicit than judgement or inference and involves no passage from premise to conclusion; consciousness of the object and sensing of the sense-data arise together and can only be distinguished by subsequent analysis. It is, however, not easy to square this with the various psychological processes which occur in perceiving. S.19 gives the blue-print for another, in which "reference to" an external object is substituted for "taking for granted" and understood behaviouristically, but this was never worked out in detail.

If one adopts the percept approach, the problem is to explain how perceptual consciousness is psychologically conditioned. One famous answer is given by the Gestalt Psychologists, that this conditioning is physiological and below the level of consciousness; it is due to various organizing forces and automatic adjustments in the brain and sense organs. Attempts to work this out in detail and to obtain experimental justification of the postulation of such forces led to much controversy and to a variety of modified theories. Other suggestions are that there is interpretation of perceptions, i.e. of more basic forms of perceptual consciousness, or that the psychological processes, while really physiological and unconscious, have to be discussed as if they were conscious, i.e. that to talk of interpretation of sense-data is to describe unconscious brain processes as if they were above the level of consciousness. These answers can hardly be understood, let alone evaluated, without a considerable study of the psychological evidence; hence no representative selections have been included, but references are given in the Bibliography.

It should be noted that this controversy is within a dualist context, i.e. the content of immediate experience is distinguished from external objects and their properties, and the question is whether this content can primarily be described as sense-data (colour patches, sounds, etc.) or as percepts, i.e. ostensible objects or scenes. Interpretation theories are often supported by an assumption about the causal processes in perceiving, namely that the basic immediate conscious experience must resemble the pattern of stimulation of the sense organs. This is attacked in S.5, but it should be noted that the philosophical Sense-datum Theory does not depend on this assumption, for it claims that sense-data are revealed by an analysis of perceptual consciousness, especially in cases of illusions and distorted perception.

Realism

Whether it is concluded that the immediate data in perceptions are sense-data or percepts, the fundamental problem is: what is their relationship to external physical objects? The main types of answer from a sense-datum point of view are outlined rather despairingly in S.12.

A notorious traditional answer was that of Representative Realism (or the Representative Theory) advanced by Descartes, Locke (S.14) and others; this was that the relation is a causal one in which the effects (ideas = sense-data) represent their causes (properties of external objects), i.e. resemble them in certain respects. Perception is to be understood strictly as the awareness of these ideas; our knowledge of the external world is thus an inference from patterns and sequences of ideas or is an intuitive assumption justifiable by subsequent reasoning. Modern analogies of "representing" are the relation between a map or radar screen and the region they cover, or between television or cinema pictures and the studio events reproduced; but traditionally it was interpreted in accordance with the associated doctrine of Primary and Secondary Qualities. As Locke stated this, external objects possess primary qualities (spatio-temporal ones mostly, e.g. shape, size, motion or rest) which cause ideas resembling them, and secondary qualities which cause ideas of colour, smell, taste, sound, warmth, etc.: in the latter case the ideas do not resemble the qualities which are really texture or molecular motion, i.e. arrangements of the primary qualities of the minute parts. Berkeley and later theorists restate this in terms of the sensible qualities of ideas or sense-data; primary qualities (shape, size, etc.) characterize both ideas and objects; secondary qualities (colour, warmth, etc.) characterize only ideas.

Representative Realism has important merits:

(1) It is the easiest inference from the scientific account of the causal processes up to the brain in all perceiving, and fits other scientific evidence. Thus colour-blindness and deafness are due to defects in the sense organ which affect all subsequent stages in the causal transmission, so that the resultant sense-data are different from normal. That electrical stimulation of the brain causes sensations of colour, smell, etc., according to place of stimulation, seems to confirm the theory, and it can easily accommodate the time-lag in perception. Further, by holding that representation does not amount to resemblance in the case of secondary qualities it can be made to fit the distinction between "the world as we see it" (i.e. the sense-data grouped as ostensible objects) and the scientific account of material objects, which is in terms of colourless, tasteless, smell-less electrons.

(2) It accounts for illusions, dreams, images, hallucinations, and the relativity of perception. The relativity and many illusions result from changes in the stimulation of the sense organs due to distance, media, angle of sight, etc.; such changes affect all that follows and so vary the sense-data

caused. Other illusions are due to misinterpretation of sense-data. In imagery and dreams the brain activity which occurs in corresponding perceptions is reactivated as the result of internal causes and so brings about the recurrence of similar sense-data. (The re-activation may only be partial and the resultant data may be altered by the mind consciously or unconsciously.) Hallucinations are imagery also; since the images are of a similar character to normally perceived data and are due to a similar immediate cause in the brain, it is easy to see how they may merge in integrated or triggered hallucinations, or how perception may be imaginatively supplemented. The standard explanation of "phantom limbs," that they are sensations caused by irritation, at the stump, of nerves normally coming from the amputated limb, is also accommodated; as perception is confined strictly to the effects of the causal chain, interference with it *en route* may readily deceive us.

(3) The theory has also traditionally been part of the widely accepted Interactionist or Dualist account of the relation of mind and body: body affects mind in perception, mind affects the body in voluntary action. Not all who accept that theory realize that they are saddled with Representative Realism.

But it has also certain defects which some regard as overwhelming:

(A) If, as it claims, our perceiving is strictly awareness of the mental ideas or sense-data, it is difficult to see how we can break out of the circle of sense-data and observe external objects. How can we tell what these objects are like, indeed how do we know that there are such objects? If we try to verify the existence of the table by touching it, we simply obtain more sense-data—tactile ones—and if we see our hands touching the table we are only having visual data. Whenever we try to peer round the barrier of ideas we just get more ideas. This difficulty undermines the analogies and evidence for the theory. Representation is conceived of as something like mapping or photographing, but we know a map or a photograph resembles a scene because we can observe both and compare them, while *ex hypothesi* we can never strictly observe both objects and ideas to compare them. Observing objects is just observing sense-data, so we do not *know* that objects and sense-data resemble in primary but not in secondary qualities.

(B) It is often said that the theory not only leads to scepticism but is actually self-refuting, cutting off the branch on which it sits. Its premises and evidence assume that we discover the action of the objects on the sense organs by observing them; its conclusion denies that we can do this—all our perception is of ideas. However there would only be self-refutation if the conclusion contradicted the premises, which it need not do if carefully stated. If one supposes that by means of ideas one gains knowledge of objects and their primary qualities, then the premises of the theory are not undermined. But there is scepticism, for since our direct awareness is limited to ideas we do not *know* and can only surmise that there are external objects or what they are like.

(C) Even though the theory need not be self-refuting it is open to the charge of circularity if considered as an attempt to explain perceiving. It appears simply to transfer perceiving as ordinarily conceived (i.e. as a face-to-face confrontation) from outside to inside the person: perceiving external objects is now put forward as perceiving private replicas of them, for we look at maps and television pictures in just the same way as we look at the countryside. Even if we say perceiving objects is achieved by means of perceiving sense-data, there is the same duplication of perceiving which is thus "explained" in terms of itself. (The S.11 criticism applies here too.)

(D) The primary and secondary quality distinction is usually regarded as unsatisfactory for the reasons advanced by Berkeley (S.20). But neither he nor Locke realized that the main basis of the distinction is that primary qualities are measurable and so are objective and independent of perceptual relativity in a way that secondary qualities are not (*see* S.15); nor of course did they know of the neurological argument for the distinction (p. 11).

Critical Realism is an attempt to keep the benefits of Representative Realism but avoid its defects (*see* S.19). It claims that the root of the troubles of Representative Realism lay in its failure to analyze perceiving or perceptual knowledge: accepting the ordinary notion of perceiving as "intuiting," i.e. a direct awareness or confrontation, and finding that on account of the causal processes and of illusions such awareness was not of external objects, Locke concluded that it must be of intra-mental ideas and so imprisoned us within the circle of such ideas. But the more reasonable conclusion would be that this ordinary notion of perceiving is wrong and that a more careful analysis is needed. This will show that an essential feature of perceiving, even as ordinarily understood, is that it is the way we discover the existence and nature of external objects, i.e. it is in fact a claim, often justified, to knowledge. Furthermore, though involving an intuition or direct awareness, perceiving is much more than this. It involves also an active external reference, as is in fact implied by the knowledge-claim: we *refer* an intuited datum or "character complex" to an external object, i.e. we explicitly judge that it is, or is the character of, an external object, or we unreflectingly take it to be this, or again we immediately react to it as if it were an external object. These different modes of reference are differently stressed by different writers, but the point seems to be that they occur in varying degrees according to circumstances. Sometimes our perception is an explicit identification or judgement, or at least it issues immediately in one, e.g. we say "Here's our bus" or "There's Tommy"; more often we just see that it is Tommy without formulating any judgement; or again our perception that it is our bus and our starting to go and catch it seem indistinguishable—reference to the external object is manifest in an immediate physical response.

There is some similarity between this "reference of an intuited datum to an external object," and the "taking for granted that a sense-datum belongs to a material object" of Price's Sense-datum Theory, especially as both stress that no

distinction between datum and object is drawn by the percipient at the time. But there is a difference in starting point
and emphasis. Price began with sense-data, treating them as
distinct existents and willing to allow that material objects
consisted of them; the Critical Realists began with knowledge
of external objects, and the datum distinguished within it
was regarded by some of them as a purely logical essence and
by others as a purely mental content very difficult to isolate
even subsequently from the associated reference (this second
group is the one represented here. Ss. 18 and 19); also reference is wider than taking for granted, covering both bodily reactions and identification of the datum with the external
object. In order to stress the relative subordination of the datum they spoke of perceiving external objects "by means of
the datum," "guided," or "mediated" by it.

Since Critical Realism can agree that the datum is "generated," it can share in the advantages of Representative
Realism; and yet it seems able to avoid the latter's worst
faults. There is no self-refutation, for perceiving is from the
start always perception of external objects by means of the
intuited data, an analysis which does not deny that we perceive such objects. There is no duplication or circularity, for
the direct awareness of the datum is not a replica of perceiving; in so far as it can be distinguished at all it is much
less complex than perceiving, for it involves no reference to
or identification with external objects.

Moreover there need be no scepticism. True that in perceiving we only *take* the datum to be an external object or its
properties, and this may of course be erroneous. In a sense it
is always erroneous in that the datum or content never is the
object, but normally the taking or reference is correct in that
(I) we are perceiving an external object, and (II) the intuited
characters do also characterize the external object so far as
primary qualities are concerned; to that extent we are perceiving actual properties or at least projections of them. In
general, the claim that perceiving is thus far veridical and
amounts to knowledge, is said to be the best hypothesis to

explain the order and nature of our sense experiences (cp. S. 18: Locke had made an unsuccessful attempt at this kind of justification—see pp. 190 ff.).

Unfortunately the Critical Realists were unable to turn these improvements into a comprehensive and convincing theory of perception; their impact was less than it should have been because they were unable to agree about the nature of the datum or to provide a completely plausible account of reference. The real difficulty seems to be that this part of their programme cannot be undertaken without a full investigation of the psychological processes in perception.

Phenomenalism

A more radical approach is to abandon entirely the notion of external physical objects as entities of a quite different type from sense-data; instead an attempt is made to show that they consist solely of groups or patterns of such data. The problem then arises of the fragmentariness of perception. Any material object is believed to exist for long periods when it is not observed, e.g. the furniture in an empty room, the beams in the roof, and so on, while some, e.g. rocks in Antarctica or under the ocean, may never have been observed. Yet when they are not observed such objects cause no sense-data, have no sense-data belonging to them or constituting them. Hence if material objects are reduced to actual data and consist only of them, they must cease to exist when unobserved and those never observed must never have existed; worse still, the familiar objects in the room must apparently come in and out of existence as one looks at or away from them—the blinking of a human eye can destroy them. This seems such an intolerable paradox that Berkeley, though tempted to say that material objects were simply collections of ideas, had to introduce God as their continuing basis or cause.

To avoid this unconvincing substitution of unobserved divine causes for unobserved material ones, Mill suggested that what continues to exist during the gaps are possible sense-data; material objects thus consist of "groups of permanent possibilities of sensation." (S.22). This view, later known as Phenomenalism, is not very plausible as it stands, but has been influential in suggesting ways of avoiding Representative Realism. The immediate difficulty is to understand what these possibilities are. Strictly if only the possibility exists then nothing actual fills the gaps—to say something, e.g. an accident, is possible implies that it is not actual. This is particularly difficult in that we believe that events may have unobserved causes. Fire still boils the water when no one is in the kitchen, and the floor is supported by unobserved beams; if the fire and the beams are only possibilities when unobserved, how can they have actual effects? It might be claimed that a possible X is an actual Y, an actual entity of a different kind, e.g. the possible winner is an actual horse, but in that case once again matter would have to consist of largely unknown and unobservable entities.

A later suggestion (by Russell) was that the gap-filling entities are unsensed sense-data (or *sensibilia*)—entities just like sense-data except that they are not sensed. But again one may ask what evidence there is of this—*ex hypothesi* one cannot observe such entities, so they are just as obscure and conjectural as the unobserved external objects of Representative Realism. Further, the scientific evidence suggests that sense-data are generated, brought into being by the brain, and this seems incompatible with their pre-existence as sensibilia before being sensed. Russell therefore abandoned this view for one closer to Representative Realism (S.17).

Modern defenders of Phenomenalism see the basic problem in a different light, as one not of stating the constituents of matter but of elucidating the concept of material object, of defining it in terms of sense-data; and this they seek to achieve not by formal definition but by a "definition in use," i.e. by providing translations of statements about material objects into equivalent sets of statements about sense-data. It is thus intended to show that what is meant about talking about tables, chairs, or similar objects can be expressed solely by talking about sense-data. Sometimes this is put by saying that material objects are logical constructions out of sense-data. The underlying position is in essence that of Hume (S. 21), that all we *know* to exist are sense-data occurring in various patterns or sequences, but one main difference is in claiming that these regular patterns are not something to be supplemented by imagination but are actually what we refer to indirectly by talking of such objects. Material objects are in fact co-ordinating concepts, devices which enable us to group and correlate our sense experiences, to identify and refer to patterns in them.

The other main difference is in the linguistic presentation, the attempt to elucidate the concept by translation into a set of equivalent statements. This is in accordance with the linguistic approach contemporary with the hey-day of Phenomenalism, in which it was held that material-object statements and statements about sense-data are simply two different ways of describing the same set of facts (but facts really about sense experiences, their patterns and sequences)—see Bibliography: *Sense-datum Language* for references. However, the sets of sensory statements are not only a translation but have a special form also. In so far as the object is observed they are all categorical, but when it is unobserved they are hypothetical. Thus "I see a book on the table" = "I have sense-data XYZ," where XYZ might stand for "of a rectangular red solid-seeming shape on a flat brown expanse." But "There is a book on the table in the next room" = "If you were in the next room you would have sense-data XYZ." This introduces the notion of possibility which was not in Hume and which earlier Phenomenalism expressed so unplausibly. It has the great advantage of expressing the possibility of sense-data in the hypothetical form of the statement without suggesting that possible data are somehow constitutents, perhaps the sole ones, of actual objects. Also of interest is that this approach was anticipated but not developed by Berkeley, (S.20, pp. 248 and 260) and Mill, (S. 22, p. 281).

The result is an ingenious theory which transforms the

problem of producing a viable alternative to Representative Realism. If successful it would be an enormous theoretical economy; it would enable the facts of experience to be accounted for solely in terms of one type of existent, namely sense-data, without any need to go beyond them and postulate other orders of material existence behind them. Also it provides a way of dealing with unobserved entities in physics, suggesting that electron-statements are equivalent to, or are logical constructions out of, sets of statements about physicists' observations. But note that in this case the data for the construction are observations of material objects, the construction thus being at a different level; also electrons, unlike tables and chairs, are agreed to be unobservable.

All the same the theory faces many difficulties, some of which are discussed in S.23.

(1) No fully equivalent translation of a material-object statement into a set of sense-datum ones seems possible. The set would have to be enormously large, perhaps infinite, to include every possible perception of the object from every point of view. Furthermore there can be no full mutual entailment of original and translation. On the one hand there might be some illusion or hallucination in which the sense-datum statements would be true and yet the material-object statement false: there might be all the red book-like data and yet it might be a box got up to look and feel like a book. This can no doubt be ruled out in practice by getting enough data, especially those resulting from tests like opening the book, but it is doubtful how far results in such tests are really part of the *meaning* of the material-object statement and so are true features of the translation. On the other hand the material-object statement might be true and the sensory ones false. There might be a book on the table and yet you might not get sense-data of it—the light might fail; you might be taken ill suddenly or be careless and inattentive; the book might be covered up by other objects, etc. There is a large range of standing conditions which would have to be stated to ensure the truth of the sense-datum statement. This is par-

ticularly so if the object is a small one: "there is a needle in this haystack"—if you look would you get the needle-like data?

(2) The difficulty in dealing with causal processes, especially unobserved ones, still remains. Ayer attempts an answer, (S.23) but many find it unconvincing. So much depends on one's analysis of causation; if one adopts the Humean regularity view ("C causes E" means only a constant conjunction: "whenever C, then E"), then conversely the correlation of sense-data should be causal; and so the translation of "a beam under the floor supports it" as "if, i.e., whenever, you have under-floor sense-data you have beam sense-data" suggests that under-floor sense-data cause beam sense-data, which is far from the original. On the other hand, if "C causes E" means more than this, e.g. that C exerts some force on E, then the translation into correlations of sense-data is not equivalent.

(3) In general Realists feel that Phenomenalism is inadequate and superficial. It deals only with effects, with sequences of sense-data which occur *because* there are continuing physical objects; it cannot *explain* the sequences of sense-data to which it reduces the external world. If we take any situation where two or more people see the same thing, e.g. if a coin is handed from one person to another, then it is not enough to say that this simply means that given one set of sense-data another occurs. This would make the sequences of sense-data incredible coincidences: why do people's sense-data agree in this situation when they do not in a dream or imaginary one? If I only imagine that I am paying you why don't you get sense-data of receiving the money as you do when I really pay you? The common-sense and realist answer seems obvious—because in the one case there is a continuing material object exchanged, while in dreams and imagination there is not. This is well illustrated in S.18.

One may conclude then that Phenomenalism has difficulties quite as serious in their way as those of Representative Realism or Critical Realism. Hence the impetus to the modern attempt to counter the argument from illusion and restore a

Direct Realism, a direct observation of external objects without the mediation of sense-data. But this in its turn cannot counter the scientific evidence or provide a satisfactory explanation of hallucinations. There is, however, one consolation from this apparent impasse—it presents a challenge that renders the study of perception an intriguing and stimulating field of philosophical endeavour.

Part I
The Problems

1. THE ROAD TO EPISTEMOLOGICAL DUALISM

A. O. LOVEJOY

Arthur Oncken Lovejoy (1873–1962) was one of the most prominent of the American Critical Realists. This passage is taken, with slight abridgment, from his Paul Carus Lectures, *The Revolt Against Dualism* (1929), pp. 16–23.

Philosophers have often begun by provisionally assuming that they know nothing whatever except the passing immediate datum, and have then sought to determine, by reflecting upon the nature or implications of this, how much knowledge of existents which are not immediate data they must, or may, suppose themselves to possess. This was, of course, essentially the method of Descartes, though he applied it confusedly and inconsistently. But it is not the natural road to epistemological dualism. That road starts from the position of natural realism—from the assumption that we already have certain information about realities which are not *merely* our immediate, private, and momentary data; and it leads to the discovery, or supposed discovery, that this very assumption forbids us to believe that our acquaintance with these realities is at first hand. The time, place, context, or qualities which we have ascribed to them prove inconsistent with those which belong to the data. Not only is this the natural approach to the dualism of datum and *cognoscendum*,[1] but it is also the only approach which is at all likely to be persuasive to those averse to that theory. The argument starts from the premises of those who would, if possible, avoid its conclusion. We shall, then, not attempt an affectation of universal doubt, but shall tentatively accept the broad outlines of the picture of nature familiar to common sense and sanctioned by the older physics. We shall, in particular, not initially question the supposition that there are extended external objects, such as pennies,

31

tables, planets, and distant stars, having at least the primary and possibly also the secondary qualities; having determinable positions in a space like that of visual and tactual perception, whether or not it is identical with it; capable of motion and causal interaction; acting, by means of processes in space, upon our sense organs; and thereby conditioning the presence in our experience of the data which, whether or not identical with the objects, are our sources of information about them. When these natural assumptions are provisionally adopted, there nevertheless prove to be at least five familiar aspects of experience in which it seems plain that the object of our knowing must be different in the time or place or mode of its existence, or in its character, from the perceptual or other content which is present to us at the moment when we are commonly said to be apprehending that object, and without which we should never apprehend it at all.

(1) Intertemporal cognition, the knowing at one time of things which exist or events which occur at another time, seems a patent example of a mode of knowledge which we are under the necessity of regarding as potentially genuine and yet as mediate. When I remember, for example, not only is there a present awareness distinct from the past memory-object (that alone would imply only the duality of act and content), but the present awareness manifestly has, and must have, a compresent content. But the past event which we say the memory is *of* cannot be this compresent content. . . . The duality of the memory-image and the bygone existence to which it refers seems to be inherent in what we *mean* by remembrance; if the two were one our intertemporal knowing would defeat its own aim of apprehending the beyond, by annulling its beyondness. The very wistfulness of memory implies such duality; the past, in being known, still inexorably keeps its distance. Plainest of all is it that a man's own *ex-periencing* of yesterday, the event of his then *having* an experience, does not seem to him, in being remembered, to become today's experiencing. Common sense, however much inclined in its more self-confident moments to believe in direct perception, has never, I suppose, believed in direct memory;

it has been well aware that what is present in retrospection is a duplicate which somehow and in some degree discloses to us the character, without constituting the existence, of its original.

(2) The second reason for dualism has not, it is true, like some of the others, always been discoverable by the simplest reflection upon everyday experience. But the fact upon which it rests has long been one of the elementary commonplaces of physical science; and the probability of it had suggested itself to acute minds long before its verification. There had at times occurred to him, wrote Bacon in the *Novum Organum* (II, 46), "a very strange doubt," a *dubitatio plane monstrosa*, "namely, whether the face of a clear and starlight sky be seen at the instant at which it really exists, and not rather a little later; and whether there be not, as regards our sight of heavenly bodies, a real time and an apparent time *(tempus visum)*, just as there is a real place and an apparent place taken account of by astronomers." For it has appeared to him "incredible that the images or rays of the heavenly bodies could be conveyed at once to the sight through such an immense space and did not rather take some appreciable time in travelling to us." Unfortunately for his reputation Lord Bacon was able to overcome his doubt by invoking against it several bad reasons, which need not be here recalled; but his subtler medieval namesake had not only propounded but embraced and defended the same conjecture three centuries earlier. Roemer's observation in 1675, through which it became established as one of the fundamental theorems of empirical science, is not usually mentioned in the histories of philosophy; but the omission merely shows how badly the history of philosophy is commonly written, for the discovery was as significant for epistemology as it was for physics and astronomy. It appeared definitely to forbid that naïvely realistic way of taking the content of visual perception to which all men at first naturally incline. The doctrine of the finite velocity of light meant that the sense from which most of our information about the world beyond our epidermal surfaces is derived never discloses anything which (in Francis Bacon's phrase)

"really exists" in that world, at the instant at which it indubitably exists in perception. It is with a certain phase in the history of a distant star that the astronomer, gazing through his telescope at a given moment, is supposed to become acquainted; but that phase, and perhaps the star itself, have, ages since, ceased to be; and the astronomer's present sense-data—it has therefore seemed inevitable to say—whatever else they may be, are not identical with the realities they are believed to reveal. They might perhaps be supposed to be identical with the peripheral effect produced by the light-ray on its belated arrival at the eye—in other words, with the retinal images; but two present and inverted retinal images *here* are obviously not the same as one extinct star formerly existing elsewhere, and the duality of datum and object would therefore remain. This particular hypothesis, moreover, is excluded by the now familiar fact established by the physiological psychologists, that there is a further lag—slight, but not theoretically negligible—in the transmission of the neural impulse to the cortical center, and therefore—since the percept does not appear until the impulse reaches the brain—a difference in time between the existence of a given pair of retinal images, or any other excitation of peripheral nerve-endings, and the existence of the corresponding percept. Never, in short, if both the physiologists and the physicists are right, can the datum or character-complex presented in the perception of a given moment be regarded as anything but the report of a messenger, more or less tardy and more or less open to suspicion, from the original object which we are said to know by virtue of that perception.

(3) Another class of empirical facts which are familiar, in their simpler forms, to all men have seemed by the plainest implication to show that perceptual content, even though it appears as external to the physical organs of perception, is not identical with the particular objects about which it is supposed to convey information. It is commonly assumed that the object, or objective, of a given perception can, first of all, be identified, at least roughly, by its position in space and time. What I am "perceiving" at a certain moment is the

ink-bottle two feet away from my hand or the star a hundred
light-years distant. Even if the position is defined only vaguely,
the thing is at least supposed to be (or have been) "out there"
somewhere. This identification of the object referred to is,
obviously, possible only by means of the same perception;
yet, assuming such identification, experience shows that what
I perceive is determined by events or conditions intervening
in space and time between that object and my so-called perception of it. The qualities sensibly presented vary with
changes which appear to occur, not in the place where the
object is supposed to exist, but in regions between it and the
body itself, and, in particular, in the very organs of perception.
The examples are trite: a man puts a lens before his eyes, and
the size or shape or number or perceived distance of the
objects presented is altered; he puts certain drugs into his
stomach, and the colors of all the perceived objects external
to his body change; he swallows other drugs in sufficient quantity and sees outside his body objects which no one else can
see, and which his own other senses fail to disclose. The discovery of this primary sort of physical relativity, which is
really one of the most pregnant of philosophical discoveries,
begins in infancy with the earliest experience of the illusions
of perspective, or the observation that the objects in the visual
field change their spatial relations when looked at with first
one eye and then the other. . . . The evidence of this dependence of the nature of what is perceived upon happenings
which, as themselves experienced, do not happen in the right
place to permit them to be regarded as changes in the *cognoscendum* itself, has constantly increased with the progress of
the sciences of optics, neurocerebral physiology, and psychology; the eventual determination of the character of the
percept has been removed farther and farther, not only from
the external object, but even from the external organ of
sense.[2] As Professor Dewey remarked (*Experience and Nature*,
1st ed., p. 333) "it is pure fiction that a 'sensation' or peripheral excitation, or stimulus, travels undisturbed in solitary
state in its own coach-and-four to either the brain or consciousness in its purity. A particular excitation is but one of an

avalanche of contemporaneously occurring excitations, peripheral and from proprioceptors; each has to compete with
others, to make terms with them; what happens is an integra-
tion of complex forces." And even in the earliest and easiest
phases of this discovery, the variability of the percept with
conditions extrinsic to the object to be perceived manifestly
affects those attributes by which the very identity of the
individual object should be defined: it is not colors only but
shapes, not shapes only but perceived positions, that prove to
be functions of the processes spatially and temporally inter-
venient between the object and the perception, and therefore
not attributable to the former. Thus what is actually perceived
could be regarded only as the terminal effect of a more or
less long and complex causal series of events happening at
different places and times, only at the perceptually inaccessible
other end of which series the *cognoscendum* was supposed to
have—or rather, to have had—its being. Aside from any
empirical evidences of the sort mentioned, it has apparently
seemed to many minds virtually axiomatic that, if the *cognoscendum* in perception is conceived (as it is in ordinary thought
and in most physical theory) as a "causal object" acting upon
the bodily organs of perception in the determination of the
character of the content experienced, that which is acted *upon*
must also have a part—must, indeed, have the last and decisive
word—in determining the character of that content. How
under these circumstances the exterior causal object could be
known at all is an obviously difficult question; this argument
for epistemological dualism, and especially the role assigned in
it to the organs of perception, gives rise to that "crux of realistic theories" which Mr. C. A. Strong has very precisely expressed: "to explain how a sensation which varies directly only
with one physical object, the nervous system, can yet vary with
another physical object sufficiently to give knowledge of it"
(*Mind*, XXXI, 1922, p. 308). But with these ulterior difficulties we are not for the moment concerned; whatever *their*
solution, they obviously do not annul the difficulty, for any
realistic philosophy, of identifying the end-term with the initial
term of the physico-physiological causal series.

(4) This physical and physiological conditionedness of the data manifestly implies that the contents of the experience of percipients having different spatial and physical relations to a postulated external object cannot be wholly identical. But this implication is independently confirmed and extended through that communication and comparison of experiences which is supposed to be possible through language. While the many knowers are dealing with what is said to be one and the same object—and if they are not doing so are not achieving what is meant by knowledge—they notoriously are not experiencing the same sensible appearances. There is an assumed identity in the region of space at which the observers are all gazing, and this serves for the requisite antecedent identification of the common *cognoscendum*; but what they severally find occupying this supposedly single locus consists of character-complexes which are not merely diverse but (according to the logic almost universally accepted until recently) contradictory. So long as it is assumed either that there are certain sets of sensible qualities—e.g., two or more colors—which are incompatible, i.e., cannot both occupy the same place or the same surface of a material object at the same time, or that there are in nature "things" which at a given moment have a single and harmonious outfit of geometrical and other properties, the conclusion has seemed inevitable that the many discrepant appearances cannot "really" inhabit the one place or be the one thing at that place. So soon as the dimmest notion that there is such a phenomenon as perspective distortion dawned upon men, they began *eo ipso* to be epistemological dualists. It is of course conceivable, so far as the present consideration goes, that *one* of the discordant appearances might be identical with the object-to-be-known or with some part of it; but even so, since all the other observers are also supposed to be apprehending the object, *their* apprehension, at least, must be mediated through data which are *not* identical with it. Nor does it seem a probable hypothesis that, while almost all perception is mediate, a few privileged observers now and then attain direct access to the object.

(5) Finally, the experience of error and illusion, however

difficult it may be to render philosophically intelligible, seems
to have at least one direct and obvious implication: namely,
that the thing which at any moment we err about—otherwise
than by mere omission—cannot be a thing which is immediately present to us at that moment, since about the latter
there can be no error. It at least is what it is experienced as.
In so far as *cognoscendum* and content are identified, error
is excluded; in so far as the possibility of error is admitted,
cognoscendum and content are set apart from one another.
It may perhaps seem that this reasoning applies only to the
cases in which there is error, and that in true judgments (or
in veridical perception) the content may still be the same as
the *cognoscendum*. And if the term "true judgments" includes
the mere awareness of an immediate datum, then in such
judgments there is in fact no duality. But these constitute, at
best, only a tiny part of the subject-matter of our claims to
potential knowledge, the range of our possible judgments at
any given time; and it is, indeed, an obviously inconvenient
use of language to call them judgments at all. For the most
part we are occupied, when judging, with matters conceived
to be so related to us that we are not, from the very nature
of that relation, necessarily immune against error; doubt as to
the validity of our judgments about them is assumed to be not
meaningless. But where error is *conceivable,* the relation
between content and *cognoscendum* must be the same as in
the case of actual error. The generic nature of judgments-
potentially-erroneous must be conceived in such a way as to
permit the genus to have both judgments actually true and
judgments actually false as its species—and to make it intelligible that the latter are aiming at the same mark as the
former without hitting it. But a judgment is about something
in particular; it has to do with a specific portion of reality.
Since in actually erroneous judgments it is impossible that
that portion can be the immediate datum, error must consist
in attributing some character now present in perception or
imagery, or represented by a verbal symbol, to *another* locus
in reality, where it in fact is not present; and the species of

actually true judgments will correspondingly be defined as the attribution of some such character to another locus in reality where it in fact *is* present.

EDITOR'S NOTES

[1] Lovejoy translates *cognoscendum* "thing-to-be-known-if-possible" (see p. 12 of his book); chief examples of such things are external physical objects.

[2] Cp. Koffka in S.5, p. 82 ff.

2. THE NEUROLOGICAL APPROACH

LORD BRAIN

Lord Brain, formerly Sir Russell Brain, is an outstanding British neurologist, and was President, for 1964, of the British Association for the Advancement of Science. He has a keen interest in the philosophy of his subject, and this selection comes from a lecture first published in *Philosophy*, XXI, 1946, pp. 133 ff., and reprinted as Chapter I of his book *Mind, Perception and Science* (Blackwell, Oxford, 1951).

Physiological Idealism. In so far as neurologists base any theory of knowledge upon their observations, they seem usually to adopt physiological idealism.[1] The neurologist observes the brains of animals and of other people. From the behaviour of both, and from the answers which patients give to his questions, he discovers that, when an object is perceived, a series of events occurs successively in time, beginning with an event in the object and ending with an event in the subject's brain. If the series is interrupted at any point between the object and the cerebral cortex (brain surface) of the subject, the object is not perceived. If the relevant area of the cortex is destroyed, the object again is not perceived. But if the relevant area of the cortex is electrically stimulated while the subject is conscious, sense-data of a kind aroused by an object are perceived by the subject. Thus it is held that the event immediately preceding, or perhaps synchronous with, the perception of the object is an event of a physico-chemical kind in the subject's cerebral cortex. The cortical neurones are normally excited in the way just described from the external world, but if they should exceptionally be excited in some other way—for example, by electrical stimulation or by an epileptic discharge—the appropriate sense-data would still be experienced. The only independently necessary condition for the awareness of sense-data, to use Broad's term[2] is thus an event in the cerebral cortex. This might be true and yet the awareness of sense-data might still be compatible with the possession by sense-data of some status in the world external to the subject's brain. But the neurologist goes on to argue that this cannot be so for reasons which are important enough to deserve detailed consideration, whether or not his conclusion from them is right.

Let us examine the account which the neurophysiologist gives of the causation of sense-data. I shall take my first illustration from hearing, because the physics of sound is easier to understand than that of light. A tuning-fork is struck or a whistle is blown, or in some other way the air is made to vibrate, and a series of waves with a frequency of, let us say, 4,000 vibrations a second is propagated through the air. It strikes the observer's ear and a portion of the cochlea, attuned to this particular frequency, is caused to vibrate at the same rate. So far the subject has heard nothing. The vibration of this part of the cochlea starts a series of nerve-impulses in a certain fibre or fibres of the auditory nerve. No nerve-fibre in the body can carry impulses at so fast a rate. The frequency with which nerve-impulses can follow one another along a nerve depends upon the electrochemical structure of nervous tissue and is never more than 1,500 a second, and often much less. We learn this by recording electrically the response of nerves to their appropriate stimuli. The auditory nerve-fibre therefore conducts impulses at its accustomed rate, and, by a series of relay paths, the impulses reach the auditory area of the cerebral cortex in the temporal lobe. Electro-encephalography enables us to detect its arrival there, and in the experimental animal we can record simultaneously the frequency of the sound-stimulus, and the electrical response which it evokes in the auditory cortex. These are entirely dissimilar. Frequencies of stimulus ranging from 100 to 16,000 vibrations a second evoke the same kind of electrical response from the auditory cortex; namely, a single deflection lasting from 1/20 to 1/55 of a second. But the auditory stimuli of different frequencies excite different nerve fibres conveying impulses to different areas of the cortex. In the dog the cortical foci responsive to high frequencies are located in front and those for low frequencies behind, and successive octaves are arranged at equal intervals along the cortex. Similar observations have been made on the cat, and since they depend upon certain properties of nervous tissue and structure, there is no reason to think that man is essentially different. Now the difference in pitch of two sounds is correlated with a difference in their frequencies, but no such difference is to be found in the events in the nervous system upon which the discrimination of their respective sense-data depends. These have neither the frequencies of the stimuli nor do they differ from each other in frequency. They differ only in that the nervous impulses travel by different paths and reach different destinations in the cerebral cortex; and this seems to be true not only of the difference between one sound and another, but also of that between nervous impulses evoked by auditory, visual and olfactory stimuli. As Adrian[3] says: "The quality of the sensation seems to depend on the path which the impulses must travel, for apart from this there is little to distinguish the messages from different receptors."

Thus, according to neurophysiology, the observer is like a deaf housemaid who sits in her kitchen and watches the indicators of the electric bells. There are different bell-pushes (receptors) outside the front door and the back door and in the various rooms, but similar currents travel along similar wires, and the only difference she can detect is that different indicators move. Being paralysed as well as deaf she never answers the bell except by pressing another one!

The facts of neurophysiology are held to mean that sense-data are "really" located either in the cerebral cortex or in the mind of the observer. It is then necessary to inquire why a coloured patch which is "really" in my brain or in my mind appears to be outside me on a table in the room. The physiological idealist replies by invoking a process which he calls "projection." The colour is "really" in my brain, but I "project" it in some way on to the table.

For various reasons it is difficult to believe that such a process occurs. Some of the objections have often been pointed out. The physiological idealist, it has been well said, is an idealist in respect to other people's sense-data and a realist in respect to his own. For, if all sense-data are states of his brain, this must also be true of the sense-data derived from his own body; and his brain itself, if, as is not impossible, he could see it in a mirror in the course of an operation, must be reduced to an activity of itself. No doubt he will try and save the situation by maintaining that his sense-data give him information concerning objects which exist independently of his awareness of them. But it is difficult to see how he could ever arrive at this conclusion if his sense-data were nothing but states of his own brain. How does the deaf and paralysed housemaid, who was born in the kitchen and has never been outside it, know that the electric bell indicators give her information as to what is happening at the front door or the back door? How does she know that anything exists outside the kitchen? These are well-known philosophical objections to physiological idealism. There is one difficulty, however, which neurophysiology itself raises.

Let us suppose that we are watching an observer looking at a circle. There is a sense-datum or a group of sense-data which are circular. Light waves, which in their grouping maintain a circular relationship, travel from the object to the eyes of the observer. On a circular area on each of his two retinae disturbances are set up which excite nervous impulses which travel through his optic nerves, tracts, and radiations to the visual areas of the cerebral cortex. Only when the nervous impulses reach the cortex does the observer see the circle. If physiological idealism is true we might expect to find that there is something circular about the events at the cerebral cortex, for it is these, we are told, which are "projected" on to the outside world when we perceive a circle. Nothing of the sort is true. The area of cortical excitation which exists when we perceive a circle is divided into two halves, one in each cerebral hemisphere. Pathways connecting them exist, but these appear to play no part in our perception of the two halves of a circle as one whole, for this still occurs when the connecting pathway (the corpus callosum) is divided. Neither half is semicircular; it is roughly the shape of , the closed end lying in front and the open end behind. The right half of the circle is represented in the left cerebral hemisphere and vice versa, and the lower quadrant is represented above the upper. There is another complication. We saw that a circular nervous disturbance occurred in each retina; thus each half of the circle has a double representation in the nervous system, and, though the pathways for the two corresponding halves—that is, the two right halves and the two left halves—come to be close together behind the optic chiasma, and are represented in the same area of the cerebral cortex, there is no anatomical point at which they fuse, as Sherrington demonstrated in his experiments with flicker. Finally, since the two halves of the circle are represented in cortical areas lying parallel to each other, the cortical disturbance is three-dimensional.

Thus when we perceive a two-dimensional circle we do so by means of an activity in the brain which is halved, reduplicated, transposed, inverted, distorted, and three-dimensional. If physiological idealism is to be really physiological it must admit that its theory of projection breaks down because the circle which is said to be projected from the cerebral cortex never existed there at all.

Realism.[4] Now let us turn to a consideration of some alternative theories—those which have in common the belief that sense-data in some way exist independently of our awareness of them, and compose or help to compose objects, and that thus our perception of objects involves and depends upon our discovery or selection of sense-data and not our creation of them. This view seems to me to encounter difficulties as formidable as those which confront physiological idealism. Let us consider some of them.

However little interest realist philosophers may take in the causal aspects of perception, they all seem to accept the view that it must be, at any rate theoretically, possible to give a causal account of perception, which shall relate events occurring in the object to events in the brain of the observer and finally to events in his consciousness. Thus when I perceive a brown patch there are wave-lengths of a given frequency, nervous impulses, and so on, even though it may be difficult or impossible to say how this series of events is related to awareness of a brown sense-datum. Now between one colour and another, between brown and green, black and white, there are differences of quality by which we distinguish them; there is also something in common, colouredness, which enables us to group them together. But suppose instead of a brown patch we consider a black patch. What are the wavelengths and frequency of black light? Of course there are none. Black is a sense-datum of the same kind as brown, or even white: in fact they shade into one another so that it may be impossible to say where one ends and the other begins—but no causal account can be given of our perception of black in terms of excitations proceeding from the object. Indeed, the perception of black depends upon the absence of such visual excitations. It also depends upon the integrity of the visual part of the cerebral cortex. Seeing black is not the same as not seeing white or any other colour. If one-half of the visual cortex is destroyed so that the subject fails to see half of his visual field it does not appear black to him. He merely fails to see it, and may even be unaware that it is lost. I hope a realist philosopher will give us an account of the ontological status of a black sense-datum when it is not being perceived, and, in particular, its relationship to its non-existent substratum in the physical world. I suspect that it will prove to belong to the family of sense-data comprising that famous non-existent black cat in the dark room. And if a black sense-datum is to be regarded as in some way generated or created by the brain or the mind, what reason have we for thinking that this is not equally true of a brown or blue sense-datum, for it would seem that external excitation does not necessarily determine the quality of a sense-datum. Indeed, our experience of dreams should have taught us that, for we experience visual sense-data when asleep in a dark room.

This brings me to another class of sense-data which need have no external excitation; namely, hallucinations. Realist philosophers treat these as "wild" sense-data. Price, referring to pink rats, says: "Three things are indubitably real: the

sensing, the sense-datum, and the act of perceptual consciousness. Only one thing is not real—the material thing
which is the object of his perceptual consciousness."[5] But the
only conditions either dependently or independently necessary
for the perception of hallucinations are states of the subject's
body. I cannot discover any evidence for the view that the
pink rats exist unperceived as wild sense-data, and that perceiving them is a process of catching them in the trap of consciousness. It is a relief to know that Price thinks that the wild
sense-data may be "fleeting entities," but, if so, how do they
come into existence apart from the process which leads to
their being perceived?

Let us turn now to another kind of hallucinations—the
phantom limb. It is well known that a person who has lost a
limb may continue to experience the feeling that it is there,
and this is called a "phantom limb."[6] The limb is felt to be
where in fact it is not: it may even be felt to be in a part of
space occupied by another solid object. "Wild" sense-data,
in the realist view, do in fact exist at that spot, but these
cannot be caused by events occurring where they are experienced in the phantom limb: they must be generated in some
other part of the body. They possess, however, qualitative
and spatial characteristics indistinguishable from those which
are caused by events occurring where they are experienced.
What reason, then, have we for thinking that the qualitative
and spatial characteristics of sense-data related to a limb which
is really there are not similarly generated elsewhere; for
example, in the brain or the mind of the observer?

The Role of the Body in Perception. The part played by
the body in our perception of the external world is of the
greatest importance, and is much neglected by realist philosophers. Whitehead[7] alone among recent philosophers seems
to me to give due weight to it. Let us begin by considering
a relatively simple experience. I am holding a stone in my
hand and I perceive that it feels smooth, hard, cold and of a
certain shape. Realism maintains that in doing so I am aware
of sense-data simultaneously and successively, and that these

sense-data belong to the object and exist either as actual or obtainable sense-data independently of my perceiving them. Now Price has observed what he calls "a curious point" about touch. "All normal tactual sense-data," he says, "belong to two objects at once; namely, to the object which we are touching, and to our own body or some part of it"[8] I should prefer to say that tactile sense-data may belong to either. Suppose that I stroke someone's skin with a fine wisp of cotton-wool, and ask what he feels. He may reply "a tickling sensation" or "a piece of wool." In the first case he is describing a sense-datum in his skin, in the second he is referring it to an object. But it may be said in the second case he is merely inferring that the sense-datum in his skin has been caused by an object with which previous experience has made him familiar. But take another example. When my hand has been exposed to cold air, I say, "My hand is cold," but when I grasp a stone I say, "This stone is cold." In each case what I am experiencing is a cold sense-datum, but in the one case I feel it in my hand and in the other case as belonging to an object. How do I perceive the size, shape, and solidity of the stone? The touch and pressure sense-data which contact with the object evokes in my fingers are localized and distinguished as relating to different parts of the skin. Furthermore, my fingers themselves will be bent or straightened and separated to a greater or less extent; and each successive movement and posture of any finger arouses sense-data from the tendons and joints. If you move your fingers when your eyes are closed you are aware of these sense-data as originating in and referring to your fingers; but if you are holding an object in your hand these sense-data become fused with those just described and are felt as collectively conveying awareness of the size, shape, and solidity of the object. Thus all the sense-data which are said to belong to an object when it is handled can in suitable conditions be experienced as belonging to the body.

But the body is present in our perceptions in a more elusive and less perceptible fashion. The realist usually starts from awareness of sense-data. Thus Price says that when we see a tomato "something is red and round then and there I cannot doubt." It is, then, assumed that we can go on to consider this red and round something as an entity independent of its then-and-thereness. Most realist philosophers, I suppose, would maintain that the red patch is or is composed of sense-data, and that its thereness is not. But how do I arrive at the awareness that the red patch is "there"? Because the images which it throws on my two retinae are slightly different, because the axes of my eyes are at a certain angle and certain ocular muscles are contracted or relaxed. All these states of my body cause nervous impulses to reach my brain. They, however, would tell me little if I did not also receive impulses from my labyrinths, which vary according to the position of my head in space, and from the muscles and joints of my neck, which indicate the position of my head in relation to my body. In other words, the spatial setting of the red patch is derived from my body: and the proof of this is that when this bodily machinery goes wrong I no longer see the red patch "there." I see two red patches, or the red patch goes round and round, or though I see it, I simply do not know where it is, and cannot find my way to it. Hence my awareness of the red patch depends to a surprising extent upon nervous impulses from my body, some of which remain unconscious though others give rise to recognizable somatic sense-data. We can consider the red patch as an isolated sense-datum but we cannot experience it so, and, in so far as we consider it so, our consideration is remote from experience. The total experience of "a red patch there" contains subjective somatic sense-data inextricably intermingled with it.

In an attack of migraine the patient experiences visual hallucinations of scintillating lights seen to one or other side. These are caused by a disturbance at the visual cortex on one side. Let such a patient during the attack lie with closed eyes in a dark room. If he turns his eyes to the right the hallucinatory figure appears to move to the right and similarly in any other direction. Thus, nervous impulses from the eye muscles evoked by the movement of the eyes determine where a hallucination originating at the visual cortex shall be seen.

There is another example which beautifully illustrates how perception and causal investigation may aid each other. If I am in a completely dark room with my eyes closed I see a black expanse which seems to be very near me if not actually behind my eyelids. If now I open my eyes, the black expanse appears to be outside me at some distance. Where I perceive the black sense-datum therefore depends upon nervous impulses from the muscles which open and close my eyes, since nothing else has changed.

Electro-encephalography shows that, when the eyes are closed, there is a steady electrical rhythm detectable over the visual cortex. This is abolished by opening the eyes in a completely dark room. Opening the eyes thus causes an electrical change in the visual cortex contemporary with the spatial change perceived in the black sense-datum, though, be it noted, there is no change in anything outside the body.

There are other objections to realism which seem to me serious, but I will mention only one. Astronomical distances are so great that light takes many years to travel to us from distant stars. The star which I now see may have ceased to exist since it sent out the light rays which are striking my retina. In what sense, other than a causal one, can my sense-datum be said to belong to a non-existent star? This is an extreme but not a special instance, for the same is true of all perception. All physical impulses upon which perception depends take time to reach us from all objects. The speed of light is so great relative to terrestrial distances that we can usually neglect it, but the fact remains that I can never see anything but the immediate past of any object I look at. Sound travels slowly in relation to the speed of modern aeroplanes; hence this discrepancy becomes of practical importance. The aeroplane which I hear in one place has now moved to another. I am hearing its past. This is true even of bodily sensation, since a nervous impulse takes a measureable time

to travel from the sense organ to the brain. I can feel only
the immediate past of any part of my own body except the
brain. Sense-data, then, are part of my present, but how can
they form part of physical objects of whose present I can
know nothing and which may even have ceased to exist?

NOTES

1 This is a version of the theory usually called by philosophers
Representative Realism or the Representative Theory.—ED.

2 C. D. Broad, *Scientific Thought* (London, 1927) p. 501—
BRAIN

3 E. D. Adrian, *The Basis of Sensation* (London, 1938).—BRAIN

4 Again there is a difference in terminology from normal philosophical usage. The views criticized here are Phenomenalist and
quasi-Phenomenalist versions of the Sense-datum Theory. Lord
Brain's objections would also condemn Naïve Realism or other
forms of Direct Realism which regard seen colour-expanses as
literally parts of physical objects; but they support Dualist types
of Realism, e.g. Representative or Critical Realism.—ED.

5 H. H. Price, *Perception* (London, 1932) p. 147—BRAIN (S.13
p. 175 below—ED.)

6 See also S.3 p. 54—ED.

7 A. N. Whitehead, *Process and Reality*, (Cambridge, 1939),
pp. 89, 104–5, 167–8, 178.—BRAIN

8 Price, *op. cit.*, p. 229—BRAIN

A few of Lord Brain's technical notes have been omitted.

3. HALLUCINATIONS

LORD BRAIN

In this passage an attempt is made to give all the data concerning hallucinations that a philosophical theory of perception needs to take into account. It comes, by courtesy of the copyright owners and publishers, from Sir Russell Brain: *The Nature of Experience,* pp. 11–22 of the 1959 Riddell Memorial Lectures delivered at the University, Newcastle upon Tyne, and published by the Oxford University Press, London.

I shall begin by describing some common visual experiences, and then turn to the illusions and hallucinations produced by drugs and disease of the nervous system. In doing so I shall use the word "see" as it is actually used by those who describe these experiences. I shall leave for subsequent discussion whether in such circumstances the word "see" is rightly used.

There are different kinds of visual after-image, but one will be sufficient for our present purpose. Hanging on the wall opposite me is a picture with a black frame. I look at it steadily for a few seconds, and then without closing my eyes look to one side. I now see against the wall a white rectangle, which is the same shape and size as the picture frame, but is white instead of black. This white rectangle lasts for a few seconds before fading away. While it lasts, if I either turn my eyes without turning my head, or turn my head and my eyes at the same time, I see the white rectangle in a different position in relation to the opposite wall, namely, in the direction in which I am at the time looking. Furthermore, if I tilt my head, the white rectangle also becomes titled and is now seen at an angle to the black picture frame. Finally, if during the experience of the white rectangle I close my eyes, I continue to see it, and if I then move my head, the white rectangle is again seen in a different position

51

in relation to the position of my body, but no longer in relation to my visual experience of the wall opposite, since, my eyes being closed, I have none.

Now let us turn to some accounts of visual hallucinations. The following quotations are taken from the account of his experiences given by a man who had taken lysergic acid.[1] "Then my attention became preoccupied with the dull, gold stars on the lamp shade. These stars began to be filled with colour; they *lived* with colour. One star, I now saw, was a very small (and wholly attractive) *turtle* on its back, its body a maze of distinct colours—the colours which must actually be involved in the gold paint itself. These little turtles—stars— or highwaymen with two huge pistols!—lived and moved in their firmament of illumined paper. . . . Then my eyes went to the whitish-gold distempered wall above, where the lamplight fell. The wall began to be covered with an incredibly beautiful series of patterns—embossed, drawn, painted, but *continuously changing*. More colour. Indescribable colour. And all the colours, all the patterns, *were in the wall* in any case—only we don't usually see them, for we haven't eyes to. . . . Looking at my bright blue pyjamas on the bed eight feet away, I saw that the blue was *edged with flame*: a narrow flickering, shifting nimbus, incredibly beautiful, which it filled me with delight to watch. Clear flame; golden-scarlet. Then I understood that this flame *was music*, that I was *seeing sound*."

Here is the account given by another observer of his experience under the influence of mescaline.[2] "I received two subcutaneous injections between nine and ten in the morning. . . . At about 11 a.m. changes in the *colour* of objects were noted and the increased intensity of after-images became disturbing. With closed eyes, visions of moving constantly changing patterns appeared and attracted the whole attention. Oriental tapestry, mosaic-like wall-papers, kaleidoscopic-coloured geometric patterns, lines in brilliant luminescent colours, or in black and white, etc. . . . The colours of real objects appeared more pure, more clean, untarnished by dirt. . . . There were also visual hallucinations unconnected with my conscious thinking, especially friendly animals, little demons and dwarfs, fairy-tale ornaments and mythology from the aquarium such as one sees sometimes on the walls of inns. The faces of people around me were slightly distorted as if drawn by a cartoonist, often with the emphasis on some small, humorous, but, nevertheless, rather characteristic feature."

Writers on the philosophical aspects of perception rarely concern themselves with illusions or hallucinations involving any other sense than vision, but if we are to learn about the status of hallucinations in general this is unduly restricting, and may be actually misleading, if there turn out to be certain features peculiar to hallucinations in the sphere of vision which, in the absence of information about other forms of hallucinations, might be taken to be characteristic of hallucinations in general. Let me, therefore, now describe the experiences of two patients who suffered from hallucinations of smell. One experienced what he described as "a smell of rubber burning" which would last for hours at a time. He said: "I would wake up at night and smell burning, and I woke my wife and said there is something on fire—and I'd heard of a beam in those old farmhouses smouldering for days. And then," he went on, "I realized it wasn't the house that was on fire—it was me!" I asked him how he discovered this, and he replied: "Well, when I went somewhere else and found I could still smell it." Another patient had her first attack of hallucination of smell while driving her car. Thinking the car battery was leaking she stopped the car to look at it. And here is the account which another patient gave me of her experience of a buzzing in the ears. "It sounded like the bombers coming over during the war. It was a long time before I found out it was me."

Disease of the brain may produce illusions and hallucinations over the whole range of sensory experience which do not differ in character from those which can be produced by the administration of drugs. Let me now quote a few examples of illusions and hallucinations occurring as part of the manifestations of an epileptic attack or elicited by electrical stimulation of the brain in the fully conscious patient.[3] First, here is an account of a visual illusion as part of an epileptic attack recorded by his doctor. "While I was visiting him this evening the patient said: "Wait a minute. You are getting bigger. The nurse is standing beside you. She is getting bigger. Watch me!' I asked, 'Are you having an attack now?' No reply." Then follows a description of the attack. And here is an account of an hallucination of hearing. "In these later attacks, she heard voices which seemed to be coming from her right. They were not the voices of her children. Indeed, she said she could not hear her children speak to her during an attack. Once, on getting up at night to go to the bathroom, she heard music. She thought it came from the radio in the living room. It was a song she had frequently heard on the radio. She could not hear the words." Another patient said that she would hear music at the beginning of her seizure "and the music was always the same, a lullaby her mother had sung, 'Hushabye my baby.' " When this patient's brain was stimulated she said "I hear people coming in; I hear music now, a funny little piece." Stimulation was continued. She became more talkative than usual, explaining that the music was something she had heard on the radio, that it was the theme song of a children's programme.

Now consider some illusions and hallucinations arising in connexion with awareness of the body. The simplest and commonest of these is the "phantom limb," which is the name for the persistent feeling of the presence of a limb which had been amputated. Phantom limbs must have been known to humanity ever since injury or warfare led to the loss of a part of the body. This strange experience is not limited to limbs, but can apply to many parts, including the nose or a tooth. The phenomenon interested Descartes, and Nelson, after losing his arm, had a phantom one, which for some reason he regarded as a proof of the existence of the soul. Of course a phantom limb can only be felt and not seen, but the feeling may be so convincing that a man who has a phantom leg may fall down because he attempts to stand on it. The subject may feel that he is able to move his phantom limb, and it may be the site of severe and persistent

pain. In most cases a painless phantom limb gradually
shortens and after a time disappears into the amputation
stump.

But amputation is not the only cause of phantom limbs. If
certain sensory nerve-paths between a normal limb and the
brain are interrupted, the patient may feel that he has a
second limb in a different place from the real one. Suppose
this happens in the case of an arm. Since the interruption of
the nerve-paths takes away the feeling from his arm, he now
says that he has one arm which he can see, but not feel, and
another arm which he can feel, but not see.

Drugs which cause hallucinations may produce the most
bizarre effects upon the subject's awareness of his body. One
who has taken mescaline said: "I felt my body particularly
plastic and minutely carved. At once I had a sensation as if
my foot was being taken off. Then I felt as if my head had
been turned about 180 degrees. . . . My feet turned spirals and
scrolls, my jaw was like a hook and my chest seemed to melt
away."[4] Not only may the body feel enlarged; it may enter
into a complicated scene. One subject, also under mescaline
and lying with his arms crossed, said: "My right arm is a
street with a group of toy soldiers. My left arm goes across
the street like a bridge and carries a railway."[5]

To complete this account of the perceptual changes produced by mescaline intoxication I must mention the occurrence of synaesthesiae, that is the irradiation of sensation
from one sense to another. For example, one subject found
that the colours of his visual hallucinations were altered by
changes in the rhythm of the music being played on the
radio. Mayer-Gross quotes an experience of a subject under
mescaline which illustrates what he calls not only "the peculiar
result of the synaesthetic perception, but also the inadequacy
of ordinary language for such experiences." "What I see, I
hear; what I smell, I think. I am music, I am the lattice-work.
I see an idea of mine going out of me into the lattice-work. . . .
I felt, saw, tasted and smelled the noise of the trumpet, was
myself the noise. . . . Everything was clear and absolutely
certain. All criticism is nonsense in the face of experience."

But lest it be thought that these results of the administration of drugs are quite remote from the experiences of normal people, let me quote Grey Walter's[6] observations on the effect of exposing normal individuals to a flickering light. At certain frequencies around ten per second some subjects see whirling spirals, whirlpools, explosions, Catherine wheels which do not correspond to any causal physical event. There may be organized hallucinations, and all sorts of emotions are experienced. Sometimes the sense of time is lost or disturbed. One subject said that he had been "pushed sideways in time"—yesterday was at one side, instead of behind, and tomorrow was off the port bow.

If I am to give a comprehensive account of hallucinations, that is to provide all the data which a philosophical explanation of them needs to take into account, there are some further points which I must add. An hallucination may be present to one sense, but not to another, as in the case of a phantom limb. Perhaps the best-known example of this is Macbeth's dagger.

> Is this a dagger which I see before me
> The handle toward my hand? Come, let me clutch thee.
> I have thee not, and yet I see thee still.
> Art thou not, fatal vision, sensible
> To feeling as to sight? or art thou but
> A dagger of the mind, a false creation,
> Proceeding from the heat-oppressed brain?

Similar experiences are common in psychiatry. On the other hand an hallucination may be present to more than one sense. For example, a person may think that he sees a coin on the floor. He may then stoop and pick up the hallucinatory coin and say that he can feel its milled edge with his finger. Or he may say that he sees a human figure and that the figure speaks to him, and he can hear its words. Probably the most elaborate hallucinatory experiences are those of so-called apparitions. Smythies[7] gives an excellent summary of the characteristics of these hallucinations. He says:

> The hallucinated object or person purports to be a physical object—i.e. it looks and behaves very like a physical

object or person. And "an apparition" usually looks solid, throws a proper shadow, gets smaller as it moves away from the observer, moves round the room with respect of the furniture, gets dimmer as it moves into the more dimly lit parts of the room, may speak to the observer or even touch him. In nearly one half of the reported cases the "apparition" has been seen by more than one observer at the same time—i.e. there are collective hallucinations. These features of this class of hallucinations may be summarized by stating that the internal and external organization of the hallucination *approaches* that of veridical perception. An "apparition" may be so "life-like" as to be frequently confused with the biological person it purports to be. They frequently satisfy the criteria by which we judge what is and what is not a veridical perception and are accepted as members of the class of veridical perceptions—at any rate for a time—although this membership is usually cancelled by subsequent experience, as when the apparition suddenly disappears or information is later obtained that the person hallucinated was actually at that time in a distant part of the country.

I have given a by no means exhaustive account of the rich variety of hallucinatory experiences, but I have described enough to be able to draw attention to certain points. First, no hard-and-fast line can be drawn introspectively between normal perception, illusions, and hallucinations. The subject under the influence of mescaline or lysergic acid describes modifications in the appearance of the objects around him. "The wall began to be covered with an incredibly beautiful series of patterns." "Looking at my bright blue pyjamas . . . I saw that the blue was edged with flame." "The colours of real objects appeared more fine." "The faces of people around me were slightly distorted." These experiences merge into others in which the change involved the nature of the object itself. "These stars (on the lampshade) began to be filled with colour. . . . One star, I now saw, was a very small (and wholly attractive) *turtle*. . . . These little turtles—stars—or highwaymen with two huge pistols!—lived and moved in their firmament of illumined paper." From this a step takes us to visual hallucinations which seem independent of any object in the environment—animals, demons, and dwarfs, for example—and finally to "visions" of coloured patterns seen with closed eyes.

Secondly, in describing illusions and hallucinations the subjects, whether normal or abnormal, frequently use the words "see," "hear," and "smell" and not the phrases "seem to see," "seem to hear," and "seem to smell." When I am describing my own experience of visual after-images it seems natural to say that I see them. I do not mean by that that I believe that I am seeing any physical object, but that the after-images have a sensory quality in common with the seeing of the object which has immediately preceded them, that they are describable in similar terms in respect of colour and spatial extension, and moreover they have some relationship to my eyes since they move when I move my eyes. Similarly the patient who had a visual illusion in an epileptic attack did not say: "You seem to be growing bigger," but "You are growing bigger." Thus the patient describing an illusion often uses the same terms with which he describes the reality. He does not discriminate the illusion as a sensory experience from the reality as a sensory experience, and he describes both in the same way. How, then, does he distinguish between them when he does so? By reasoning. He compares the appearance or behaviour of the illusory object with what he knows is its normal appearance or behaviour, and concludes that he is experiencing an illusion.

Thirdly, both the drug-induced illusions and the hallucinatory "apparitions" show that these abnormal experiences are often associated with a modification of normal perception such that the abnormal appearance is integrated into the subject's perception of his environment. When an apparition hides from view an object in front of which it is standing, or opens and passes through a door known to be locked, it provides the strongest evidence that the sense-data comprising the apparition and those comprising the environment possess the same perceptual status, and that those events, whatever they may be, which are causing the subject to see the apparition are at the same time appropriately modifying his perception of the rest of his environment. Perhaps I should add at this point that I am concerned with these phenomena purely as hallucinations and express no views as to the epistemological status of apparitions.

Now although there are many hallucinatory states which present themselves with the same sensory vividness as veridical perceptions, and of which the subject naturally, and in my view appropriately, says "I see," "I hear," or "I smell" so-and-so, there are other experiences which are usually and appropriately described by the subject with the words "I seemed to see," "I seemed to hear," or "I seemed to smell." The commonest example of this is a dream. If we relate our dreams, we commonly do so in some such words as Bottom's: "Methought I was,—and methought I had,—." Our account of our dreams is usually retrospective, though I do not know whether philosophers in their dreams give themselves an account of their experiences. But although in our dreams most of us have experiences which we describe in visual terms— and in what other terms could we discuss, for example, whether an object seen in a dream is coloured or not?—we do, looking back on a dream in memory, regard it as having a sensory quality which distinguishes it from a waking experience. And the same applies to visual imagery and visual memory in a subject who had these faculties strongly developed. However vividly he may see an object in his memory or in his imagination he is never likely to make the mistake of thinking he is seeing it in reality: he will recognize that he is seeing it in his "mind's eye." No doubt the perceptual character of the experience is only one reason for this: the subject knows that he is himself responsible for remembering, or for imagining, in a way in which he is not responsible for the appearance of things he perceives or his hallucinations. However, there are disorders of sleep in which the subject, who may be described as half-awake, fails to distinguish between the events of his dream and the reality of his environment which he also perceives. He may then, as it were, act out his dream in his ordinary surroundings.

This, though rare in adults, is by no means uncommon in a child awakening from a nightmare. In some mental disorders, too, the patient's fantasies may not have the vivid perceptual external location of hallucinations, but rather the quality of dreams or imagination mingling with the everyday environment. Thus, while there are many perceptual experiences in which a hallucination has sensory qualities indistinguishable to the subject from veridical perceptual experiences and which are naturally, and appropriately, described in the same terms, there are also both normal and abnormal mental states in which images may play a part which are not naturally or appropriately so described.

AUTHOR'S NOTES

[1] R. H. Ward, *A Drug-taker's Notes* (London, 1957).

[2] W. Mayer-Gross, "Experimental Psychoses and other Mental Abnormalities produced by Drugs," *British Medical Journal*, ii (1951), p. 317.

[3] The following quotations are taken from W. Penfield and H. Jasper's *Epilepsy and the Functional Anatomy of the Human Brain* (London, 1954).

[4] Quoted by E. Guttmann in "Artificial Psychoses produced by Mescaline," *Journal of Mental Science*, lxxxii (1936), p. 203.

[5] Quoted by Mayer-Gross (2) above.

[6] W. Grey Walter, *The Living Brain* (London, 1953), p. 68.

[7] J. R. Smythies, "A Logical and Cultural Analysis of Hallucinatory Sense Experience," *Journal of Mental Science*, cii (1956), p. 336.

4. COLOURS AND LIGHT WAVES

HERMANN VON HELMHOLTZ

Hermann von Helmholtz (1821–1894) was one of the most brilliant and versatile scientists of the nineteenth century. He made substantial contributions to physiology and to several branches of physics, and invented the opthalmoscope; but he is noted above all for his outstanding work on the physics and physiology of the senses, especially his treatise *Physiological Optics*. Not content with original research, he was well versed in mathematics and the philosophy of science and was a most successful popularizer of scientific knowledge. In this selection we have his own statement of the famous Young-Helmholtz theory of colour vision, together with his general reflections on the philosophical significance of the relation of colour to light-waves. There is no universally agreed theory of colour vision, but this one, with extensions, is widely held; and if modern research shows the facts are a little more complex that Helmholtz indicates, the complexities only reinforce his philosophical conclusions. The selection is taken from his *Popular Lectures on Scientific Subjects,* translated by E. Atkinson, P. H. Pye-Smith and others (Longmans, Green and Co., 1889).

Those undulations which strongly affect our eyes, and which we call light, excite the impression of different colours, according to the length of the waves. The undulations with the longest waves appear to us red; and as the length of the waves gradually diminishes they seem to be golden yellow, yellow, green, blue, violet, the last colour being that of the illuminating rays which have the smallest wave-length. This series of colours is universally known in the rainbow. We also see it if we look towards the light through a glass prism, and a diamond sparkles with hues which follow in the same order. In passing through transparent prisms, the primitive beam of white light, which consists of a multitude of rays of various colour and various wave-lengths, is decomposed by the different degree of refraction of its several parts; and thus each of its component hues appears separately.

When several of these colours are mixed together, they give the impression of a new colour, which generally seems more or less white. If they were all mingled in precisely the same proportions in which they are combined in the sunlight, they would give the impression of perfect white. According as the rays of greatest, middle, or least wave-length predominate in such a mixture, it appears as reddish-white, greenish-white, bluish-white, and so on.

Everyone who has watched a painter at work knows that two colours mixed together give a new one. Now, although the results of the mixture of coloured light differ in many particulars from those of the mixture of pigments, yet on the whole the appearance to the eye is similar in both cases. If we allow two different coloured lights to fall at the same time upon a white screen, or upon the same part of our retina, we see only a single compound colour, more or less different from the two original ones. The most striking difference between the mixture of pigments and that of coloured light is, that while painters make green by mixing blue and yellow pigments, the union of blue and yellow rays of light produces white.[1] The number of hues which we can recognize is much smaller than that of the various possible combinations of rays with different wave-lengths which external objects can convey to our eyes. The retina cannot distinguish between the white which is produced by the union of scarlet and bluish-green light, and that which is composed of yellowish-green and violet, or of yellow and ultramarine blue, or of red, green, and violet, or of all the colours of the spectrum united. All these combinations appear identically as white; and yet, from a physical point of view, they are very different. In fact, the only resemblance between the several combinations just mentioned is, that they are indistinguishable to the human eye. For instance, a surface illuminated with red and bluish-green light would come out black in a photograph; while another lighted with yellowish-green and violet would appear very bright, although both surfaces alike seem to the eye to be simply white. Again, if we successively illuminate coloured objects with white beams of light of various composition, they will appear different coloured. And whenever we decompose two such beams by a prism, or look at them through a coloured glass, the difference between them at once becomes evident.

Other colours, also, especially when they are not strongly pronounced, may, like pure white light, be composed of very different mixtures, and yet appear indistinguishable to the eye, while in every other property, physical or chemical, they are entirely distinct.

Newton first showed how to represent the system of colours distinguishable to the eye in a simple diagrammatic form; and by the same means it is comparatively easy to demonstrate the law of the combination of colours. The primary colours of the spectrum are arranged in a series around the circumference of a circle, beginning with red, and by imperceptible degrees passing through the various hues of the rainbow to violet. The red and violet are united by shades of purple, which on the one side pass off to the indigo and blue tints, and on the other through crimson and scarlet to orange. The middle of the circle is left white, and on lines which run from the centre to the circumference are represented the various tints which can be produced by diluting the full colours of the circumference until they pass into white. A colour-disc of this kind shows all the varieties of hue which can be produced with the same amount of light.

It will now be found possible so to arrange the places of the several colours in this diagram, and the quantity of light which each reflects, that when we have ascertained the resultants of two colours of different known strength of light (in the same way as we might determine the centre of gravity of two bodies of different known weights), we shall then find their combination-colour at the "centre of gravity" of the two amounts of light. That is to say, that in a properly constructed colour-disc, the combination-colour of any two colours will be found upon a straight line drawn from between them; and compound colours which contain more of one than of the other component hue, will be found in that portion nearer to the former, and further from the latter.

We find, however, when we have drawn our diagram, that those colours of the spectrum which are most saturated[2] in nature and which must therefore be placed at the greatest distance from the central white, will not arrange themselves in the form of a circle. The circumference of the diagram presents three projections corresponding to the red, the green, and the violet, so that the colour circle is more properly a triangle, with the corners rounded off as seen in the diagram. The continuous line represents the curve of the colours of the spectrum, and the small circle in the middle the white. At the corners are the three colours I have mentioned, and the sides of the triangle show the transitions from red through yellow into green, from green through bluish-green and ultramarine to violet, and from violet through purple to scarlet.

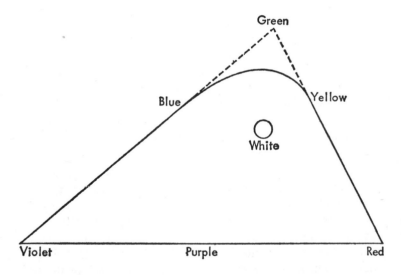

Newton used the diagram of the colours of the spectrum (in a somewhat different form from that just given) only as a convenient way of representing the facts to the eye; but recently Maxwell has succeeded in demonstrating the strict and even quantitative accuracy of the principles involved in the construction of this diagram. His method is to produce combinations of colours on swiftly rotating discs, painted of various tints in sectors. When such a disc is turned rapidly round, so that the eye can no longer follow the separate hues, they melt into a uniform combination-colour, and the quantity of light which belongs to each can be directly measured by the breadth of the sector of the circle it occupies. Now the combination-colours which are produced in this manner are exactly those which would result if the same qualities of coloured light illuminated the same surface continuously, as can be experimentally proved. Thus have the relations of size and number been introduced into the apparently inaccessible region of colours, and their differences in quality have been reduced to relations of quantity.[3]

I said above that a properly constructed colour-disc approaches a triangle in its outline. Let us suppose for a moment that it is an exact rectilinear triangle, as made by the dotted lines in our diagram; how far this differs from the actual conditions we shall have afterwards to point out. Let the colours red, green, and violet be placed at the corners, then we see the law which was mentioned above: namely, that all the colours in the interior and on the sides of the triangle are components of the three at its corners. It follows that *all differences of hue depend upon combinations in different proportion of the three primary colours*. It is best to consider the three just named as primary; the old ones, red, yellow, and blue are inconvenient, and were only chosen from experience of painters' colours.

We shall better understand the remarkable fact that we are able to refer all the varieties in the composition of external light to mixtures of three primitive colours, if in this respect we compare the eye with the ear.

Sound, as I mentioned before, is like light in that it spreads by waves. In the case of sound also, we have to distinguish waves of various length which produce upon our ear impressions of different quality. We recognize the long waves as low notes, the short as high-pitched, and the ear may receive at once many waves of sound—that is to say, many notes. But here these do not melt into compound notes in the same way that colours, when perceived at the same time and place, melt into compound colours. The eye cannot tell the difference, if we substitute orange for red and yellow; but if we hear the notes C and E sounded at the same time, we cannot put D instead of them, without entirely changing the impression upon the ear. The most complicated harmony of a full orchestra becomes changed to our perception if we alter any one of its notes. No accord (or consonance of several tones) is, at least for the practised ear, completely like another, composed of different tones; whereas, if the ear perceived musical tones as the eye colours, every accord might be completely represented by combining only three constant notes, one very low, one very high, and one intermediate, simply changing the relative strength of these three primary notes to produce all possible musical effects.

In reality we find that an accord only remains unchanged to the ear, when the strength of each separate tone which it contains remains unchanged. Accordingly, if we wish to describe it exactly and completely, the strength of each of its component tones must be exactly stated.

In the same way, the physical nature of a particular kind of light can only be fully ascertained by measuring and noting the amount of light of each of the simple colours which it contains. But in sunlight, in the light of most of the stars, and in flames, we find a continuous transition of colours into one another through numberless intermediate gradations. Accordingly, we must ascertain the amount of light of an infinite number of compound rays if we would arrive at an exact physical knowledge of sun or star light. In the sensations of the eye we need distinguish for this purpose only the varying intensities of three components.

The practised musician is able to catch the separate notes of the various instruments among the complicated harmonies of an entire orchestra, but the optician cannot directly ascertain the composition of light by means of the eye; he must make use of the prism to decompose the light for him. As soon, however, as this is done, the composite character of light becomes apparent, and he can then distinguish the light of separate fixed stars from one another by the dark and bright lines which the spectrum shows him, and can recognize what chemical elements are contained in flames which are met with on the earth, or even in the intense heat of the sun's atmosphere, in the fixed stars or in the nebulae. This fact that light derived from each separate source carries with it certain permanent physical peculiarities is the foundation of spectrum analysis.

There is an extremely interesting and not very uncommon defect of sight which is known as colour-blindness.[4] In this condition the differences of colour are reduced to a still more simple system than that described above; namely, to combinations of only two primary colours. Persons so affected are called *colour-blind,* because they confound certain hues which appear very different to ordinary eyes. At the same time they distinguish other colours, and that quite as accurately, or even (as it seems) rather more accurately, than ordinary people. They are usually "red-blind"; that is to say, there is no red in their system of colours, and accordingly they see no difference which is produced by the addition of red. All tints are for them varieties of blue and green, or, as they call it, yellow. Accordingly scarlet, flesh-colour, white, and bluish-green appear to them to be identical, or at the utmost to differ in brightness. The same applies to crimson, violet, and blue, and to red, orange, yellow, and green. The scarlet flowers of the geranium have for them exactly the same colour as its leaves. They cannot distinguish between the red and the green signals of trains. They cannot see the red end of the spectrum at all. Very full scarlet appears to them almost black, so that a red-blind Scotch clergyman went to buy scarlet cloth for his gown, thinking it was black.

In this particular of discrimination of colours, we find remarkable inequalities in different parts of the retina. In the first place, all of us are red-blind in the outermost part of our field of vision. A geranium-blossom when moved backwards and forwards just within the field of sight, is only recognized as a moving object. Its colour is not seen, so that if it is waved in front of a mass of leaves of the same plant it cannot be distinguished from them in hue. In fact, all red colours appear much darker when viewed indirectly.

In the second place, the middle of the retina, just around the central pit, is coloured yellow. This makes all blue light appear somewhat darker in the centre of the field of sight. The effect is particularly striking with mixtures of red and greenish-blue, which appear white when looked at directly, but acquire a blue tint when viewed at a slight distance from the middle of the field; and, on the other hand, when they appear white here, are red to direct vision. These inequalities of the retina are rectified by the constant movements of the eye. We know from the pale and indistinct colours of the external world as usually seen, what impressions of indirect vision correspond to those of direct; and we thus learn which they *would* make on us if seen directly. The result is, that only unusual combinations and unusual or special direction of attention enable us to recognize the difference of which I have been speaking.

The theory of colours, with all these marvellous and complicated relations, was a riddle which Goethe in vain attempted to solve; nor were we physicists and physiologists more successful. I include myself in the number; for I long toiled at the task, without getting any nearer my object, until I at last discovered that a wonderfully simple solution had been discovered at the beginning of this century, and had been in print ever since for anyone to read who chose. This solution was found and published by the same Thomas Young who first showed the right method of arriving at the interpretation of Egyptian hieroglyphics. He was one of the most acute men who ever lived, but had the misfortune to be too far in advance of his contemporaries.

In proceeding to explain the theory of colours proposed by him, I beg the reader to notice that the conclusions afterwards to be drawn upon the nature of the sensations of sight are quite independent of what is hypothetical in this theory.

Dr. Young supposes that there are in the eye three kinds

of nerve-fibres, the first of which, when irritated in any way, produces the sensation of red, the second the sensation of green, and the third that of violet. He further assumes that the first are excited most strongly by the waves of ether of greatest length; the second, which are sensitive to green light, by the waves of middle length; while those which convey impressions of violet are acted upon only by the shortest vibrations of ether. Accordingly, at the red end of the spectrum the excitation of those fibres which are sensitive to that colour predominates; hence the appearance of this part as red. Further on there is added an impression upon the fibres sensitive to green light, and thus results the mixed sensation of yellow. In the middle of the spectrum, the nerves sensitive to green become much more excited than the other two kinds, and accordingly green is the predominant impression. As soon as this becomes mixed with violet the result is the colour known as blue; while at the most highly refracted end of the spectrum the impression produced on the fibres which are sensitive to violet light overcomes every other.

Just as the difference of sensation of light and warmth depends demonstrably upon whether the rays of the sun fall upon nerves of sight or nerves of feeling, so it is supposed in Young's hypothesis that the difference of sensation of colours depends simply upon whether one or the other kind of nervous fibres are more strongly affected. When all three kinds are equally excited, the result is the sensation of white light.

The phenomena that occur in red-blindness must be referred to a condition in which the one kind of nerves, which are sensitive to red rays, are incapable of excitation. It is possible that this class of fibres are wanting, or at least very sparingly distributed, along the edge of the retina, even in the normal human eye.

It must be confessed that both in men and in quadrupeds we have at present no anatomical basis for this theory of colours,[5] but Max Shultze has discovered a structure in birds and reptiles which manifestly corresponds with what we should expect to find. In the eyes of many of these animals there are found among the rods of the retina a number which contain a red drop of oil in their anterior end, that namely which is turned towards the light; while other rods contain a yellow drop, and others none at all. Now there can be no doubt that red light will reach the rods with a red drop much better than light of any other colour, while yellow and green light, on the contrary, will find easiest entrance to the rods with the yellow drop. Blue light would be shut off almost completely from both, but would affect the colourless rods all the more effectually. We may therefore with great probability regard these rods as the terminal organs of those nervous fibres which respectively convey impressions of red, of yellow, and of blue light.

It remains to reply to an objection against Young's theory of colour. I mentioned above that the outline of the colour-disc, which marks the position of the most saturated colours (those of the spectrum), approaches to a triangle in form; but our conclusions upon the theory of the three primary colours depend upon a perfect rectilinear triangle inclosing the complete colour-system, for only in that case is it possible to produce all possible tints by various combinations of the three primary colours at the angles. It must, however, be remembered that the colour-disc only includes the entire series of colours which actually occur in nature, while our theory has to do with the analysis of our subjective sensations of colour. We need then only assume that actual coloured light does not produce sensations of absolutely pure colour; that red, for instance, even when completely freed from all admixture of white light, still does not excite those nervous fibres alone which are sensitive to impressions of red, but also, to a very slight degree, those which are sensitive to green, and perhaps to a still smaller extent those which are sensitive to violet rays. If this is so, then the sensation which the purest red light produces in the eye is still not the purest sensation of red which we can conceive of as possible. This sensation could only be called forth by a fuller, purer, more saturated red than has ever been seen in this world.

It is possible to verify this conclusion. We are able to

produce artificially a sensation of the kind I have described. This fact is not only important as a complete answer to a possible objection to Young's theory, but is also, as will readily be seen, of the greatest importance for understanding the real value of our sensations of colour. In order to describe the experiment I must first give an account of a new series of phenomena.

The process of fatigue as the result of nervous action takes place in the eye as well as other organs. When the entire retina becomes tired, as when we spend some time in the open air in brilliant sunshine, it becomes insensible to weaker light, so that if we pass immediately into a dimly lighted room we see nothing at first; we are blinded, as we call it, by the previous brightness. After a time the eye recovers itself, and at last we are able to see, and even read, by the same dim light which at first appeared complete darkness.

It is thus that fatigue of the entire retina shows itself. But it is possible for separate parts of that membrane to become exhausted, if they alone have received a strong light. If we look steadily for some time at any bright object, surrounded by a dark background—it is necessary to look steadily in order that the image may remain quiet upon the retina, and thus fatigue a sharply defined portion of its surface,—and afterwards turn our eyes upon a uniform dark-grey surface, we see projected upon it an *after-image* of the bright object we were looking at just before, with the same outline but with reversed illumination. What was dark appears bright, and what was bright dark, like the first negative of a photographer. By carefully fixing the attention, it is possible to produce very elaborate after-images, so much so that occasionally even printing can be distinguished in them. This phenomenon is the result of a local fatigue of the retina. Those parts of the membrane upon which the bright light fell before are now less sensitive to the light of the dark-grey background than the neighbouring regions, and there now appears a dark spot upon the really uniform surface, corresponding in extent to the surface of the retina which before received the bright light.

(I may here remark that illuminated sheets of white paper are sufficiently bright to produce this after-image. If we look at much brighter objects—at flames, or at the sun itself—the effect becomes complicated. The strong excitement of the retina does not pass away immediately, but produces a direct or positive after-image, which at first unites with the negative or indirect one produced by the fatigue of the retina. Besides this the effects of the different colours of white light differ both in duration and intensity, so that the after-images become coloured, and the whole phenomenon much more complicated.)

It is possible to produce a partial fatigue of the retina in another way. We may tire it for certain colours only, by exposing either the entire retina, or a portion of it, for a certain time (from half a minute to five minutes) to one and the same colour. According to Young's theory, only one or two kinds of the optic nerve fibres will then be fatigued, those namely which are sensitive to impressions of the colour in question. All the rest will remain unaffected. The result is, that when the after-image arising from the perception of red, for example, appears upon a grey background, the uniformly mixed light of the latter can only produce sensations of green and violet in the part of the retina which has become fatigued by red light. This part is made red-blind for the time. The after-image accordingly appears of a bluish-green, the complementary colour to red.

It is by this means that we are able to produce in the retina the pure and primitive sensations of saturated colours. If, for instance, we wish to see pure red, we fatigue a part of our retina by the bluish-green of the spectrum, which is the complementary colour of red. We thus make this part at once green-blind and violet-blind. We then throw the after-image upon the red of as perfect a prismatic spectrum as possible; the image immediately appears in full and burning red, while the red light of the spectrum which surrounds it, although the purest that the world can offer, now seems to the unfatigued part of the retina less saturated than the after-image, and looks as if it were covered by a whitish mist.

We have already seen enough to answer the question whether it is possible to maintain the natural and innate conviction that the quality of our sensations, and especially our sensations of sight, give us a true impression of corresponding qualities in the outer world. It is clear that they do not. The question was really decided by Johannes Müller's deduction from well-ascertained facts of the law of specific nervous energy. Whether the rays of the sun appear to us as colour, or as warmth, does not at all depend upon their own properties, but simply upon whether they excite the fibres of the optic nerve, or those of the skin. Pressure upon the eyeball, a feeble current of electricity passed through it, a narcotic drug carried to the retina by the blood are capable of exciting the sensation of light just as well as the sunbeams. The most complete difference offered by our several sensations, that, namely, between those of sight, of hearing, of taste, of smell, and of touch—this deepest of all distinctions, so deep that it is impossible to draw any comparison of likeness, or unlikeness, between the sensations of colour and of musical tones— does not, as we now see, at all depend upon the nature of the external object, but solely upon the central connections of the nerves which are affected.[6]

We now see that the question whether within the special range of each particular sense it is possible to discover a coincidence between its objects and the sensations they produce is of only subordinate interest. What colour the waves of ether shall appear to us when they are perceived by the optic nerve depends upon their length. The system of naturally visible colours offers us a series of varieties in the composition of light, but the number of those varieties is wonderfully reduced from an unlimited number to only three. Inasmuch as the most important property of the eye is its minute appreciation of locality, and as it is so much more perfectly organized for this purpose than the ear, we may well be content that it is capable of recognizing comparatively few differences in quality of light; the ear, which in the latter respect is so enormously better provided, has scarcely any power of appreciating differences of locality. But it is certainly matter for astonishment to anyone who trusts to the direct information of his natural senses, that neither the limits within which the spectrum affects our eyes nor the differences of colour which alone remain as the simplified effect of all the actual differences of light in kind, should have any other demonstrable import than for the sense of sight. Light which is precisely the same to our eyes, may in all other physical and chemical effects be completely different. Lastly, we find that the unmixed primitive elements of all our sensations of colour (the perception of the simple primary tints) cannot be produced by any kind of external light in the natural unfatigued condition of the eye. These elementary sensations of colour can only be called forth by artificial preparation of the organ, so that, in fact, they only exist as subjective phenomena. We see, therefore, that as to any correspondence in kind of external light with the sensations it produces, there is only one bond of connection between them, a bond which at first sight may seem slender enough but is in fact quite sufficient to lead to an infinite number of most useful applications. This law of correspondence between what is subjective and objective in vision is as follows:—

Similar light produces under like conditions a like sensation of colour. Light which under the conditions excites unlike sensations of colour is dissimilar.

When two relations correspond to one another in this manner, the one is a *sign* for the other. Hitherto the notions of a "sign" and of an "image" or representation have not been carefully enough distinguished in the theory of perception; and this seems to me to have been the source of numberless mistakes and false hypotheses. In an "image" the representation must be of the same kind as that which is represented. Indeed, it is only so far an image as it is like in kind. A statue is an image of a man, so far as its form reproduces his: even if it is executed on a smaller scale, every dimension will be represented in proportion. A picture is an image or representation of the original, first, because it represents the colours of the latter by similar colours, secondly, because it represents a part of its relations in space—those, namely, which belong to perspective—by corresponding relations in space.

Functional cerebral activity and the mental conceptions which go with it may be "images" of actual occurrences in the outer world, so far as the former represent the sequence in time of the latter, so far as they represent likeness of objects by likeness of signs—that is, a regular arrangement by a regular arrangement.

This is obviously sufficient to enable the understanding to deduce what is constant from the varied changes of the external world and to formulate it as a notion or a law. But not only uneducated persons who are accustomed to trust blindly to their senses, even the educated, who know that their senses may be deceived, are inclined to demur to so complete a want of any closer correspondence in kind between actual objects and the sensations they produce than the law I have just expounded. For instance, natural philosophers long hesitated to admit the identity of the rays of light and of heat, and exhausted all possible means of escaping a conclusion which seemed to contradict the evidence of their senses.

We must not be led astray by confounding the notions of a *phenomenon* and an *appearance*. The colours of objects are phenomena caused by certain real differences in their constitution. They are, according to the scientific as well as to the uninstructed view, no mere appearance, even though the way in which they appear depends chiefly upon the constitution of our nervous system. A "deceptive appearance" is the result of the normal phenomena of one object being confounded with those of another. But the sensation of colour is by no means a deceptive appearance. There is no other way in which colour can appear; so that there is nothing which we could describe as the normal phenomenon, in distinction from the impressions of colour received through the eye.

Here the principal difficulty seems to me to lie in the notion of *quality*. All difficulty vanishes as soon as we clearly understand that each quality or property of a thing is, in reality, nothing else but its capability of exercising certain effects upon other things. These actions either go on between similar parts of the same body, and so produce the differences of its aggregate conditions; or they proceed from one body upon another, as in the case of chemical reactions; or they produce their effect on our organs of special sense, and are there recognized as *sensations,* as those of sight, with which we have now to do. Any of these actions is called a "property," when its object is understood without being expressly mentioned. Thus, when we speak of the "solubility" of a substance we mean its behaviour towards *water;* when we speak of its "weight," we mean its attraction to *the earth;* and in the same way we may correctly call a substance "blue," understanding, as a tacit assumption, that we are only speaking of its action upon a *normal eye.*

But if what we call a property always implies an action of one thing on another, then a property or quality can never depend upon the nature of one agent alone, but exists only in relation to, and dependent on, the nature of some second object, which is acted upon.[7] Hence, there is really no meaning in talking of properties of light which belong to it absolutely, independent of all other objects, and which we may expect to find represented in the sensations of the human eye. The notion of such properties is a contradiction in itself. They cannot possibly exist, and therefore we cannot expect to find any coincidence of our sensations of colour with qualities of light.

EDITOR'S NOTES

[1] The difference is due to the absorption of light by paints. Yellow paint looks yellow because it absorbs blue light and reflects red and green whose combined effect on the percipient is that of yellow light, i.e. a yellow sense-datum; blue paint absorbs yellow and red light, so that when blue and yellow paint are mixed, only green light is unabsorbed and reflected.

[2] The saturation of a colour is its purity of tint; the more saturated it is, the less it is diluted with white light; red, for example, is more saturated than pink, for pink is red diluted with white. All natural colours show some dilution.

[3] Does this introduction of numerical values spoil the primary-secondary quality distinction? [Cf. S.15] Probably not, for one

measures and compares not colours but coloured *areas* on the disc and hence degrees of sensory excitation.

[4] This explanation needs to be considered with the Young-Helmholtz theory outlined later. Several different forms of colour-blindness occur; their causation is a matter of controversy and no one theory of colour vision seems to explain all satisfactorily. Some authorities, supporting Young-Helmholtz, claim that the two most common forms (in both of which red and green are not distinguished) are due to failure of the red receptors to react to stimuli or of the red and green receptors to react differentially; in much rarer cases the violet mechanism fails (and blue is not seen properly), and there may be a partial failure of red or green which reduces ability to match colours. Others state that in one kind of red/green blindness yellow is actually seen (not green called yellow, as Helmholtz suggests) and claim that this requires the "opponens-pairs" theory (of Hering or Ladd-Franklin); on this there are still three kinds of receptors, but one causes red or green sense-data according to stimulation, one yellow or blue, and one black or white; in common colour-blindness the first is faulty. In contrast, recent experiments by Land suggest that all sensed colours can be produced by a combination of two wave-lengths of light (or two bands of wave-lengths) not three; but his experiments are not generally regarded as ruling out the tri-chromatic theories.

[5] There is now said to be evidence of red-sensitive and green-sensitive pigments in the cones of the fovea of the eye, but no blue- or violet-sensitive one has yet been found.

[6] Sound waves (compression waves in air) of course differ appreciably from the electro-magnetic waves responsible for light and heat, and the stimuli for smell and taste differ even more greatly. The real point seems to be that the impulses travelling along nerves from the sense organs to the brain are of the same basic type in each case [see S.2 p. 42].

[7] Cf. S.16

Special references on colour. Besides the general Scientific and Psychological Works mentioned in the Bibliography (p. 304), note: (1) an up-to-date and fact-filled survey of the science of colour is Robert W. Burnham, R. M. Hanes, and C. J. Bartleson: *Color: A Guide to the Basic Facts and Concepts* (New York: Wiley 1963); (2) the reference for Land's experiments is E. H. Land, "Experiments in Color Vision," *Scientific American*, Vol. 200, No. 5 (May 1959), pp. 84–99; (3) their philosophical significance is discussed by J. J. C. Smart in an article "Colours" in *Philosophy*, XXXVI (1961), pp. 128 ff. and in his book, *Philosophy and Scientific Realism* (London, 1963).

5. WHY DO THINGS LOOK AS THEY DO?

KURT KOFFKA

Kurt Koffka (1886–1941) was a leader of the Gestalt psychologists who have made a great impact on the psychological study of perception. In this passage we have a stimulating statement from outside philosophy of issues which face, or should face, any philosophy of perception. The first answer he criticizes is that of Naïve Realism; the second contains an assumption to which Representative Realism is prone, while even modern discussions of the argument from illusion often fail to take account of the facts about constancy that he adduces; and lastly we get a psychological slant on the age-old question of the relation of sensation and perception. The selection comes with some abridgement from Koffka's well-known *Principles of Gestalt Psychology* (London: Routledge and Kegan Paul, 1935), pp. 76–89 and 95–6.

The first answer. Why do things look as they do? A first answer would be: things look as they look because they are what they are.

Although this answer seems banal, it is not only utterly inadequate, but in many cases literally wrong. Let us single out a few aspects of behavioural things and compare them with the real ones. The pen with which I am writing is a unit in my behavioural environment and so is the real pen in the geographical.[1] So far, so good. But if our proposition were true, to be a real unit would be a necessary and sufficient condition for a thing to be also a behavioural unit. But it is easy to show that it is neither necessary nor sufficient. If it were a necessary condition, it would mean: to every unit in my behavioural field there corresponds a unit in the geographical environment; for if behavioural units could exist without corresponding geographical ones, then the existence of the latter would no longer be necessary for the existence of the former. Nothing, however, is easier to point out than behavioural units to which no geographical units correspond. Look at Fig. 1. In your behavioural field it is a unit, a cross; in reality, in the geographical environment, there is no cross, there are just eleven dots in a certain geometrical arrangement, but there is no connection between them that could make them a unit. This is, of course, true of all pictures, equally true of the stellar constellations like Charles's Wain, a case which Köhler has chosen as an illustration of this point.

FIG. 1

If the visible existence of real units were the *sufficient* condition for the appearance of a behavioural unit it would mean that whenever our eyes were directed on a physical unit, we should perceive a behavioural one. But this is not true either. Certainly, in most cases, this correspondence exists, but there are exceptions. As a matter of fact, it is possible to interfere with the real units in such a way that they will no longer look like units, an effect which we try to produce when we want to conceal certain well-known objects. If a gun is covered with paint in such a way that one part of it will "fuse" with the bole of a tree, another with the leaves, a third with the ground, then the beholder will no longer see a unit, the gun, but a multiplicity of much less important objects. Camouflage was an art well developed during the war, when even big ships were destroyed as real units in the behavioural world of the scouting enemy. Thus existence of a real unity is neither the necessary nor the sufficient cause of behavioural unity.

If we choose size as the aspect in which we should find correspondence we see at once that no direct relation between real and apparent size can exist, for the moon looks large on the horizon and small on the zenith. And even for the aspect of motion it is easy to prove that the existence, within the field of vision, of real motion is neither a necessary nor a sufficient condition for the perception of motion. It is not a necessary condition, for we can see motion when no real motion occurs, as on the cinematographic screen, but neither is it sufficient, for apart from the fact that too slow and too fast real motions produce no perception of motion, there are many cases where the apparently moving object is really at rest, as the moon that seems to float through the clouds.

We forbear discussing other aspects because our material is sufficient to prove the first answer to our question wrong. That things are what they are does not explain why they look as they look.

Before we discuss another answer to our question we may for a moment consider what it would mean if the first answer were right. If things looked as they do because they are what they are, then the relation between the behavioural and the geographical environment would be simple indeed. Then for all practical purposes we could substitute the latter for the former. Conversely, since we know that the answer is wrong, we must guard against this confusion, which is not as easily avoided as one might think. To show how a disregard of our warning has influenced psychological theory, we will formulate our conclusion in still another manner. If things looked as they do because they are what they are, then perception would not contain in its very make-up a cognitive problem. Perception would, barring certain unusual conditions, be cognitive of the geographical environment. A cognitive problem might arise in the field of generalized thought, but as long as we remained in the field of direct perception we ought to be face to face with objective reality. The proposition, included in many philosophical systems, that the senses cannot lie, is a special form of this more general idea. To be sure the existence of special cases where perception was deceptive was generally admitted. But these cases were treated as exceptions to the general rule, and for this reason the so-called geometric optical illusions received so much attention in the development of psychology. And when one reads the older literature on the subject, and some of the recent too, one will find explanations of this kind: if of two equal lines, one looks longer than the other, then we must look for special conditions which mislead our *judgement* about the relative length of these lines. Remove these distracting circumstances and the judgement will be correct, the normal state of affairs, in which the behavioural world corresponds to the geographical one, will be re-established. That is to say, illusory perceptions were not accorded the same rank as non-illusory ones; they presented a special problem, whereas the normal appearance presented no problem at all. This distinction between two kinds of perception, normal and illusory, disappears as a psychological distinction as soon as one becomes thoroughly aware of the fallacy which it implies, much as it may remain as an epistemological distinction. For each thing we have to ask the same question, "Why does it look as it does?" whether it looks "right" or "wrong."

These last considerations ought to have shown that our refutation of the first answer is not so banal as might have been thought. At the start it might well have been argued: How can the first answer be right, when the geographical things are not in direct contact with the organism? When I see a table, this table *qua* table does not affect my senses at all; they are affected by processes which have their origin in the sun or an artificial source of light, and which are only modified by the table before they excite the rods and cones in our retinae. Therefore, these processes, the light waves, and not the geographical objects, are the direct causes of our perceptions, and consequently we cannot expect a very close relationship between behavioural and geographical things. For the light waves do not depend only upon the things *qua* things, but also upon the nature of the source of light (which only in the case of self-luminous bodies belongs to them as their own property) and on the position of the things with regard to our own bodies. This last relation is regulated by the laws of perspective, the first by laws of light absorption and reflection. But perspective, light absorption, and reflection remain outside our organisms. The retinae receive a pattern of excitations, and it can make no difference to the retinae how these excitations have been produced. If, without a table and even without light (for instance, by electrical stimulation of the rods and cones), we could produce the same pattern of excitation with the same curvature of the lenses which is ordinarily produced on our retinae when we fixate a table, then the person on whose retinae these excitations were produced should and would see a table. This leads us to introduce a new terminological distinction. The causes of the excitations of our sense organs are called stimuli. We see now that this word has two different meanings which must be clearly distinguished from each other: on the one hand the table in the geographical environment can be called a stimulus for our perception of a table; on the other hand the excitations to which the light rays coming from the table give rise are called the stimuli for our perception. Let us call the first the *distant* stimulus, the second the *proximal* stimuli. Then we can say that our question why things look as they do must find its answer not in terms of the distant, but of the proximal stimuli. . . .

The second answer thus is: things look as they do because the proximal stimuli are what they are. Now in its broadest interpretation this proposition is certainly true, but the interpretation usually given to it is distinctly limited and therefore false. In the widest interpretation our proposition means no more than this: any change in the proximal stimulation will, provided it be not too small, produce *some* change in the look of things, but *what kind* of change in the behavioural world will follow upon a change in the proximal stimulation cannot be derived from our proposition; whereas in the narrower interpretation the proposition also contains implicitly a statement about the kind of this change. Two objects project retinal images of different size on our retinae and appear to be at the same distance. Then the one which corresponds to the larger retinal image will look larger. We see two adjacent surfaces at an equal distance in front of us, the one looks a lighter, the other a darker grey; then the retinal image corresponding to the former will contain more light than that of the latter. From these examples two conclusions might be drawn: the larger the retinal image, the larger the perceived object, and the greater the intensity of the image the more white will the object look; consequently when I change the stimulus corresponding to one object by making it smaller, the object should look smaller too, and if I reduce the intensity of stimulation the object should look blacker. These conclusions, which have been actually accepted as axioms of sense psychology, will seem very plausible. But neither do they follow from our examples, nor are they true. They do not follow from our examples because they only take in a part of the conditions of these examples and they are continually contradicted by the facts. Look at a white surface and then reduce the illumination of this surface; for a long time the surface will remain white, and only when you have reduced your illumination to a very low point will it become greyish. As a matter of fact a surface which still looks white under a low illumination may send much less light into our eyes than a black surface in good illumination. Disregard for the moment such plausible explanations as that when the light is decreased the pupil dilates so as to allow more of the incoming light to fall on our retinae, and that simultaneously the sensitivity of our retinae increases so as to make the effect of light greater. Both these factors, which are admittedly real, have been ruled out as sufficient explanations of our effect, so for simplicity's sake we neglect them altogether in our present discussion. Have we then shown that a change in the stimulus, in our case a diminution of light, has no effect at all on the look of things? If we had, we should have contradicted our general interpretation of the proposition: things look as they do because the proximal stimuli are what they are, an interpretation which we have accepted. But we have shown no such thing; we have only shown that the particular effect which would follow from the narrower interpretation of our proposition has failed to materialize. But there is an effect notwithstanding. For when the illumination is reduced, we become aware of a *darkening* of the *room*. Comparing this case with our former example we see that a change in the intensity of the retinal image may have at least two different effects: it may make the particular object look whiter or blacker, or it may make the whole room appear brighter or darker.

And the same is true of our other example. Look at the moon, particularly when it is at the horizon, and compare its size with that of a shilling held at arm's length. You will find the moon looking very much larger, whereas the retinal image of the shilling is larger than that of the moon. At the same time you see the moon at a much greater distance. Therefore decrease in size of a retinal image may either produce a shrinking or a receding of the corresponding object in the behavioural environment.

Two old experiments confirm this conclusion. In both, the observer looks monocularly at a screen with a circular hole in it. At some distance behind the screen there is a well-illuminated homogeneous white wall part of which is visible through the hole. In the first experiment a taut vertical black thread between the screen and the wall passes through the centre of the circle exposed by the hole. This thread is attached to stands which can be moved backwards and forwards in a sagittal line from the observer in such a way that the thread, whatever its distance from the hole, divides the circle into equal halves, the stands being invisible behind the screen. A movement of the thread has then no other effect than an increase or decrease of the width of its retinal image, apart from a possible blurring due to insufficient accommodation. Under these conditions the observer sees, as a rule, a sagittal motion of a thread with *constant* thickness, and not an increase or decrease of the thickness of an immovable thread. In the second experiment there is no thread at all, and the room is totally dark so that the light circular hole is the only visible object in it. The variable is this time the opening of the hole itself which is made by an iris diaphragm which can be opened or closed. The retinal conditions are still simpler than in the first case, the retinal area on which the light falls increasing or decreasing. Accompanying these retinal changes the observers see either a forward or backward movement of the light circle, or its expansion or contraction, or finally a joint effect in which expansion and approach, contraction and recession, are combined.

We can now present our argument in a more generalized form. If the answer, things look as they do because the proximal stimuli are what they are, were true in the narrower sense, two propositions should hold: (1) Changes in the proximal stimulation unaccompanied by changes of the distant stimulus-object should produce corresponding changes in the *looks* of the behavioural object, and (2) any change in the distant object which produces no effect in the proximal stimulation should leave the looks of the behavioural object unchanged.

That (1) is not true follows from the example we have discussed. A white surface continues to look white, a black one black even when the proximal stimulation to which they give rise varies over a very wide range; my pencil looks no bigger when I hold it in my hand than when it is at the other end of my desk, when its retinal image may be less than half the size of the image of the pencil in my hand; the seat of a chair looks rectangular, although its retinal image will be rectangular in a negligibly small number of occasions only. In other words the behavioural things are conservative; they do not change with every change of the proximal stimulation by which they are produced. The constancy of real things is to a great extent preserved in the constancy of the *phenomenal* things despite variations in their proximal stimuli.[2]

When we compare this argument with the one given in our discussion of the first answer which explained the look of behavioural things by the nature of the real things, we are struck with a somewhat curious relation between the two answers: According to the first, the correspondence between real and behavioural things should have been much better than it really is, and according to the second, it should be much worse.

Let us now turn to the second point. It is quite true that changes of the distant stimuli unaccompanied by any change in the proximal stimulation can have no effect on the look of things. . . . And yet the proposition of our point (2) does not tell us the whole truth, because its conversion is no longer true. The conversion of our proposition (2) would be: no change can occur in the looks of things without corresponding changes in the proximal stimuli. But this is not true. Fig. 2 will not preserve its appearance when you continue to look at it: if you see at first a black cross on white, you will later see a white cross on black, and these two phases will alternate. Puzzle pictures, reversible perspectives demonstrate the same fact, and so does the experiment with the iris diaphragm described above in which the observer may at one time see a displacement, at another time

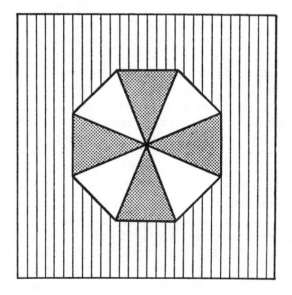

FIG. 2

a change of the size of the hole. From this we must draw the conclusion that the looks of things cannot alone depend upon the proximal stimulation, even if this dependence is considered in the broadest sense, but also upon sets of other conditions which must lie within the real organism.

Finally, many of the arguments used to disprove the first answer apply equally well to the second. Since the mosaic of proximal stimulation possesses no unity, the unity within our behavioural world cannot be explained by a corresponding unity in the proximal stimulation. And the argument derived from the cinema applies to proximal stimulation as well as to distant, so that, in this respect, the second answer is in the same boat with the first. . . .

The interpretation hypothesis. Things do not look as they ought to on the ground of pure proximal stimulation, and they differ from such an expectation by looking more like the distant stimuli, like the things with which we have real dealings. Therefore it was assumed that the *real* properties of things, that the distant stimuli, have something to do with the looks of things after all. The answer, that things look as they do because the proximal stimulation is what it is, had to be supplemented by the first answer, viz., that the fact that things are what they are must be included also in a final explanation. Current theory was, in this way, a sort of combination of our two answers, in which the second answer accounted for the immediate effect, the first for a secondary one. For according to this way of thinking, in dealing with things we acquire experience about them, and this experience enters our whole perception. Thus, according to this view, we must really distinguish between two kinds of behavioural fields, a primary and a secondary one, the field of sensations and the field of perceptions. The original primary field, the field of sensations, corresponded completely to the proximal stimuli; for this primary field the answer that it looked as it did because the proximal stimuli were what they were was true in a very narrow sense. But experience has changed this primary field and has substituted for it the secondary by virtue of the numberless experiences which we have had.

Let us see how this theory worked. In 1920 Jaensch explained Wundt's experiment of the approaching and receding thread whose motion we perceive, in the following manner: "In the case of the thread, judgement can rest only upon a change in the magnitude of the retinal dimensions which accompanies the alteration of the thread's distance, and although this change is too small to be directly noticed as a change of magnitude, still it must determine the judgement of distance." Several features of this explanation are worth noting. First it distinguishes between *effects* which can be directly noticed—even if they are not noticed at the time—, viz. the change of the apparent thickness of the thread corresponding to a change of breadth in the retinal image, and *judgements* determined by such directly noticeable effects, viz. the greater or smaller distance of the thread. If we express this distinction by saying: the increasing thickness of the behavioural thread means, is interpreted as, approach, its decreasing thickness as recession, then we see that this is a clear-cut example of the "meaning theory" which Köhler has discussed with great brilliance in his book. What, so any un-biassed person ought to ask, is the reason for distinguishing in Wundt's experiment between a sensory, though unnoticed, breadth and a judgemental distance? Admittedly, experience presents us only with one fact, the change of distance; admittedly, because the change of breadth is called unnoticed, i.e. unexperienced; neither do we experience this movement as a judgement, but as a change of the same palpability as a change of width which we may experience at another time. That this particular change of distance is interpreted by Jaensch as a judgement is due to the fact that the proximal stimulation changed in breadth, and therefore implies the relation between proximal stimulation and the behavioural field assumed in the second answer. Thus we see the circular nature of this interpretation: in order to call the experienced change of distance a judgement, Jaensch must assume that a change of breadth in the retinal image produces primarily a change of breadth in the perceived object; but in order to reconcile this assumption with the observed facts he must interpret the actual experience of changed distance as a judgement. The general name for this assumption is "constancy hypothesis," we shall call the other the interpretation hypothesis. Then we can say: the interpretation hypothesis presupposes the constancy hypothesis, but also the latter the former. . . .[3]

There is another point in Jaensch's explanation that deserves a special comment; the direct sensory experience is, according to him, too small to be noticed! And yet it is supposed to determine a judgement. This removes the last vestige of plausibility from this theory. We could at least understand what is meant by a judgement based on a perceived sensory experience. In the particular case under discussion the process would then be like this: the observer experiences a change in the thickness of the thread; he has learned, we do not know how, that often such a change is not a real change of the thread but merely due to a change of its position with regard to himself. Therefore he judges that in the present case too the thread has moved without changing its volume. I say that such a description would at least have a meaning, even though it must appear as a pure construction unsupported by facts which contain nothing of such an inferential judgement. But now the change of thickness is assumed to be unnoticed. Since I cannot judge about something I am not aware of, the term judgement must have a meaning different from the ordinary one; in fact it can have no definite meaning any more over and above the very general one: non-sensory process. But then it will not explain anything. For though we can understand how a judgement based upon a sensory experience may lead to a certain interpretation of this experience—we see smoke and we judge there must be a fire—we do not understand how a non-sensory process produces out of an unnoticed sensory process a noticed datum which has all the direct characteristics of a sensory process and is different from the non-noticed one.

Furthermore, the assumption of the non-noticed sensory experience is necessary only because of the constancy hypothesis which derives the looks of things from a universal point-to-point relation with the proximal stimulation. Without the constancy hypothesis we would not assume unnoticed experiences, and without unnoticed experiences we could not preserve the constancy hypothesis. . . .

Let us return to the constancy of size. We saw that diminution of the retinal image instead of producing a shrinkage of the seen object may arouse the perception of its recession with conservation of its apparent size. If this effect is to be explained as a matter of perception and not of sensation, then the assumption must be that originally any diminution of the retinal image would produce a shrinkage of the seen object and that experience only can teach the organism that an object that seems to grow smaller need not really be shrinking. Or otherwise expressed: if of two objects the larger is so much further away from the animal that its retinal image is smaller then, according to this view, originally the animal would see the larger as smaller and would only learn that it is bigger. We should then expect that it ought to be quite easy to find animals who would mistake large objects at a greater distance for small objects; we need only select animals which have not had much time to learn and have no great intelligence; for the acquisition of such knowledge as is implied in the theory is surely a high-grade achievement. But this expectation has not been fulfilled. Thus human infants show a remarkable constancy of size. An infant of eleven months, e.g., who had been trained to select the larger of two boxes standing side by side, continued in her choice when the larger box had been removed to a distance at which its retinal image was less than 1/15 of the area of the retinal image of the smaller, nearer box, which corresponds to a proportion of 4: 1 in linear dimension in favour of the smaller box. I doubt whether this result would have been foreseen by the defenders of the meaning theory. Once it has been obtained they are of course prepared to say that it proves the intelligence of the infant sufficiently great and the time he has lived sufficiently long to gain the necessary experience. Perhaps the faith of these psychologists will not be shaken either by Köhler's experiments published in 1915, which yielded the same results with chimpanzees. Although the species of animal used was sub-human the animals were older than the infants, and the greater time might compensate for the lower intelligence—an explanation tenable only as long as experiments with much younger chimpanzees have not disproved it. But such an experiment is hardly necessary, since Götz has proved that chicks only three months old show constancy of size in their behaviour. Since chicks choose spontaneously the larger grains first, it was not difficult to train them consistently to peck first at the larger of two simultaneously presented grains. For the purpose of the experiment it was necessary to go beyond this and train them to peck at the bigger grains *only,* a result that was safely though not quite so easily accomplished. Then in critical experiments the two grains were so deposited that the smaller was 15 cm. distant from the chick emerging from the door of an antechamber to the food box, whereas the bigger grain was at a greater distance. The chicks chose consistently the bigger one up to a distance of 73 cm., between the two grains; only at greater distances did they peck the smaller one. Now objectively the proportion of the visible areas of the grains was 4:5, the proportion of their linear dimensions therefore 2: 2.24; the fact that the chicks were so easily trained to select the bigger ones first, proves therefore a high degree of discrimination. But the results of the critical experiments are truly astounding, for in them the animals selected as the bigger a grain whose retinal image was but about 1/30 of the area of the smaller, corresponding to a linear proportion of 1:5.5! Chicks must be geniuses if they can discover in the first three months of their lives that something that looks smaller is really bigger. Since we do not believe that they are endowed with such miraculous gifts we must conclude that they select the bigger because it looks bigger, even when, within wide but definite limits, its retinal image is smaller.

Our conviction is strengthened when we learn, without going into details, that so-called brightness-constancy has been proved to exist in infants, chimpanzees and chickens, i.e.

trained to select the whiter or blacker of two objects, they will continue to do so when the blacker object reflects more light than the whiter. . . .

We have adduced these various experiments which show the inadequacy of the interpretation theory. We might have taken a simpler course by showing directly how meaning does not account for constancy of size. I look at the bare hills that rise from the valley and on one of them I perceive a tiny object moving about. I know that it is a man: this tiny object in my field of vision *means* a man. Or I stand on the Chrysler Building in New York and look down into the street. I see hurrying ant-like creatures and tiny cars, but I do not doubt for a moment that these ants are men and women and the toys real automobiles and tramway cars. The meaning is as clear as it can be, but it does not affect in the slightest the size of the objects which carry this meaning. Thus the interpretation theory explains too much: since the meaning is there, the interpretation theory implies that the sizes should be there also, but they are not!

We can summarize our discussion in this way: if "meaning" as employed by the interpretation theory has any assignable meaning, then it is neither the necessary nor the sufficient condition of discrepancies between the pattern of the proximal local stimuli and the perceived objects—not necessary because these discrepancies appear under conditions where we can exclude meaning, not sufficient because they fail to appear where meaning is clearly present. Thus the interpretation theory and the constancy hypothesis with which it is inextricably connected have to disappear from our system for good.[4]

EDITOR'S NOTES

[1] For Koffka the geographical environment is the external world as it actually is, and the behavioural environment is that world as it appears to the percipient and so as it influences his behaviour. This corresponds to the philosophical distinction between external objects and the contents (or objects) of perceptual consciousness.

[2] This phenomenon, usually called *object constancy,* applies to shape, size, brightness, and colour; many examples are given in psychological textbooks. It must be clearly distinguished from the *constancy hypothesis,* the name Koffka gives to the assumption that sense-data resemble the pattern of stimulation of the sense-organs. (For another objection to the constancy hypothesis see S.2 p. 43; the brain pattern is presumably even more "proximal"!) Object constancy means that statements of the relativity of perception and the argument from illusion need care; only from extreme angles or at large distances or with marked changes of light can it be claimed that the look (and so the sense-data) of a thing differs from its real properties.

[3] Some philosophers reach an interpretation hypothesis—viz. that we interpret, or take sense-data to be (properties of) external objects—without embracing the constancy hypothesis. This is because they avoid questions of the causation of perception and claim to detect normally unnoticed sense-data as the result of an analysis of perception guided by the argument from illusion. Hence their sense-data usually embody the results of object-constancy adjustments. But if sense-data do exhibit constancy, Koffka's question becomes "why do sense-data look as they do?," i.e. why do they mostly but not always exhibit the actual characteristics of the external objects? It is not easy, however, to describe what is seen in the thread experiment in terms of sense-data; should one say "receding data"? Is the recession really a datum? If so are the data really incorrigible, for in a well-known more recent version of the experiment a stationary balloon inflated and then deflated a little seems to advance and recede?

[4] Koffka then proceeds to give his own answer, but as it takes up virtually the whole of his book it cannot be reproduced here. Like the other Gestalt psychologists he holds that the behavioural world or content of perceptual consciousness is due to the whole field of stimulation and to its organization: i.e. (*a*) one must take into account not only stimulation due to the object seen but also that due to its background; (*b*) the whole field is grouped or organized so that some elements in it go together making forms or figures (*Gestalten* in German), while others are subordinate. Considerable experimental evidence was adduced to support this and develop laws of field organization. Certainly (*a*) seems plausible: if the object alone is seen and the background cut off by a screen, object-constancy does not hold—apparent size and shape vary according to the laws of perspective, while apparent brightness varies according to amount of illumination. Some automatic grouping or organization seems plausible too. Difficulties are: (1) what is the mechanism of these organizations and adjustments—do they occur in the brain or sense organs or both,

or are they mental in some way? In so far as the adjustments are admitted as fact this difficulty does not affect the Gestalt psychologists' answer, though they did introduce some speculative explanations of them which are not widely accepted. (2) What is the extent of the organization? To oust the interpretation theory completely one would have to show that all the facts are covered by "organization." But there are many psychological features of perception which fit the interpretation theory better, e.g. (a) it is generally held that perception of depth and distance depends on the use of "cues" (though this is denied by some, e.g. J. J. Gibson), (b) the "behavioural environment" does depend a good deal on learning and past experience and on imaginative supplementation (cf. Introduction, p. 12). However, these questions can only be pursued with a full investigation of the psychological evidence, discussions of which are listed in the Bibliography.

Part II
The Sense-datum Theory

6. THE INTRODUCTION OF SENSE-DATA

G. E. Moore

Besides being a leader of the British revolt against Idealism and father of modern Analytical Philosophy, George
Edward Moore (1873–1958) introduced sense-data into
philosophy in his lectures of 1910. The lectures were not
published, however, until 1953, when they appeared as
Some Main Problems of Philosophy (London, George
Allen & Unwin, Ltd.; New York, The Macmillan Company), from pp. 29–38 of which this passage is taken. A
few repetitions, more helpful to the original student audience
than to the reader, have been cut out. The notes represent Moore's second thoughts in 1952.

My first question is, then: What exactly is it that happens
when (as we should say) we *see* a material object? And I
should explain, perhaps, to avoid misunderstanding, that I
do not mean to say anything at all about the bodily processes
which occur in the eye and the optic nerves and the brain.
I have no doubt, myself, that these bodily processes *do* occur,
when we see; and that physiologists really do *know* a great
deal about them. But all that I shall mean by "seeing," and
all that I wish to talk about, is the mental occurrence—the
act of consciousness—which occurs (as is supposed) as a
consequence of or accompaniment of these bodily processes.
This mental occurrence is known to us in a much more simple
and direct way than are the complicated physiological processes which go on in our eyes and nerves and brains. A man
cannot directly observe the minute processes which go on in
his own eyes and nerves and brain when he sees; but all of
us who are not blind can directly observe this mental occurrence, which we mean by seeing.
And I wish to illustrate what I have to say about seeing
by a direct practical example; because, though I dare say
many of you are perfectly familiar with the sort of points
I wish to raise, it is, I think, very important for every one,

in these subjects, to consider carefully single concrete instances, so that there may be no mistake as to exactly what it is that is being talked about. Such mistakes are, I think, very apt to happen, if one talks merely in generalities; and moreover one is apt to overlook important points. I propose therefore, to hold up an envelope in my hand, and to ask you all to look at it for a moment; and then to consider with me exactly what it is that happens, when you see it: *what* this occurrence, which we call the *seeing* of it, *is*.

I hold up this envelope, then: I look at it, and put it down again. Now what has happened? We should certainly say (if you have looked at it) that we all *saw* that envelope, *the same* envelope; *I* saw it, and you all saw it. And by the *it*, which we all saw, we mean an object, which, at any one of the moments when we were looking at it, occupied just *one* of the many places that constitute the whole of space. Even during the short time in which we were looking at it, it may have moved—occupied successively several different places; for the earth, we believe, is constantly going round on its axis, and carrying with it all the objects on its surface, so that, even while we looked at the envelope, it probably moved and changed its position in space, though we did not see it move. But at any *one* moment, we should say, this *it*, the envelope, which we say we all saw, was at some *one* definite place in space.

But now, what happened to each of us, when we saw that envelope? I will begin by describing *part* of what happened to me. I saw a patch[1] of a particular whitish colour, having a certain size, and a certain shape, a shape with rather sharp angles or corners and bounded by fairly straight lines. These things; this patch of a whitish colour, and its size and shape I did actually see. And I propose to call these things, the colour and size and shape, *sense-data*,[2] things *given* or presented by the senses—given, in this case, by my sense of sight. Many philosophers have called these things which I call sense-data, *sensations*. They would say, for instance, that that particular patch of colour was a sensation. But it seems to me that this term "sensation" is liable to be misleading. We should certainly say that I *had* a sensation, when I saw that colour. But when we say that I *had* a sensation, what we mean by a "sensation" is my *seeing* of the colour, not the colour which I saw. It is very unnatural to say that I *had* the colour, that I *had* that particular whitish-grey or that I *had* the patch which was of that colour. What I certainly did *have* is the experience which consisted in my seeing the colour and the patch. And when, therefore, we talk of *having* sensations, I think what we mean by "sensations" is the experiences which consist in apprehending certain sense-data, *not* these sense-data themselves. I think, then, that the term "sensation" is liable to be misleading, because it may be used in two different senses: *either* for the colour which I saw or for the experience which consisted in my seeing it. And it is, I think, very important to distinguish these two things. In the first place, it is, I think, quite *conceivable* that the patch of colour which I saw may have continued to exist after I saw it: whereas, of course, when I ceased to see it, my seeing of it ceased to exist. I will illustrate what I mean, by holding up the envelope again, and looking at it. I look at it, and I again see a sense-datum, a patch of a whitish colour. But now I immediately turn away my eyes, and I no longer see that sense-datum: my seeing of it has ceased to exist. But I am by no means sure that the sense-datum—that very same patch of whitish colour which I saw—is not still *existing* and still there. I do not say, for certain, that it is: I think very likely it is not. But I have a strong inclination to believe that it is. And it seems to me at least *conceivable* that it should be still existing, whereas my seeing of it certainly has ceased to exist. Secondly, it seems to me *conceivable*—here again I do not say it is true but conceivable—that some sense-data— this whitish colour for instance—are in the place in which the material object—the envelope is. It seems to me *conceivable* that this whitish colour is really on the surface of the material envelope. Whereas it does not seem to me that my *seeing* of it is in that place. My seeing of it is in another place—somewhere within my body. Here, then, are two reasons for distinguishing between the *sense-data* which I see, and my *seeing* of them. And it seems to me that both of these two very different things are often meant when people talk about "sensations." In fact, when you are reading any philosopher who is talking about sensations (or about sense-*impressions* or *ideas* either), you need to look very carefully to see which of the two he is talking about in any particular passage—whether of the sense-data themselves or of our apprehension of them: you will, I think, almost invariably find that he is talking now of the one and now of the other, and very often that he is assuming that what is true of the one must be true also of the other—an assumption which does not seem to be at all justified. I shall therefore always talk of *sense-data,* when what I mean is such things as this colour and size and shape or the patch which is *of* this colour and size and shape, which I actually see. And when I want to talk of my seeing of them, I shall expressly call this the seeing of sense-data; or, if I want a term which will apply equally to all the senses, I shall speak of the *direct apprehension of* sense-data. Thus when I see this whitish colour, I am *directly apprehending* this whitish colour: my seeing of it, as a mental act, an act of consciousness, just consists in my direct apprehension of it;—so too when I hear a sound, I directly apprehend the sound; when I feel a toothache I directly apprehend the ache: and all these things—the whitish colour, the sound, and the ache are *sense-data.*

To return, then, to what happened to us, when we all saw the same envelope. Part, at least, of what happened to me, I can now express by saying that I saw certain sense-data; I saw a whitish patch of colour, of a particular size and shape. And I have no doubt whatever that this is part, at least, of what happened to all of you. You also saw certain sense-data; and I expect also that the sense-data which you saw were more or less similar to those which I saw, and of a shape similar at least in this that it had rather sharp corners and was bounded by fairly straight lines. But now, what I want to emphasize is this. Though we all did (as we should say) see *the same* envelope, no two of us, in all probability, saw exactly the *same sense-data.* Each of us, in all probability, saw, to begin with, a slightly different shade of colour. All these colours may have been whitish; but each was probably at least slightly different from all the rest, according to the way in which the light fell upon the paper, relatively to the different positions you are sitting in; and again according to differences in the strength of your eye-sight, or your distance from the paper. And so too, with regard to the size of the patch of colour which you saw: differences in the strength of your eyes and in your distance from the envelope probably made slight differences in the size of the patch of colour, which you saw. And so again with regard to the shape. Those of you on that side of the room will have seen a rhomboidal figure, while those in front of me will have seen a figure more nearly rectangular. Those on my left will have seen a figure more like this which you in front now see, and which you see is different from *this* which you then saw. And those in front of me will have seen a figure like that which you on the left now see, and which, you see, is different from *this,* which you saw before. Those directly in front of me, may, indeed, have all seen very nearly the same figure—perhaps, even, exactly the same. But we should not say we *knew* that any two did; whereas we should say we did *know* that we all saw the *same* envelope. That you did all see the same envelope, would, indeed be accepted in ordinary life as a certainty of the strongest kind. Had you all seen me commit a murder, as clearly as you all saw this envelope, your evidence would be accepted by any jury as sufficient to hang me. It would be accepted, that is, that you had all seen me, *the same man,* commit a murder. And yet, in this case, as in the case of the envelope, the sense-data which you had all seen, would have been different sense-data: you could not swear in a court of law that you had all seen exactly the *same sense-data.*

Now all this seems to me to show very clearly, that, *if* we *did* all see the same envelope, the envelope which we saw was not *identical with* the sense-data which we saw: the envelope cannot be exactly the same thing as each of the sets of sense-data, which we each of us saw; for these were in all probability each of them slightly different from all the rest, and they cannot, therefore, *all* be exactly the same thing as the envelope.

But it might be said: Of course, when we say that we all saw the envelope, we do not mean that we all saw the whole of it. I, for instance, only saw *this* side of it, whereas all of you only saw *that* side. And generally, when we talk of seeing an object we only mean seeing some *part* of it. There is always more in any object which we see, than the *part* of it which we see.

And this, I think, is quite true. Whenever we talk roughly of seeing any object, it is true that, in another and stricter sense of the word *see*, we only see *a part of* it. And it might, therefore, be suggested that why we say we all saw this envelope, when we each in fact, saw a different set of sense-data, is because each of these *sets of sense-data* is, in fact, a *part* of the envelope.

But it seems to me there is a great difficulty even in maintaining that the different sense-data we all saw are parts of the envelope. What do we mean by a *part* of a material object? We mean, I think at least this. What we call a part of a material object must be something which occupies a part of the volume in space occupied by the whole object. For instance, anything which is a *part* of the envelope at any moment, must be *in* some part of the volume of space occupied by the whole envelope at that moment or *at* some point in the surfaces bounding that volume.

Are, then, any of the sense-data we saw *parts* of the envelope in this sense?

The sense-data I mentioned were these three—the colour—the whitish colour; the *size* of this colour; its *shape*.[3] And of these three it is only the colour, which could, in the sense defined, possibly be supposed to be a *part* of the envelope. The colour might be supposed to occupy a *part* of that volume occupied by the envelope—one of its bounding surfaces,[4] for instance. But the size and shape could hardly be said to *occupy* any part of this volume. What might be true of them is that the size I saw *is* the size of one surface of the envelope, and that the shape *is* the shape of this surface of the envelope.

Let us consider whether these things are so.

And first, as to the colours. Can these possibly be parts of the envelope? What we supposed is that each of you probably saw a slightly different colour. And if we are to suppose that *all* those colours are parts of the envelope, then we must suppose that *all* of them are in the same place. We must suppose that ever so many different colours all of them occupy the same surface—this surface of the envelope which you now see. And I think it is certainly difficult to suppose this, though not absolutely impossible. It is not absolutely impossible, I think, that all the different colours which you see are really all of them in the same place. But I myself find it difficult to believe that this is so; and you can understand, I think, why most philosophers should have declared it to be impossible. They have declared that none of the colours which any of us ever see are ever parts of material objects or are ever in any part of the places where material objects (if there are any material objects) are. This conclusion does, indeed, go beyond what the premises justify, even if we accept the premise that several different colours cannot all be in exactly the same place. For it remains possible that the colour, which some *one* of you sees, is really on the surface of the envelope; whereas the colours which all the rest of you see are not there. But if so, then we must say that though all of you are seeing the same side of the envelope, yet only one of you is seeing a sense-datum which is a part of that side: the sense-data seen by all the rest are *not* parts of the envelope. And this also, I think, is difficult to believe.

Now as to the size. I assumed that the sense-given sizes, which you see, are all of them probably slightly different from one another. And, if this is so, then certainly it seems to be absolutely impossible that they should *all* of them be the size of this side of the envelope. This side of the envelope can only really have *one* size; it cannot have several different sizes. But it may not seem quite clear, that you all do see different sizes; the differences between the different distances at which you are from the envelope are not so great, but what the patches of colour you all see might be, at least, of

much the same size. So I will give a hypothetical instance to
make my point clearer. Suppose this room were so large that
I could carry the envelope two or three hundred yards away
from you. The sense-given size which you would then see,
when I was three hundred yards off, would certainly be appreciably smaller than what you see now. And yet you would
still be seeing this same envelope. It seems quite impossible
that these two very different sizes should both of them be *the*
size of the envelope. So that here the *only* possibility is that
the size which you see at some *one* definite distance or set of
distances, should be the envelope's real size, *if* you ever see
its real size at all. This may be so: it may be that some one of
the sense-given sizes which we see is the envelope's real size.
But it seems also possible that none of them are; and in any
case we all see the envelope, just the same, *whether* we see its
real size or not.

And now for the shape. Here again it seems quite impossible
that *all* the shapes we see can be the envelope's real shape.
This side of the envelope can have but *one* shape: it cannot
be both rhomboidal, as is the shape which you on the left see,
and also rectangular, as is the shape seen by those in front;
the angles at its corners cannot be both right angles and also
very far from right angles. Certainly, therefore, the sense-
given shape which some of you see is *not* the shape of this
side of the envelope. But here it may be said, it is plain
enough that one of the sense-given shapes seen *is* its real shape.
You may say; The shape seen by those in front *is* its real
shape; the envelope *is* rectangular. And I quite admit that
this is so: I think we do know, in fact, that the envelope
really is *roughly* rectangular. But here I want to introduce a
distinction. There are two different senses in which we may
talk of *the* shape of anything. A rectangle of the size of this
envelope, and a rectangle of the size of this blackboard, may
both, in a sense, have exactly *the same* shape in the sense,
that all the angles of both are right angles, and that the
proportions between the sides of the one, and those between
the sides of the other, are the same. But there is another
sense in which *the* shape of a big square is obviously not *the*

same as that of a small square. We may mean by *the* shape
of a big square the actual lines bounding it; and if we mean
this, *the* shape of a big square cannot possible be the *same*
as *the* shape of a smaller one. The lines bounding the two
cannot possibly be the *same* lines. And the same thing may
be true, even when there is no difference in size between two
shapes. Imagine *two* squares, of the same size, side by side.
The lines bounding the one are *not* the same lines as those
bounding the other: though each is both *of* the same shape
and *of* the same size as the other. The difference between
these two senses in which we may talk of *the* shape of anything, may be expressed by saying that the shape of the big
square is the same *in quality*—qualitatively identical—with
that of the small square, but is not *numerically* the same—
not numerically identical: the shape of the big square is
numerically different from that of the small, in the sense that
they are *two* shapes, and not one only, of which we are
talking, though both are the same in quality: both are *squares,*
but the one is *one* square and the other is *another* square.
And now to return to the case of the envelope. Even supposing
that the sense-given shape which you in front see is rectangular, and that the real shape of the envelope is also rectangular, and that both are rectangles of exactly the same
shape; it still does not follow that the sense-given shape which
you see is *the* shape of the envelope. The sense-given shape
and the shape of the envelope, even if they are qualitatively the
same, *must* still be *two* different shapes, *numerically* different,
unless they are *of the same size.* And we saw before how
difficult it was to be sure that any of the sizes which you saw
were the *real* size of the envelope. And even if the sense-given
size which some one of you sees *is* the real size of the envelope, it still does not follow that the sense-given *shape*
which you see is numerically the same as the shape of the
envelope. The two may be numerically different, just as in the
case of two different squares, side by side, of the same shape
and size, *the* shape of the one *is* not *the* shape of the other;
they are two numerically different shapes. We may say, then,
that if those of you who see rectangular shapes, do see

rectangular shapes of different sizes, only one of these can possibly be *the* shape of the envelope: all the others may be *of* the same shape—the same in quality—but they cannot be *the* shape of the envelope. And even if some *one* of you does see a shape, which is of the same size as *the* shape of the envelope, as well as being of the same shape (and it is very doubtful whether any of you does) it would yet be by no means certain that this sense-given shape which you saw was *the* shape of the envelope. It might be a shape *numerically* different from *the* shape of the envelope, although exactly similar both in shape and size. And finally there is some reason to suppose that none of the sense-given shapes which any of you see are *exactly* the same, even in quality, as *the* shape of the envelope. The envelope itself probably has a more or less irregular edge; there are probably ups and downs in the line bounding its side, which you at that distance cannot see.

Of the three kinds of sense-data,[5] then, which you all of you saw, when I held up the envelope, the following things seem to be true. First, as regards the colour, no one of you can be sure that the exact colour which you saw was really a part of the envelope. Then as regards the size, no one of you can be sure that the size which you saw was the real size of the envelope. And finally as regards the shape, no one of you can be sure that the shape which you saw was really of exactly the same shape as that of the envelope; still less can you be sure that it *was the* shape of the envelope, that the bounding lines which composed it were numerically the same bounding lines as those which enclosed the envelope. And not only can none of you be sure of these things. As regards the sizes and shapes which you saw, it seems quite certain that some of you saw sizes and shapes which were *not* the real size and shape of the envelope; because it seems quite certain that some of you saw sizes and shapes different from those seen by others, and that these different sizes and shapes cannot possibly *all* be *the* size and shape of the envelope. And as regards the colours it seems fairly certain, that the colours which you saw cannot all have been *in* the envelope; since it seems fairly certain that you all saw slightly different colours, and it is difficult to believe, though not absolutely impossible, that all these different colours were really in the same place at the same time.

This seems to be the state of things with regard to these sense-data. They seem, in a sense, to have had very little to do with the real envelope, if there *was* a real envelope. It seems very probable that *none* of the colours seen was really a part of the envelope; and that *none* of the sizes and shapes seen were the size or the shape of the real envelope.

AUTHOR'S NOTES

[1] I am so extending the use of the word "patch" that, e.g. the very small black dot which I directly apprehend when I see a full-stop, or the small black line which I directly apprehend when I see a hyphen, are, each of them, in the sense in which I am using the word, a "patch of colour."

[2] I should now make, and have for many years made, a sharp distinction between what I have called the "patch," on the one hand, and the colour, size, and shape, *of* which it is, on the other; and should call, and have called, *only* the patch, *not* its colour, size, or shape, a "sense-datum."

[3] I had here forgotten that one of the sense-data mentioned was the *patch* which *has* that colour and shape and size—the *patch* which, I should now say, is the *only* "sense-datum," having to do with the envelope, which I then saw.

[4] I should now say that any part of the *surface* of a volume is *not* a part of the volume, because it is not itself a volume.

[5] The *patch* itself, which *has* that colour and shape and size, again forgotten! [Moore's argument could still be adapted to urge that the sense-datum (the patch) was not identical in colour, shape, or size with the envelope.—ED.]

7. THE GIVEN

H. H. PRICE

Professor Price (1899–   ) is a well-known exponent of the Sense-datum Theory who has presented it in its most highly developed form in his *Perception* (Methuen, London, 1932). Both this selection (which consists in pp. 1–5 and 18–19) and Selection 13 are taken from that book.

Every man entertains a great number of beliefs concerning material things, e.g. that there is a square-topped table in this room, that the earth is a spheroid, that water is composed of hydrogen and oxygen. It is plain that all these beliefs are based on sight and on touch (from which organic sensation cannot be separated): based upon them in the sense that if we had not had certain particular experiences of seeing and touching, it would be neither *possible* nor *reasonable* to entertain these beliefs. Beliefs about imperceptibles such as molecules or electrons or X-rays are no exception to this. Only they are based not directly on sight and touch, but indirectly. Their direct basis consists of certain other beliefs concerning scientific instruments, photographic plates, and the like. Thus over and above any intrinsic uncertainty that they themselves may have, whatever uncertainty attaches to these more basic beliefs is communicated to them. It follows that in any attempt either to analyse or to justify our beliefs concerning material things, the primary task is to consider beliefs concerning perceptible or "macroscopic" objects such as chairs and tables, cats and rocks. It follows, too, that no theory concerning "microscopic" objects can possibly be used to throw doubt upon our beliefs concerning chairs or cats or rocks, so long as these are based directly on sight and touch. Empirical science can never be more trustworthy than perception, upon which it is based; and it can hardly fail to be *less* so, since among its non-perceptual premises there can hardly fail to be some which are neither self-evident nor demonstrable. Thus the not uncommon view that the world which we perceive is an illusion and only the "scientific" world of protons and electrons is real, is based upon a gross fallacy, and would destroy the very premises upon which science itself depends.

My aim in this book is to examine those experiences in the way of seeing and touching upon which our beliefs concerning material things are based, and to inquire in what way and to what extent they justify these beliefs. Other modes of sense-experience, e.g. hearing and smelling, will be dealt with only incidentally. For it is plain that they are only auxiliary. If we possessed them, but did not possess either sight or touch, we should have no beliefs about the material world at all, and should lack even the very conception of it. Possessing sight or touch or both, we can use experiences of these other senses as signs of obtainable but not at the moment actual experiences of seeing or touching, and thereby gain indirectly information which these inferior senses in themselves provide no hint of.

It may appear to some people that science, particularly physiology, can answer these questions for us. But it should already be clear that this is a mistake. Thus if it be said that when a man sees something, e.g. a tomato, light rays emanating from the object impinge upon his retina and this stimulates the optic nerve, which in turn causes a change in the optic centres in his brain, which causes a change in his mind: there are two comments to be made.

1. No doubt this is in fact a perfectly true account, but what are our *grounds* for believing it? Obviously they are derived from observation, and mainly if not entirely from visual observation. Thus the physiologist has not explained in the least how visual observation justifies a man in holding a certain belief about a tomato, e.g. that it is spherical. All he has done is to put forward certain *other* beliefs concerning a retina and a brain. Those other beliefs have themselves to be justified in exactly the same way as the first belief, and we are as far as ever from knowing what way that is. Instead of answering our question, we have found another instance of

it. Nor is this result surprising. Since the premises of physiology are among the propositions into whose validity we are inquiring, it is hardly likely that its conclusions will assist us.

2. In any case, science only professes to tell us what are the *causes* of seeing and touching. But we want to know what seeing and touching themselves *are*. This question lies outside the sphere of science altogether.

Thus there is no short cut to our goal. We must simply examine seeing and touching for ourselves and do the best we can. What, then, is it to see or to touch something? Let us confine ourselves to sight for the moment and return to the instance of the tomato.

When I see a tomato there is much that I can doubt. I can doubt whether it is a tomato that I am seeing, and not a cleverly painted piece of wax. I can doubt whether there is any material thing there at all. Perhaps what I took for a tomato was really a reflection; perhaps I am even the victim of some hallucination. One thing however I cannot doubt: that there exists a red patch of a round and somewhat bulgy shape, standing out from a background of other colour-patches, and having a certain visual depth, and that this whole field of colour is directly present to my consciousness. What the red patch is, whether a substance, or a state of a substance, or an event, whether it is physical or psychical or neither, are questions that we may doubt about. But that something is red and round then and there[1] I cannot doubt. Whether the something persists even for a moment before and after it is present to my consciousness, whether other minds can be conscious of it as well as I, may be doubted. But that it now *exists*, and that *I* am conscious of it—by me at least who am conscious of it this cannot possibly be doubted. And when I say that it is "directly" present to my consciousness, I mean that my consciousness of it is not reached by inference, nor by any other intellectual process (such as abstraction or intuitive induction), nor by any passage from sign to significate. There obviously must be some sort or sorts of presence to consciousness which can be called "direct" in this sense, else we should have an infinite regress. Analogously, when I am in the situations called "touching something," "hearing it," "smelling it," etc., in each case there is something which at that moment indubitably exists—a pressure (or prement patch), a noise, a smell; and that something is directly present to my consciousness.

This peculiar and ultimate manner of being present to consciousness is called *being given*, and that which is thus present is called a *datum*. The corresponding mental attitude is called *acquaintance, intuitive apprehension*, or sometimes *having*. Data of this special sort are called *sense-data*. And the acquaintance with them is conveniently called *sensing*; though sometimes, I think, this word is used in another sense. It is supposed by some writers that sense-data are mental events, and these writers appear to think that the word "sensing," if used at all, ought to mean the coming-into-being of sense-data, not the intuitive apprehension of them. (For their coming-into-being will then be a mental process.) This seems to be a very inconvenient usage. We need some word for the intuitive apprehension of sense-data. We cannot say "perceiving" (for that, we shall see, has at least two other meanings already).[2] And "sensing" is the obvious word to use. At any rate in this book we shall always use it in this sense. When we have occasion to speak of the process which is the coming-into-being of a sense-datum we shall call it *sense-datum-genesis*.

It is true that the term "given" or "datum" is sometimes used in a wider and looser sense to mean "that, the inspection of which provides a premise for inference." Thus the data of the historian are the statements which he finds in documents and inscriptions; the data of the general are the facts reported by his aircraft and his intelligence service; the data of the detective are the known circumstances and known results of the crime, and so on. But it is obvious that these are only data relatively and for the purpose of answering a certain question. They are really themselves the results of inference, often of a very complicated kind. We may call them data *secundum quid*. But eventually we must get back to something which is a datum *simpliciter*, which is not the result of any previous intellectual process. It is with data *simpliciter,* or rather with one species of them, that we are concerned.

How do sense-data differ from other data, e.g. from those of memory or introspection? We might be tempted to say, in the manner in which they come to be given, viz. as a result of the stimulation of a sense organ. This will not do. For first, the sense organs are themselves material things, and it seems quite likely that the term "material thing" cannot be defined except by reference to sense-data; and if so we should have a vicious circle. And secondly, even though we doubted the existence of all material things, including our own body and its organs, it would still be perfectly obvious that sense-data differ from other sorts of data. The only describable differentia that they seem to have is this, that they lead us to conceive of and believe in the existence of certain material things, whether there are in fact any such things or not. (Visual and tactual sense-data do this directly, and others indirectly, as explained above.) But it seems plain that there is also another characteristic common and peculiar to them, which may be called "sensuousness." This is obvious on inspection, but it cannot be described.

Does sensing differ from other forms of intuitive apprehension? Or is there only one sort of intuitive apprehension, and does the difference between (say) sensing, remembering, and the contemplation of mental images lie only in the nature of the apprehensa? The question is difficult, nor does it seem very important. Perhaps we may say that there are two sorts of intuitive apprehension, one directed upon *facts,* e.g. the fact that I am puzzled or was puzzled, or again the fact that $2 + 2 = 4$, or that courage is good: another directed upon *particular existents,* e.g. this colour-patch or this noise or that visual image, or again upon this feeling of disgust and that act of wondering. The first is apprehension *that,* the second is apprehension *of.* The term *acquaintance* is properly reserved for the second, and we shall so use it in future.

Are there several different sorts of acquaintance, e.g. sensing, self-consciousness, and contemplation of mental images? I cannot see that there are. The difference seems to be wholly on the side of the data. If so, *a fortiori* there are not different kinds of sensing. Visual sensing will simply be the acquaintance with colour-patches, auditory sensing the acquaintance with sounds, and so on; the acquaintance being the same in each case. No doubt there will be different kinds of *sense-datum-genesis*, just as there are different kinds of sense-data. And if any one likes to use the term "visual sensing"[3] to mean the genesis of colour-patches and "auditory sensing" to mean the genesis of noises, he may; and of course he is then entitled to say that there *are* different kinds of sensing. But this has not the slightest tendency to show that there are different kinds of sensing in *our* sense of the word (which is also the usual one).

[Some pages containing a reply to older criticisms of the notion of a "given" are omitted here.]

In conclusion we may point out that the admission that there are sense-data is not a very large one; it commits us to very little. It may be worth while to mention explicitly a number of things which we are *not* committed to.

1. We are not committed to the view that sense-data *persist*[4] through the intervals when they are not being sensed. We have only to admit that they *exist* at the times when they are being sensed.

2. We are not committed to the view that several minds can be acquainted with the *same* sense-datum. We have only to admit that every mind is acquainted with *some* sense-data from time to time.

3. We are not committed to any view about what is called "the status" of sense-data in the universe, either as regards the *category* they fall under, or as regards their relations with other types of existent entities. They may be events, or substances, or states of substances. They may be physical; i.e. they may be parts of, or events in, material objects such as chairs and tables or (in another theory) brains. They may be

mental as Berkeley and many others have held. They may be neither mental nor physical.

4. We are not committed to any view about their *origin*. They may originate as a result of processes in material objects, or of mental processes, or of both. Or again, it may be that the boot is on the other leg: it may be that they are the ultimate constituents of the universe, and material things (perhaps minds as well) may be just collections of them; in which case they "just are," and have no origin and no explanation, since everything else is explained by reference to them.

Thus the term sense-datum is meant to be a *neutral* term. The use of it does not imply the acceptance of any particular theory. The term is meant to stand for something whose existence is indubitable (however fleeting), something from which all theories of perception ought to start, however much they may diverge later.

And I think that all past theories have in fact started with sense-data. The ancients and the Schoolmen called them *sensible species*. Locke and Berkeley called them *ideas of sensation*, Hume, *impressions*, Kant, *Vorstellungen*. In the nineteenth century they were usually known as *sensations*, and people spoke of visual and auditory sensations when they meant colour-patches and noises; while many contemporary writers, following Dr. C. D. Broad, have preferred to call them *sensa*.

All these terms have the defect of begging questions. If we speak of *sensible species* we assume that sense-data are physical, a sort of effluences flying off the external objects into our sense-organs. If we use terms like *idea, impression,* and *sensation* we commit ourselves to the view that sense-data are mental events. *Sensum* is very much the best. But it is generally used to mean a "third kind" of entity, neither mental nor physical. And although we are not at present in a position to assert that sense-data are physical or that they are mental, neither are we in a position to deny either of these alternatives. (Thus "sense-data are sensa" is not a tautology, but a synthetic proposition.)

NOTES

[1] "There" means "In spatial relations to other colour-patches present to my consciousness at the same time."—PRICE

[2] The two senses of the word "perceive" to which Price refers may be illustrated by supposing that a man with double vision looks at one bottle. In one sense of the word "perceive" he can be said to perceive two bottles, but in the more usual sense he perceives one. The point is that "X perceives Y" in this ordinary sense implies two things: (a) that X is conscious (*perceptually conscious*) of Y, and (b) that Y is present to his senses. In seeming to perceive Y only condition (a) holds. One can therefore conveniently speak of perceptual consciousness as the state of mind present in perceiving and in seeming to perceive—the man with double vision is perceptually conscious of two bottles, the normal man of only one—and discuss such consciousness without unwanted implications about its veridicality, i.e. about what is actually present to the senses (as in *Introduction* p. 14). Price, however, uses the term more narrowly for the non-sensuous element in perceiving and seeming to perceive: for him the state of mind in either of these (i.e. in the wide sense of perceptual consciousness) consists in sensing plus the (narrower) non-sensuous perceptual consciousness, which he identifies as "taking for granted" (see S.13). But this usage does not allow for those who claim that the consciousness in perceiving (and seeming to perceive) is not analysable into sensuous and non-sensuous elements—ED.

[3] The substitution of "seeing" for visual sensing, "hearing" for auditory sensing, etc. would make confusion even worse confounded. For in the ordinary sense of the word, *see,* what I see is not a colour-patch, but a material thing, e.g. a table or a tomato. Likewise *hear, smell,* etc. are in ordinary usage ambiguous. I hear the train, or I hear a noise. I smell the rose, or I smell a smell.—PRICE

[4] Or more strictly, that there are persistent *sensibilia* which become sense-data temporarily when they are sensed. Cf. Mr. Bertrand Russell's *Mysticism and Logic*, p. 148.—PRICE

8. HARD AND SOFT DATA

Bertrand Russell

Bertrand Russell (1872–   ), the best-known of contemporary British philosophers, was, like Moore, a pioneer of sense-datum analysis. This passage comes from *Our Knowledge of the External World* (Reissued by George Allen & Unwin, Ltd., London, 1922) pp. 75–88, an early work (date 1914) in which he sought to show how our whole conception of the external world could be built up out of patterns of "hard data" (i.e., mostly, sense-data), of which alone we are absolutely certain. Compare the radical theories of Part IV.

The first thing that appears when we begin to analyse our common knowledge is that some of it is derivative, while some is primitive; that is to say, there is some that we only believe because of something else from which it has been inferred in some sense, though not necessarily in a strict logical sense, while other parts are believed on their own account, without the support of any outside evidence. It is obvious that the senses give knowledge of the latter kind: the immediate facts perceived by sight or touch or hearing do not need to be proved by argument, but are completely self-evident. Psychologists, however, have made us aware that what is actually given in sense is much less than most people would naturally suppose, and that much of what at first sight seems to be given is really inferred. This applies especially in regard to our space-perceptions. For instance, we unconsciously infer the "real" size and shape of a visible object from its apparent size and shape, according to its distance and our point of view. When we hear a person speaking, our actual sensations usually miss a great deal of what he says, and we supply its place by unconscious inference; in a foreign language, where this process is more difficult, we find ourselves apparently grown deaf, requiring, for example, to be much nearer the stage at a theatre than would be necessary in our own country. Thus the first step in the analysis

116

of data, namely, the discovery of what is really given in sense, is full of difficulty. We will, however, not linger on this point; so long as its existence is realized, the exact outcome does not make any very great difference in our main problem.

The next step in our analysis must be the consideration of how the derivative parts of our common knowledge arise. Here we become involved in a somewhat puzzling entanglement of logic and psychology. Psychologically, a belief may be called derivative whenever it is caused by one or more other beliefs, or by some fact of sense which is not simply what the belief asserts. Derivative beliefs in this sense constantly arise without any process of logical inference, merely by association of ideas or some equally extra-logical process. From the expression of a man's face we judge as to what he is feeling: we say we *see* that he is angry, when in fact we only see a frown. We do not judge as to his state of mind by any logical process: the judgement grows up, often without our being able to say what physical mark of emotion we actually saw. In such a case, the knowledge is derivative psychologically; but logically it is in a sense primitive, since it is not the result of any logical deduction. There may or may not be a possible deduction leading to the same result, but whether there is or not, we certainly do not employ it. If we call a belief "logically primitive" when it is not actually arrived at by a logical inference, then innumerable beliefs are logically primitive which psychologically are derivative. The separation of these two kinds of primitiveness is vitally important to our present discussion.

When we reflect upon the beliefs which are logically but not psychologically primitive, we find that, unless they can on reflection be deduced by a logical process from beliefs which are also psychologically primitive, our confidence in their truth tends to diminish the more we think about them. We naturally believe, for example, that tables and chairs, trees and mountains are still there when we turn our backs upon them. I do not wish for a moment to maintain that this is certainly not the case, but I do maintain that the question whether it is the case is not to be settled offhand on any supposed ground of obviousness. The belief that they persist is, in all men except a few philosophers, logically primitive, but it is not psychologically primitive; psychologically, it arises only through our having seen those tables and chairs, trees and mountains. As soon as the question is seriously raised whether, because we have seen them, we have a right to suppose that they are there still, we feel that some kind of argument must be produced, and that if none is forthcoming, our belief can be no more than a pious opinion. We do not feel this as regards the immediate objects of sense: there they are, and as far as their momentary existence is concerned, no further argument is required. There is accordingly more need of justifying our psychologically derivative beliefs than of justifying those that are primitive.

We are thus led to a somewhat vague distinction between what we may call "hard" data and "soft" data. This distinction is a matter of degree, and must not be pressed; but if not taken too seriously, it may help to make the situation clear. I mean by "hard" data those which resist the solvent influence of critical reflection, and by "soft" data those which, under the operation of this process, become to our minds more or less doubtful. The hardest of hard data are of two sorts: the particular facts of sense, and the general truths of logic. The more we reflect upon these, the more we realize exactly what they are, and exactly what a doubt concerning them really means, the more luminously certain do they become. *Verbal* doubt concerning even these is possible, but verbal doubt may occur when what is nominally being doubted is not really in our thoughts, and only words are actually present to our minds. Real doubt, in these two cases, would, I think, be pathological. At any rate, to me they seem quite certain, and I shall assume that you agree with me on this. Without this assumption, we are in danger of falling into that universal scepticism which is as barren as it is irrefutable. If we are to continue philosophizing, we must make our bow to the sceptical hypothesis, and, while admitting the elegant terseness of its philosophy, proceed to the consideration of other hypotheses which, though perhaps not certain, have at least as good a right to our respect as the hypothesis of the sceptic.

Applying our distinction of "hard" and "soft" data to psychologically derivative but logically primitive beliefs, we shall find that most, if not all, are to be classed as soft data. They may be found, on reflection, to be capable of logical proof, and they then again become believed, but no longer as data. As data, though entitled to a certain limited respect, they cannot be placed on a level with the facts of sense or the laws of logic. The kind of respect which they deserve seems to me such as to warrant us in hoping, though not too confidently, that the hard data may prove them to be at least probable. Also, if the hard data are found to throw no light whatever upon their truth or falsehood, we are justified, I think, in giving rather more weight to the hypothesis of their truth than to the hypothesis of their falsehood. For the present, however, let us confine ourselves to the hard data, with a view to discovering what sort of world can be constructed by their means alone.

Our data now are primarily the facts of sense (i.e. of *our own* sense-data) and the laws of logic. But even the severest scrutiny will allow some additions to this slender stock. Some facts of memory—especially of recent memory— seem to have the highest degree of certainty. Some introspective facts are as certain as any facts of sense. And facts of sense themselves must, for our present purposes, be interpreted with a certain latitude. Spatial and temporal relations must sometimes be included, for example in the case of a swift motion falling wholly within the specious present. And some facts of comparison, such as the likeness or unlikeness of two shades of colour, are certainly to be included among hard data. Also we must remember that the distinction of hard and soft data is psychological and subjective, so that, if there are other minds than our own—which at our present stage must be held doubtful—the catalogue of hard data may be different for them from what it is for us.

Certain common beliefs are undoubtedly excluded from

hard data. Such is the belief which led us to introduce the distinction, namely, that sensible objects in general persist when we are not perceiving them. Such also is the belief in other people's minds: this belief is psychologically derivative from our perception of their bodies, and is felt to demand logical justification as soon as we become aware of its derivativeness. Belief in what is reported by the testimony of others, including all that we learn from books, is of course involved in the doubt as to whether other people have minds at all. Thus the world from which our reconstruction is to begin is very fragmentary. The best we can say for it is that it is slightly more extensive than the world at which Descartes arrived by a similar process, since that world contained nothing except himself and his thoughts.

We are now in a position to understand and state the problem of our knowledge of the external world, and to remove various misunderstandings which have obscured the meaning of the problem. The problem really is: Can the existence of anything other than our own hard data be inferred from the existence of those data? But before considering this problem, let us briefly consider what the problem is *not*.

When we speak of the "external" world in this discussion, we must not mean "spatially external," unless "space" is interpreted in a peculiar and recondite manner. The immediate objects of sight, the coloured surfaces which make up the visible world, are spatially external in the natural meaning of this phrase. We feel them to be "there" as opposed to "here"; without making any assumption of an existence other than hard data, we can more or less estimate the distance of a coloured surface. It seems probably that distances, provided they are not too great, are actually given more or less roughly in sight; but whether this is the case or not, ordinary distances can certainly be estimated approximately by means of the data of sense alone. The immediately given world is spatial, and is further not wholly contained within our own bodies, at least in the obvious sense. Thus our knowledge of what is external in this sense is not open to doubt.

Another form in which the question is often put is: "Can

we know of the existence of any reality which is independent of ourselves?" This form of the question suffers from the ambiguity of the two words "independent" and "self." To take the Self first: the question as to what is to be reckoned part of the Self and what is not, is a very difficult one. Among many other things which we may mean by the Self, two may be selected as specially important, namely (1) the bare subject which thinks and is aware of objects, (2) the whole assemblage of things that would necessarily cease to exist if our lives came to an end. The bare subject, if it exists at all, is an inference, and is not part of the data; therefore, this meaning of Self may be ignored in our present inquiry. The second meaning is difficult to make precise, since we hardly know what things depend upon our lives for their existence. And in this form, the definition of Self introduces the word "depend," which raises the same questions as are raised by the word "independent." Let us therefore take up the word "independent," and return to the Self later.

When we say that one thing is "independent" of another, we may mean either that it is logically possible for the one to exist without the other, or that there is no causal relation between the two such that the one only occurs as the effect of the other. The only way, so far as I know, in which one thing can be *logically* dependent upon another is when the other is *part* of the one. The existence of a book, for example, is logically dependent upon that of its pages: without the pages there would be no book. Thus in this sense the question, "Can we know of the existence of any reality which is independent of ourselves?" reduces to the question, "Can we know of the existence of any reality of which our Self is not part?" In this form, the question brings us back to the problem of defining the Self; but I think, however the Self may be defined, even when it is taken as the bare subject, it cannot be supposed to be part of the immediate object of sense; thus in this form of the question we must admit that we can know of the existence of realities independent of ourselves.

The question of causal dependence is much more difficult.

To know that one kind of thing is causally independent of another, we must know that it actually occurs without the other. Now it is fairly obvious that, whatever legitimate meaning we give to the Self, our thoughts and feelings are causally dependent upon ourselves, i.e. do not occur when there is no Self for them to belong to. But in the case of objects of sense this is not obvious; indeed, as we saw, the common-sense view is that such objects persist in the absence of any percipient. If this is the case, then they are causally independent of ourselves; if not, not. Thus in this form the question reduces to the question whether we can know that objects of sense, or any other objects not our own thoughts and feelings, exist at times when we are not perceiving them. This form, in which the difficult word "independent" no longer occurs, is the form in which we stated the problem a minute ago.

Our question in the above form raises two distinct problems, which it is important to keep separate. First, can we know that objects of sense, or very similar objects, exist at times when we are not perceiving them? Secondly, if this cannot be known, can we know that other objects, inferable from objects of sense but not necessarily resembling them, exist either when we are perceiving the objects of sense or at any other time? This latter problem arises in philosophy as the problem of the "thing in itself," and in science as the problem of matter as assumed in physics. We will consider this latter problem first.

According to some authors—among whom I was formerly included—it is necessary to distinguish between a sensation, which is a mental event, and its object, which is a patch of colour or a noise or what not. If this distinction is made, the object of the sensation is called a "sense-datum" or a "sensible object." Nothing in the problems to be discussed in this book depends upon the question whether this distinction is valid or not. If it is not valid, the sensation and the sense-datum are identical. If it is valid, it is the sense-datum which concerns us in this book, not the sensation. For reasons explained in *The Analysis of Mind* (e.g. p. 141ff.) I have come to regard the distinction as not valid, and to consider the sense-datum identical with the sensation. But it will not be necessary to assume the correctness of this view in what follows.

When I speak of a "sensible object" it must be understood that I do not mean such a thing as a table, which is both visible and tangible, can be seen by many people at once, and is more or less permanent. What I mean is just that patch of colour which is momentarily seen when we look at the table, or just that particular hardness which is felt when we press it, or just that particular sound which is heard when we rap it. Both the thing-in-itself of philosophy and the matter of physics present themselves as causes of the sensible object as much as of the sensation (if these are distinct). What are the common grounds for this opinion?

In each case, I think, the opinion has resulted from the combination of a belief that *something* which can persist independently of our consciousness makes itself known in sensation, with the fact that our sensations often change in ways which seem to depend upon us rather than upon anything which would be supposed to persist independently of us. At first, we believe unreflectingly that everything is as it seems to be, and that, if we shut our eyes, the objects we had been seeing remain as they were though we no longer see them. But there are arguments against this view, which have generally been thought conclusive. It is extraordinarily difficult to see just what the arguments prove; but if we are to make any progress with the problem of the external world, we must try to make up our minds as to those arguments.

A table viewed from one place presents a different appearance from that which it presents from another place. This is the language of common sense, but this language already assumes that there is a real table of which we see the appearances. Let us try to state what is known in terms of sensible objects alone, without any element of hypothesis. We find that as we walk round the table, we perceive a series of gradually changing visible objects. But in speaking of "walking round the table," we have still retained the hypothesis that there is a single table connected with all the appearances. What we ought to say is that, while we have those muscular and other sensations which make us say we are walking, our visual sensations change in a continuous way, so that, for example, a striking patch of colour is not suddenly replaced by something wholly different but is replaced by an insensible gradation of slightly different colours with slightly different shapes. This is what we really know by experience, when we have freed our minds from the assumption of permanent "things" with changing appearances. What is really known is a correlation of muscular and other bodily sensations with changes in visual sensations.

But walking round the table is not the only way of altering its appearance. We can shut one eye, or put on blue spectacles, or look through a microscope. All these operations, in various ways, alter the visual appearance which we call that of the table. More distant objects will also alter their appearance if (as we say) the state of the atmosphere changes—if there is fog or rain or sunshine. Physiological changes also alter the appearances of things. If we assume the world of common sense, all these changes, including those attributed to physiological causes, are changes in the intervening medium. It is not quite so easy as in the former case to reduce this set of facts to a form in which nothing is assumed beyond sensible objects. Anything intervening between ourselves and what we see must be invisible: our view in every direction is bounded by the nearest visible object. It might be objected that a dirty pane of glass, for example, is visible, although we can see things through it. But in this case we really see a spotted patchwork: the dirtier specks in the glass are visible, while the cleaner parts are invisible and allow us to see what is beyond. Thus the discovery that the intervening medium affects the appearances of things cannot be made by means of the sense of sight alone.

Let us take the case of the blue spectacles, which is the simplest, but may serve as a type for the others. The frame of the spectacles is of course visible, but the blue glass, if it is clean, is not visible. The blueness, which we say is in the glass, appears as being in the objects seen through the glass. The glass itself is known by means of the sense of touch. In order to know that it is between us and the objects seen through it, we must know how to correlate the space of touch with the space of sight. This correlation itself, when stated in terms of the data of sense alone is by no means a simple matter. But it presents no difficulties of principle, and may therefore be supposed accomplished. When it has been accomplished, it becomes possible to attach a meaning to the statement that the blue glass, which we can touch, is between us and the object seen, as we say, "through" it.

But we have still not reduced our statement completely to what is actually given in sense. We have fallen into the assumption that the object of which we are conscious when we touch the blue spectacles still exists after we have ceased to touch them. So long as we are touching them, nothing except our finger can be seen through the part touched, which is the only part where we immediately know that there is something. If we are to account for the blue appearance of objects other than the spectacles, when seen through them, it might seem as if we must assume that the spectacles still exist when we are not touching them; and if this assumption really is necessary, our main problem is answered: we have means of knowing of the present existence of objects not given in sense, though of the same kind as objects formerly given in sense.

It may be questioned, however, whether this assumption is actually unavoidable, though it is unquestionably the most natural one to make. We may say that the object of which we become aware when we touch the spectacles continues to have effects afterwards, though perhaps it no longer exists. In this view, the supposed continued existence of sensible objects after they have ceased to be sensible will be a fallacious inference from the fact that they still have effects. It is often supposed that nothing which has ceased to exist can continue to have effects, but this is a mere prejudice, due to a wrong conception of causality. We cannot, therefore, dismiss our present hypothesis on the ground of *a priori* impossibility, but must examine further whether it can really account for the facts.

It may be said that our hypothesis is useless in the case when the blue glass is never touched at all. How, in that case, are we to account for the blue appearance of objects? And more generally, what are we to make of the hypothetical sensations of touch which we associate with untouched visible objects, which we know would be verified if we chose, though in fact we do not verify them? Must not these be attributed to permanent possession, by the objects, of the properties which touch would reveal?

Let us consider the more general question first. Experience has taught us that where we see certain kinds of coloured surfaces we can, by touch, obtain certain expected sensations of hardness or softness, tactile shape, and so on. This leads us to believe that what is seen is usually tangible, and that it has, whether we touch it or not, the hardness or softness which we should expect to feel if we touched it. But the mere fact that we are able to infer what our tactile sensations would be shows that it is not logically necessary to assume tactile qualities before they are felt. All that is really known is that the visual appearance in question together with touch, will lead to certain sensations, which can necessarily be determined in terms of the visual appearance, since otherwise they could not be inferred from it.

We can now give a statement of the experienced facts concerning the blue spectacles, which will supply an interpretation of common-sense beliefs without assuming anything beyond the existence of sensible objects at the times when they are sensible. By experience of the correlation of touch and sight sensations, we become able to associate a certain place in touch-space with a certain corresponding place in sight-space. Sometimes, namely in the case of transparent things, we find that there is a tangible object in a touch-place without there being any visible object in the corresponding sight-place. But in such a case as that of the blue spectacles, we find that whatever object is visible beyond the empty sight-place in the same line of sight has a different colour from what it has when there is no tangible object in the intervening touch-place; and as we move the tangible object in touch-space, the blue patch moves in sight-space. If now we find a blue patch moving in this way in sight-space, when we have no sensible experience of an intervening tangible object, we nevertheless infer that, if we put our hand at a certain place in touch-space, we should experience a certain touch-sensation. If we are to avoid non-sensible objects, this must be taken as the whole of our meaning when we say that the blue spectacles are in a certain place, though we have not touched them, and have only seen other things rendered blue by their interposition.

9. THE ARGUMENT FROM ILLUSION

A. J. AYER

Noted as a persuasive champion of Phenomenalism and of Logical Positivism, Professor Ayer (1910–   ) has written with admirable clarity on many topics in the Theory of Knowledge, as is shown by this passage from his *Foundations of Empirical Knowledge* (Macmillan and Company, Ltd., London, and St. Martin's Press, Inc., New York, 1940), pp. 3–11. This selection should be read with Selections 1 and 10.

Why may we not say that we are directly aware of material things? The answer is provided by what is known as the argument from illusion. This argument, as it is ordinarily stated, is based on the fact that material things may present different appearances to different observers, or to the same observer in different conditions, and that the character of these appearances is to some extent causally determined by the state of the conditions and the observer. For instance, it is remarked that a coin which looks circular from one point of view may look elliptical from another; or that a stick which normally appears straight looks bent when it is seen in water; or that to people who take drugs such as mescal, things appear to change their colours. The familiar cases of mirror images, and double vision, and complete hallucinations, such as the mirage, provide further examples. Nor is this a peculiarity of visual appearances. The same things occurs in the domains of the other senses, including the sense of touch. It may be pointed out, for example, that the taste that a thing appears to have may vary with the condition of the palate; or that a liquid will seem to have a different temperature according as the hand that is feeling it is itself hot or cold; or that a coin seems larger when it is placed on the tongue than when it is held in the palm of the hand; or, to take a case of complete hallucination, that people who have had limbs amputated may still continue to feel pain in them.

Let us now consider one of these examples, say that of the stick which is refracted in water, and see what is to be inferred. For the present it must be assumed that the stick does not really change its shape when it is placed in water. I shall discuss the meaning and validity of this assumption later on. Then it follows that at least one of the visual appearances of the stick is delusive; for it cannot be both crooked and straight. Nevertheless, even in the case where what we see is not the real quality of a material thing, it is supposed that we are still seeing something; and that it is convenient to give this a name. And it is for this purpose that philosophers have recourse to the term "sense-datum." By using it they are able to give what seems to them a satisfactory answer to the question: What is the object of which we are directly aware, in perception, if it is not part of any material thing? Thus, when a man sees a mirage in the desert, he is not thereby perceiving any material thing; for the oasis which he thinks he is perceiving does not exist. At the same time, it is argued, his experience is not an experience of nothing; it has a definite content. Accordingly, it is said that he is experiencing sense-data, which are similar in character to what he would be experiencing if he were seeing a real oasis, but are delusive in the sense that the material thing which they appear to present is not actually there. Or again, when I look at myself in the glass my body appears to be some distance behind the glass; but other observations indicate that it is in front of it. Since it is impossible for my body to be in both these places at once, these perceptions cannot all be veridical. I believe, in fact, that the ones that are delusive are those in which my body appears to be behind the glass. But can it be denied that when one looks at oneself in the glass one is seeing something? And if, in this case, there really is no such material thing as my body in the place where it appears to be, what is it that I am seeing? Once again the answer we are invited to give is that it is a sense-datum. And the same conclusion may be reached by taking any other of my examples.

If anything is established by this, it can be only that there are some cases in which the character of our perceptions makes it necessary for us to say that what we are directly experiencing is not a material thing but a sense-datum. It has not been shown that this is so in all cases. It has not been denied, but rather assumed, that there are some perceptions that do present material things to us as they really are: and in their case there seems at first sight to be no ground for saying that we directly experience sense-data rather than material things. But, as I have already remarked, there is general agreement among the philosophers who make use of the term "sense-datum," or some equivalent term, that what we immediately experience is always a sense-datum and never a material thing. And for this they give further arguments which I shall now examine.

In the first place it is pointed out that there is no intrinsic difference in kind between those of our perceptions that are veridical in their presentation of material things and those that are delusive.[1] When I look at a straight stick, which is refracted in water and so appears crooked, my experience is qualitatively the same as if I were looking at a stick that really was crooked. When, as the result of my putting on green spectacles, the white walls of my room appear to me to be green, my experience is qualitatively the same as if I were perceiving walls that really were green. When people whose legs have been amputated continue to feel pressure upon them, their experience is qualitatively the same as if pressure really were being exerted upon their legs. But, it is argued, if, when our perceptions were delusive, we were always perceiving something of a different kind from what we perceived when they were veridical, we should expect our experience to be qualitatively different in the two cases. We should expect to be able to tell from the intrinsic character of a perception whether it was a perception of a sense-datum or of a material thing. But this is not possible, as the examples that I have given have shown. In some cases there is indeed a distinction with respect to the beliefs to which the experiences give rise, as can be illustrated by my original example. For when, in normal conditions, we have the experience of seeing a straight stick, we believe that there really is a straight stick there;

but when the stick appears crooked, through being refracted
in water, we do not believe that it really is crooked; we do
not regard the fact that it looks crooked in water as evidence
against its being really straight. It must, however, be remarked
that this difference in the beliefs which accompany our perceptions is not grounded in the nature of the perceptions
themselves, but depends upon our past experience. We do not
believe that the stick which appears crooked when it stands
in water really is crooked because we know from past experience that in normal conditions it looks straight. But a child
who had not learned that refraction was a means of distortion would naturally believe that the stick really was
crooked as he saw it. The fact, therefore, that there is this
distinction between the beliefs that accompany veridical and
delusive perceptions does not justify the view that these are
perceptions of generically different objects, especially as the
distinction by no means applies to all cases. For it sometimes
happens that a delusive experience is not only qualitatively
indistinguishable from one that is veridical but is also itself
believed to be veridical, as in the example of the mirage; and,
conversely, there are cases in which experiences that are
actually veridical are believed to be delusive, as when we see
something so strange or unexpected that we say to ourselves
that we must be dreaming. The fact is that from the character of a perception considered by itself, that is, apart from
its relation to further sense-experience, it is not possible to tell
whether it is veridical or delusive. But whether we are entitled
to infer from this that what we immediately experience is
always a sense-datum remains still to be seen.

Another fact which is supposed to show that even in the
case of veridical perceptions we are not directly aware of
material things is that veridical and delusive perceptions may
form a continuous series, both with respect to their qualities
and with respect to the conditions in which they are obtained.[2]
Thus, if I gradually approach an object from a distance I
may begin by having a series of perceptions which are delusive in the sense that the object appears to be smaller than
it really is. Let us assume that this series terminates in a

veridical perception. Then the difference in quality between this perception and its immediate predecessor will be of the same order as the difference between any two delusive perceptions that are next to one another in the series; and, on the assumption that I am walking at a uniform pace, the same will be true of the difference in the conditions on which the generation of the series depends. A similar example would be that of the continuous alteration in the apparent colour of an object which was seen in a gradually changing light. Here again the relation between a veridical perception and the delusive perception that comes next to it in the series is the same as that which obtains between neighbouring delusive perceptions, both with respect to the difference in quality and with respect to the change in the conditions; and these are differences of degree and not of kind. But this, it is argued, is not what we should expect if the veridical perception were a perception of an object of a different sort, a material thing as opposed to a sense-datum. Does not the fact that veridical and delusive perceptions shade into one another in the way that is indicated by these examples show that the objects that are perceived in either case are generically the same? And from this it would follow, if it was acknowledged that the delusive perceptions were perceptions of sense-data, that what we directly experienced was always a sense-datum and never a material thing.

The final argument that has to be considered in this context is based upon the fact that all our perceptions, whether veridical or delusive, are to some extent causally dependent both upon external conditions, such as the character of the light, and upon our own physiological and psychological states. In the case of perceptions that we take to be delusive this is a fact that we habitually recognize. We say, for example, that the stick looks crooked because it is seen in water; that the white walls appear green to me because I am wearing green spectacles; that the water feels cool because my hand is hot; that the murderer sees the ghost of his victim because of his bad conscience or because he has been taking drugs. In the case of perceptions that we take to be veridical we

are apt not to notice such causal dependencies, since as a rule
it is only the occurrence of the unexpected or the abnormal
that induces us to look for a cause. But in this matter also
there is no essential difference between veridical and delusive
perceptions. When, for example, I look at the piece of paper
on which I am writing, I may claim that I am seeing it as it
really is. But I must admit that in order that I should have
this experience it is not sufficient that there should actually
be such a piece of paper there. Many other factors are necessary, such as the condition of the light, the distance at which
I am from the paper, the nature of the background, the state
of my nervous system, and of my eyes. A proof that they are
necessary is that if I vary them I find that I have altered the
character of my perception. Thus, if I screw up my eyes I see
two pieces of paper instead of one; if I grow dizzy the appearance of the paper becomes blurred; if I alter my position
sufficiently it appears to have a different shape and size; if
the light is extinguished, or another object is interposed, I
cease to see it altogether. On the other hand, the converse does
not hold. If the paper is removed I shall cease to see it; but
the state of the light or of my nervous system or any other
of the factors that were relevant to the occurrence of my
perception may still remain the same. From this it may be
inferred that the relation between my perception and these
accompanying conditions is such that, while they are not
causally dependent upon it, it is causally dependent upon
them. And the same would apply to any other instance of a
veridical perception that one cared to choose.

This point being established, the argument proceeds as
follows. It is held to be characteristic of material things that
their existence and their essential properties are independent
of any particular observer. For they are supposed to continue
the same, whether they are observed by one person or another,
or not observed at all. But this, it is argued, has been shown
not to be true of the object we immediately experience. And
so the conclusion is reached that what we immediately experience is in no case a material thing. According to this way
of reasoning, if some perceptions are rightly held to be

veridical, and others delusive, it is because of the different relations in which their objects stand to material things, and it is a philosophical problem to discover what these relations are. We may be allowed to have indirect knowledge of the properties of material things. But this knowledge, it is held, must be obtained through the medium of sense-data, since they are the only objects of which, in sense-perception, we are immediately aware.

Author's Notes

[1] Cf. H. H. Price, *Perception,* p. 31.
[2] Cf. *op. cit.,* p. 32.

10. A REFUTATION OF THE ARGUMENT FROM ILLUSION

J. L. AUSTIN

John Langshaw Austin (1911–1960) played a prominent part in the development of the "Linguistic" philosophy associated in recent years with Oxford University. His dominant thesis was that philosophers must pay the closest attention to ordinary language, for its abuse in philosophy leads to pervasive and unrealized errors. This led him to defend the plain man's view of perception against philosophical attacks, as is here illustrated in two passages from the posthumous reconstruction of his lectures, *Sense and Sensibilia* (The Clarendon Press, Oxford, 1962), pp. 22–32 and 46–54. The criticism is mainly directed against the "Argument from Illusion" as stated by Ayer (Selection 9).

Now I want to call attention, first of all, to the name of this argument—the "argument from *illusion*," and to the fact that it is produced as establishing the conclusion that some at least of our "perceptions" are *delusive*. For in this there are two clear implications—(a) that all the cases cited in the argument are cases of *illusions*; and (b) that *illusion* and *delusion* are the same thing. But both of these implications, of course, are quite wrong; and it is by no means unimportant to point this out, for, as we shall see, the argument trades on confusion at just this point.

What, then, would be some genuine examples of illusion? (The fact is that hardly any of the cases cited by Ayer is, at any rate without stretching things, a case of illusion at all.) Well, first, there are some quite clear cases of *optical* illusion —for instance the case we mentioned earlier in which, of two lines of equal length, one is made to look longer than the other. Then again there are illusions produced by professional "illusionists," conjurors—for instance the Headless Woman on the stage, who is made to look headless, or the ventriloquist's dummy which is made to appear to be talking.

Rather different—not (usually) produced on purpose—is the case where wheels rotating rapidly enough in one direction may look as if they were rotating quite slowly in the opposite direction. Delusions, on the other hand, are something altogether different from this. Typical cases would be delusions of persecution, delusions of grandeur. These are primarily a matter of grossly disordered beliefs (and so, probably, behaviour) and may well have nothing in particular to do with perception.[1] But I think we might also say that the patient who sees pink rats has (suffers from) delusions—particularly, no doubt, if, as would probably be the case, he is not clearly aware that his pink rats aren't real rats.[2]

The most important differences here are that the term "an illusion" (in a perceptual context) does not suggest that something totally unreal is *conjured up*—on the contrary, there just is the arrangement of lines and arrows on the page, the woman on the stage with her head in a black bag, the rotating wheels; whereas the term "delusion" *does* suggest something totally unreal, not really there at all. (The convictions of the man who has delusions of persecution can be *completely* without foundation.) For this reason delusions are a much more serious matter—something is really wrong, and what's more, wrong *with* the person who has them. But when I see an optical illusion, however well it comes off, there is nothing wrong with me personally, the illusion is not a little (or a large) peculiarity or idiosyncrasy of my own; it is quite public, anyone can see it, and in many cases standard procedures can be laid down for producing it. Furthermore, if we are not actually to be taken in, we need to be *on our guard*; but it is no use to tell the sufferer from delusions to be on his guard. He needs to be cured.

Why is it that we tend—if we do—to confuse illusions with delusions? Well, partly, no doubt the terms are often used loosely. But there is also the point that people may have, without making this explicit, different views or theories about the facts of some cases. Take the case of seeing a ghost, for example. It is not generally known, or agreed, what seeing ghosts *is*. Some people think of seeing ghosts as a case of something being conjured up, perhaps by the disordered nervous system of the victim; so in their view seeing ghosts is a case of delusion. But other people have the idea that what is called seeing ghosts is a case of being taken in by shadows, perhaps, or reflections, or a trick of the light—that is, they assimilate the case in their minds to illusion. In this way, seeing ghosts, for example, may come to be labelled sometimes as "delusion," sometimes as "illusion"; and it may not be noticed that it makes a difference which label we use. Rather, similarly, there seem to be different doctrines in the field as to what mirages are. Some seem to take a mirage to be a vision conjured up by the crazed brain of the thirsty and exhausted traveller (delusion), while in other accounts it is a case of atmospheric refraction, whereby something below the horizon is made to appear above it (illusion). (Ayer, you may remember, takes the delusion view, although he cites it along with the rest as a case of illusion. He says not that the oasis appears to be where it is not, but roundly that "it does not exist.")

The way in which the "argument from illusion" positively trades on not distinguishing illusions from delusions is, I think, this. So long as it is being suggested that the cases paraded for our attention are cases of *illusion,* there is the implication (from the ordinary use of the word) that there really is something there that we perceive. But then, when these cases begin to be quietly called delusive, there comes in the very different suggestion of something being conjured up, something unreal or at any rate "immaterial." These two implications taken together may then subtly insinuate that in the cases cited there really is something that we are perceiving, but that this is an immaterial something; and this insinuation, even if not conclusive by itself, is certainly well calculated to edge us a little closer towards just the position where the sense-datum theorist wants to have us.

So much, then—though certainly there could be a good deal more—about the differences between illusions and delusions and the reasons for not obscuring them. Now let us look briefly at some of the other cases Ayer lists. Reflections, for instance. No doubt you *can* produce illusions with mirrors, suitably disposed. But is just *any* case of seeing something in a mirror an illusion, as he implies? Quite obviously not. For seeing things in mirrors is a perfectly *normal* occurrence, completely familiar, and there is usually no question of anyone being taken in. No doubt, if you're an infant or an aborigine and have never come across a mirror before, you may be pretty baffled, and even visibly perturbed, when you do. But is that a reason why the rest of us should speak of illusion here? And just the same goes for the phenomena of perspective—again, one *can* play tricks with perspective, but in the ordinary case there is no question of illusion. That a round coin should "look elliptical" (in one sense) from some points of view is exactly what we expect and what we normally find; indeed, we should be badly put out if we ever found this not to be so. Refraction again—the stick that looks bent in water—is far too familiar a case to be properly called a case of illusion. We may perhaps be prepared to agree that the stick looks bent; but then we can see that it's partly submerged in water, so that is exactly how we should expect it to look.

It is important to realize here how familiarity, so to speak, takes the edge off illusion. Is the cinema a case of illusion? Well, just possibly the first man who ever saw moving pictures may have felt inclined to say that here was a case of illusion. But in fact it's pretty unlikely that even he, even momentarily, was actually taken in; and by now the whole thing is so ordinary a part of our lives that it never occurs to us even to raise the question. One might as well ask whether producing a photograph is producing an illusion—which would plainly be just silly.

Then we must not overlook, in all this talk about illusions and delusions, that there are plenty of more or less unusual cases, not yet mentioned, which certainly aren't either. Suppose that a proof-reader makes a mistake—he fails to notice that what ought to be "causal" is printed as "casual"; does he have a delusion? Or is there an illusion before him? Neither, of course; he simply *misreads*. Seeing after-images, too, though not a particularly frequent occurrence and not just an ordinary case of seeing, is neither seeing illusions nor having delusions. And what about dreams? Does the dreamer see illusions? Does he have delusions? Neither; dreams are *dreams.*

Let us turn for a moment to what Price has to say about illusions. He produces,[3] by way of saying "what the term 'illusion' means," the following "provisional definition": "An illusory sense-datum of sight or touch is a sense-datum which is such that we tend to take it to be part of the surface of a material object, but if we take it so we are wrong." It is by no means clear, of course, what this dictum itself means; but still, it seems fairly clear that the definition doesn't actually fit all the cases of illusion. Consider the two lines again. Is there anything here which we tend to take, wrongly, to be part of the surface of a material object? It doesn't seem so. We just see the two lines, we don't think or even tend to think that we see anything else, we aren't even raising the question whether anything is or isn't "part of the surface" of—what, anyway? the lines? the page?—the trouble is just that one line looks longer than the other, though it isn't. Nor surely, in the case of the Headless Woman, is it a question whether anything is or isn't part of her surface; the trouble is just that she looks as if she had no head.

It is noteworthy, of course, that, before he even begins to consider the "argument from illusion," Price has already incorporated in this "definition" the idea that in such cases there is something to be seen *in addition to* the ordinary things —which is part of what the argument is commonly used, and not uncommonly taken, to *prove.* But this idea surely has no place in an attempt to say what "illusion" *means.* It comes in again, improperly I think, in his account of perspective (which incidently he also cites as a species of illusion)—"a distant hillside which is full of protuberances, and slopes upwards at quite a gentle angle, will appear flat and vertical. . . . This means that the sense-datum, the colour-expanse which we sense, actually *is* flat and vertical." But why should we accept this account of the matter? Why should we say that there is *anything* we see which *is* flat and vertical, though not "part of the surface" of any material object? To speak thus is to assimilate all such cases to cases of delusion, where there *is* something not "part of any material thing." But we have already discussed the undesirability of this assimilation.

Next, let us have a look at the account Ayer himself gives of some at least of the cases he cites. (In fairness we must remember here that Ayer has a number of quite substantial reservations of his own about the merits and efficacy of the argument from illusion, so that it is not easy to tell just how seriously he intends his exposition of it to be taken; but this is a point we shall come back to.)

First, then, the familiar case of the stick in water. Of this case Ayer says (a) that since the stick looks bent but is straight, "at least one of the visual appearances of the stick is *delusive*"; and (b) that "what we see [directly anyway] is not the real quality of [a few lines later, not part of] a material thing." Well now: does the stick "look bent" to begin with? I think we can agree that it does, we have no better way of describing it. But of course it does *not* look *exactly* like a bent stick, a bent stick out of water—at most, it may be said to look rather like a bent stick partly immersed *in* water. After all, we can't help seeing the water the stick is partly immersed in. So exactly what in this case is supposed to be *delusive*? What is wrong, what is even faintly surprising, in the idea of a stick's being straight but looking bent sometimes? Does anyone suppose that if something is straight, then it jolly well has to *look* straight at all times and in all circumstances? Obviously no one seriously supposes this. So what mess are we supposed to get into here, what is the difficulty? For of couse it has to be suggested that there *is* a difficulty—a difficulty, furthermore, which calls for a pretty radical solution, the introduction of sense-data. But what is the problem we are invited to solve in this way?

Well, we are told, in this case you are seeing *something*; and what is this something "if it is not part of any material thing?" But this question is, really, completely mad. The straight part of the stick, the bit not under water, is presumably part of a material thing; don't we see that? And what about the bit *under* water?—we can see that too. We can see, come to that, the water itself. In fact what we see is *a stick partly immersed in water*; and it is particularly extraordinary that this should appear to be called in question—that a question should be raised about *what* we are seeing—since this, after all, is simply the description of the situation with which we started. It was, that is to say, agreed at the start that we were looking at a stick, a "material thing," part of which was under water. If, to take a rather different case, a church were cunningly camouflaged so that it looked like a barn, how could any serious question be raised about what we see when we look at it? We see, of course, *a church* that now *looks like a barn*. We do *not* see an immaterial barn, an immaterial church, or an immaterial anything else. And what in this case could seriously tempt us to say that we do?

Notice, incidentally, that in Ayer's description of the stick-in-water case, which is supposed to be prior to the drawing of any philosophical conclusions, there has already crept in the unheralded but important expression "visual appearances" —It is, of course, ultimately to be suggested that all we *ever* get when we see is a visual appearance (whatever that may be).

Consider next the case of my reflection in a mirror. My body, Ayer says, "appears to be some distance behind the glass"; but as it's in front, it can't really be behind the glass. So what am I seeing? A sense-datum. What about this? Well, once again, although there is no objection to saying that my body "appears to be some distance behind the glass," in saying this we must remember what sort of situation we are dealing with. It does not "appear to be" there in a way which might tempt me (though it might tempt a baby or a savage) to go round the back and look for it, and be astonished when this enterprise proved a failure. (To say that A is *in* B doesn't always mean that if you open B you will find A, just as to say that A is *on* B doesn't always mean that you could pick it off—consider "I saw my face in the mirror"; "There's a pain in my toe"; "I heard him on the radio"; "I saw the image

on the screen," etc. Seeing something in a mirror is not like
seeing a bun in a shop window.) But does it follow that, since
my body is not actually located behind the mirror, I am not
seeing a material thing? Plainly not. For one thing, I can see
the mirror (nearly always anyway). I can see my own body
"indirectly," *sc.* in the mirror. I can also see the reflection of
my own body or, as some would say, a mirror-image. And a
mirror-image (if we choose this answer) is not a "sense-
datum"; it can be photographed, seen by any number of
people, and so on. (Of course there is no question here of
either illusion or delusion.) And if the question is pressed,
what actually *is* some distance, five feet say, behind the
mirror, the answer is, not a sense-datum, but some region of
the adjoining room.

The mirage case—at least if we take the view, as Ayer does,
that the oasis the traveller thinks he can see "does not exist"—
is significantly more amenable to the treatment it is given. For
here we are supposing the man to be genuinely deluded, he
is *not* "seeing a material thing."[4] We don't actually have to
say, however, even here that he is "experiencing sense-data";
for though, as Ayer says above, "it is convenient to give a
name" to what he is experiencing, the fact is that it already
has a name—a *mirage*. Again, we should be wise not to
accept too readily the statement that what he is experiencing
is "*similar in character* to what he would be experiencing if
he were seeing a real oasis." For is it at all likely, really, to
be very similar? And, looking ahead, if we were to concede
this point we should find the concession being used against
us at a later state—namely, at the stage where we shall be
invited to agree that we see sense-data always, in normal
cases too.

[Austin now proceeds to discuss the second stage of the
argument, which seeks to show that what we (directly)
perceive is always a sense-datum. Ayer's version is given in
S.9 above. Price's version, also criticised, is found on
pp. 31–32 of his *Perception*; he makes the same point about
the indistinguishability of normal and abnormal sense-data:
"The abnormal crooked sense-datum of a straight stick

standing in water is qualitatively indistinguishable from a normal sense-datum of a crooked stick. Again a mirror image of a right-hand glove 'looks exactly like' a real left-hand glove; i.e. the two sense-data are indistinguishable, though one is abnormal, the other normal. Is it not incredible that two entities so similar in all these qualities should really be so utterly different: that the one should be a real constituent of a material object, wholly independent of the observer's mind and organism, while the other is merely the fleeting product of his cerebral processes?" He also emphasizes the continuity between abnormal and normal sense-data as one moves toward or away from an object. N.B. (1) While he talks of "normal and abnormal sense-data," Ayer talks of "veridical and delusive perception"; the two are not quite parallel in that by "perception" Ayer seems to mean the experience or awareness of an object not the object or datum itself. (2) Austin admittedly does not discuss Ayer's "final argument" pp. 132-134.]

1. It is pretty obvious, for a start, that the terms in which the argument is stated by Ayer are grossly tendentious. Price, you remember, is not producing the argument as a proof that we are always aware of sense-data; in his view that question has already been settled, and he conceives himself to be faced here only with the question whether any sense-data are "parts of the surfaces of material objects." But in Ayer's exposition the argument *is* put forward as a ground for the conclusion that what we are (directly) aware of in perception is always a sense-datum; and if so, it seems a rather serious defect that this conclusion is practically assumed from the very first sentence of the statement of the argument itself. In that sentence Ayer uses, not indeed for the first time, the term "perceptions" (which incidentally has never been defined or explained), and takes it for granted, here and throughout, that there is at any rate some kind of entities of which we are aware in absolutely all cases—namely, "perceptions," delusive or veridical. But of course, if one has already been induced to swallow the idea that every case, whether "delusive" or "veridical," supplies us with "perceptions," one is

only too easily going to be made to feel that it would be straining at a gnat not to swallow sense-data in an equally comprehensive style. But in fact one has not even been told what "perceptions" *are*; and the assumption of their ubiquity has been slipped in without any explanation or argument whatever. But if those to whom the argument is ostensibly addressed were not thus made to concede the essential point from the beginning, would the statement of the argument be quite such plain sailing?

2. Of course we shall also want to enter a protest against the argument's bland assumption of a simple dichotomy between "veridical and delusive experiences." There is, as we have already seen, *no* justification at all *either* for lumping all so-called "delusive" experiences together, *or* for lumping together all so-called "veridical" experiences. But again, could the argument run quite so smoothly without this assumption? It would certainly—and this, incidentally, would be all to the good—take rather longer to state.

3. But now let us look at what the argument actually says. It begins, you will remember, with an alleged statement of fact—namely, that "there is no intrinsic difference in kind between those of our perceptions that are veridical in their presentation of material things and those that are delusive" (Ayer), that "there is no qualitative difference between normal sense-data as such and abnormal sense-data as such" (Price). Now, waiving so far as possible the numerous obscurities in and objections to this manner of speaking, let us ask whether what is being alleged here is actually true. Is it the case that "delusive and veridical experiences" are not "qualitatively different"? Well, at least it seems perfectly extraordinary to say so in this sweeping way. Consider a few examples. I may have the experience (dubbed "delusive" presumably) of dreaming that I am being presented to the Pope. Could it be seriously suggested that having this dream is "qualitatively indistinguishable" from *actually being* presented to the Pope? Quite obviously not. After all, we have the phrase "a dream-like quality"; some waking experiences are said to have this dream-like quality, and some artists and

writers occasionally try to impart it, usually with scant success, to their works. But of course, if the fact here alleged *were* a fact, the phrase would be perfectly meaningless, because applicable to everything. If dreams were not "qualitatively" different from waking experiences, then *every* waking experience would be like a dream; the dream-like quality would be, not difficult to capture, but impossible to avoid.[5] It is true, to repeat, that dreams are *narrated* in the same terms as waking experiences: these terms, after all, are the best terms we have; but it would be wildly wrong to conclude from this that what is narrated in the two cases is *exactly alike*. When we are hit on the head we sometimes say that we "see stars"; but for all that, seeing stars when you are hit on the head is *not* "qualitatively" indistinguishable from seeing stars when you look at the sky.

Again, it is simply not true to say that seeing a bright green after-image against a white wall is exactly like seeing a bright green patch actually on the wall; or that seeing a white wall through blue spectacles is exactly like seeing a blue wall; or that seeing pink rats in D.T.s is exactly like really seeing pink rats; or (once again) that seeing a stick refracted in water is exactly like seeing a bent stick. In all these cases we may *say* the same things ("It looks blue," "It looks bent," etc.), but this is no reason at all for denying the obvious fact that the "experiences" are *different*.

4. Next, one may well wish at least to ask for the credentials of a curious general principle on which both Ayer and Price seem to rely,[6] to the effect that, if two things are not "generically the same," the same "in nature," then they can't be alike, or even very nearly alike. If it were true, Ayer says, that from time to time we perceived things of two different kinds, then "we should expect" them to be qualitatively different. But why on earth should we?—particularly if, as he suggests would be the case, we never actually found such a thing to be true. It is not at all easy to discuss this point sensibly, because of the initial absurdity in the hypothesis that we perceive just *two* kinds of things. But if, for example, I had never seen a mirror, but were told (a) that in mirrors

one sees reflections of things, and (b) that reflections of things are not "generically the same" as things, is there any reason why I should forthwith *expect* there to be some whacking big "qualitative" difference between seeing things and seeing their reflections? Plainly not; if I were prudent, I should simply wait and see what seeing reflections was like. If I am told that a lemon is generically different from a piece of soap, do I "expect" that no piece of soap could look just like a lemon? Why should I?

(It is worth noting that Price helps the argument along at this point by a bold stroke of rhetoric: how *could* two entities be "qualitatively indistinguishable," he asks, if one is a "real constituent of a material object," the other "a fleeting product of his cerebral processes"? But how in fact are we supposed to have been persuaded that sense-data are *ever* fleeting products of cerebral processes? Does this colourful description fit, for instance, the reflection of my face in a mirror?)

5. Another erroneous principle which the argument here seems to rely on is this: that it *must* be the case that "delusive and veridical experiences" are not (as such) "qualitatively" or "intrinsically" distinguishable—for if they were distinguishable, we should never be "deluded." But of course this is not so. From the fact that I am sometimes "deluded," mistaken, taken in through failing to distinguish A from B, it does not follow at all that A and B must be *indistinguishable*. Perhaps I should have noticed the difference if I had been more careful or attentive; perhaps I am just bad at distinguishing things of this sort (e.g. vintages); perhaps, again, I have never learned to discriminate between them, or haven't had much practice at it. As Ayer observes, probably truly, "a child who had not learned that refraction was a means of distortion would naturally believe that the stick really was crooked as he saw it"; but how is the fact that an uninstructed child probably would not discriminate between *being refracted* and *being crooked* supposed to establish the allegation that there *is* no "qualitative" difference between the two cases? What sort of reception would I be likely to get from a professional tea-taster, if I were to say to him,

"But there can't be any difference between the flavours of these two brands of tea, for I regularly fail to distinguish between them"? Again, when "the quickness of the hand deceives the eye," it is not that what the hand is really doing is *exactly like* what we are tricked into thinking it is doing, but simply that it is *impossible to tell* what it is really doing. In this case it may be true that we can't distinguish, and not merely that we don't; but even this doesn't mean that the two cases are exactly alike.

I do not, of course, wish to deny that there may be cases in which "delusive and veridical experiences" really are "qualitatively indistinguishable"; but I certainly do wish to deny (a) that such cases are anything like as *common* as both Ayer and Price seem to suppose, and (b) that there *have* to be such cases to accommodate the undoubted fact that we are sometimes "deceived by our senses." We are not, after all, quasi-infallible beings, who can be taken in only where the avoidance of mistake is completely impossible. But if we are prepared to admit that there may be, even that there are, *some* cases in which "delusive and veridical perceptions" really are indistinguishable, does this admission require us to drag in, or even let in, sense-data? No. For even if we were to make the prior admission (which we have so far found no reason to make) that in the "abnormal" cases we perceive sense-data, we should not be obliged to extend this admission to the "normal" cases too. For why on earth should it *not* be the case that, in some few instances, perceiving one sort of thing is exactly like perceiving another?

6. There is a further quite general difficulty in assessing the force of this argument, which we (in common with the authors of our texts) have slurred over so far. The question which Ayer invites us to consider is whether two classes of "perceptions," the veridical and the delusive, are or are not "qualitatively different," "intrinsically different in kind"; but how are we supposed to set about even considering this question, when we are not told what "a perception" *is*? In particular, how many of the circumstances of a situation, as these would ordinarily be stated, are supposed to be included in

"the perception"? For example, to take the stick in water again: it is a feature of this case that part of the stick is under water, and water, of course, is not invisible; is the water, then, part of "the perception"? It is difficult to conceive of any grounds for denying that it is; but *if* it is, surely this is a perfectly obvious respect in which "the perception" differs from, is distinguishable from, the "perception" we have when we look at a bent stick *not* in water. There is a sense, perhaps, in which the presence or absence of water is not the *main thing* in this case—we are supposed to be addressing ourselves primarily to questions about the stick. But in fact, as a great quantity of psychological investigation has shown, discrimination between one thing and another very frequently depends on such more or less extraneous concomitants of the main thing, even when such concomitants are not consciously taken note of. As I said, we are told nothing of what "a perception" is; but could any defensible account, if such an account were offered, completely exclude all these highly significant attendant circumstances? And if they *were* excluded—in some more or less arbitrary way— how much interest or importance would be left in the contention that "delusive" and "veridical" perceptions are indistinguishable? Inevitably, if you rule out the respects in which A and B differ, you may expect to be left with respects in which they are alike.

I conclude, then, that this part of the philosophical argument involves (though not in every case equally essentially) (a) acceptance of a quite bogus dichotomy of all "perceptions" into two groups, the "delusive" and the "veridical"— to say nothing of the unexplained introduction of "perceptions" themselves; (b) an implicit but grotesque exaggeration of the *frequency* of "delusive perceptions"; (c) a further grotesque exaggeration of the *similarity* between "delusive" perceptions and "veridical" ones; (d) the erroneous suggestion that there *must* be such similarity, or even qualitative *identity*; (e) the acceptance of the pretty gratuitous idea that things "generically different" could not be qualitatively alike; and (f) —which is really a corollary of (c) and (a)—the gratuitous neglect of those more or less subsidiary features which often make possible the discrimination of situations which, in other *broad* respects, may be roughly alike. These seem to be rather serious deficiencies.

AUTHOR'S NOTES

[1] The latter point holds, of course, for *some* uses of "illusion" too; there are the illusions which some people (are said to) lose as they grow older and wiser.

[2] Cp. the white rabbit in the play called *Harvey*.

[3] Price, *Perception,* p. 27.

[4] Not even "indirectly," no such thing is "presented." Doesn't this seem to make the case, though more amenable, a good deal less useful to the philosopher? It's hard to see how normal cases could be said to be *very like* this.

[5] This is part, no doubt *only* part, of the absurdity in Descartes' toying with the notion that the whole of our experience might be a dream.

[6] Ayer in fact expresses qualms later: see p. 12 of his book.

11. THE "LOGICAL HOWLER" OF THE SENSE-DATUM THEORY

G. RYLE

Like his younger contemporary Austin, Professor Gilbert Ryle (1900–   ) has been one of the principal architects of the characteristic "Oxford" philosophy. He has sought, by a wealth of examples from the ordinary use of expressions, to "plot the logical geography" of our concepts of mental powers and operations. In this passage from his *The Concept of Mind* (Hutchinson & Co. Ltd., London, 1949) pp. 213–220, he attacks the faulty conceptual geography of the Sense-datum Theory.

I shall try to prove that this whole theory rests upon a logical howler, the howler, namely, of assimilating the concept of sensation to the concept of observation; and I shall try to show that this assimilation makes nonsense simultaneously of the concept of sensation and of the concept of observation. The theory says that when a person has a visual sensation, on the occasion, for example, of getting a glimpse of a horse-race, his having this sensation consists in his finding or intuiting a sensum, namely a patchwork of colours. This means that having a glimpse of a horse-race is explained in terms of his having a glimpse of something else, the patchwork of colours. But if having a glimpse of a horse-race entails having at least one sensation, then having a glimpse of colour patches must again involve having at least one appropriate sensation, which in its turn must be analysed into the sensing of yet an earlier sensum, and so on forever. At each move having a sensation is construed as a sort of espying of a particular something, often gravely called "a sensible object," and at each move this espying must involve the having of a sensation. The use of awe-inspiring words like "intuit" in no way exempts us from having to say that for a person to find, watch, listen to, peep at or savour something he must be sensitively affected; and to be sensitively affected is to have at least one sensation. So whether, as we ordinarily think, we see horse-races or whether, as we are instructed to think, we intuit colour patches, the descrying of whatever we descry involves our having sensations. And having sensations is not by itself descrying, any more than bricks are houses, or letters are words.

As has been shown earlier, there is an important logical connection between the concept of sensation and that of observing or perceiving, a connection which by itself entails that they are concepts of different kinds. There is a contradiction in saying that someone is watching or peeping at something, but not getting even one glimpse of it; or in saying that someone is listening to something, though he gets no auditory sensations. Having at least one sensation is part of the force of "perceiving," "overhearing," "savouring," and the rest. It follows that having a sensation cannot itself be a species of perceiving, finding or espying. If all clothes are concatenations of stitches, absurdity results from saying that all stitches are themselves very tiny clothes.

It has already been remarked earlier in this chapter that there are several salient differences between the concepts of sensations and those of observation, scrutinizing, detecting, and the rest, which are revealed by the uninterchangeability of the epithets by which the different things are described. Thus we can speak of the motives from which a person listens to something, but not of the motives from which he has an auditory sensation; he may show skill, patience, and method in peering, but not in having visual sensations. Conversely tickles and tastes may be relatively acute, but his inspections and detections cannot be so described. It makes sense to speak of someone refraining from watching a race or of his suspending his observation of a reptile, but it makes no sense to speak of someone refraining from feeling a pain, or suspending the tingle in his nose. Yet if having a tingle were, as the theory holds, intuiting a special object, it is not clear why this or any discomfort should not be dismissed by suspending the intuition of it.

Sensations then, are not perceivings, observings, or findings;

they are not detectings, scannings, or inspectings; they are not apprehendings, cognizings, intuitings, or knowings. To have a sensation is not to be in a cognitive relation to a sensible object. There are no such objects. Nor is there any such relation. Not only is it false, as was argued earlier, that sensations can be objects of observation; it is also false that they are themselves observings of objects.

A champion of the Sense-datum Theory might admit that, for a person to be describable as listening to a train, he must catch at least one sound and so have at least one auditory sensation, and still deny that, by admitting this point, he necessarily set his foot on the suggested Gadarene slope; he need not concede that, for a person to be describable as hearing a sound, he must have yet a prior sensation in his sensing of that sense-datum. "Having a sensation" is merely the vulgar way of reporting the simple intuiting of a special sensible object and to say that a person intuits such an object does not entail his being in any way sensitively affected. He might be an angelic and impassive contemplator of sounds and colour patches, and these might be of any degree of intensity, without anything in him being describable as more or less acute. He may come across tickles without himself being tickled, and the ways in which he becomes acquainted with smells or pains need not involve his being sensitive in any way other than that he is capable of simple detection or inspection of such things.

Such a defence in effect explains the having of sensations as the *not* having any sensations. It avoids the imputed regress by the heroic device of suggesting that sensing is a cognitive process which does not require its owner to be susceptible of stimuli, or to be describable as either highly or slightly sensitive. By construing sensation as the simple observation of special objects, it first does away with the very concept it was professing to elucidate and, in the second stage, makes nonsense of the concept of observation itself, since this concept entails the concept of sensations which are not themselves observings.

Alternatively, the Sense-datum Theory may be defended on

a different ground. It may be said that, whatever may be the logical rules governing the concepts of sensation and of observation, it remains an unchallengeable fact that in seeing I am directly presented with patchworks of colours momentarily occupying my field of view, in hearing I am directly presented with noises, in smelling with smells, and so forth. That sense-data are sensed is beyond question and independent of theory. Two-dimensional colour patches are what I see in the strictest sense of "see"; and these are not horses and jockeys, but at best the looks, or visual appearances, of horses and jockeys. If there are not two candles, then the squinter does not really see two candles, but he certainly sees two bright somethings, and these can be nothing but two proprietary "candle-looks" or sense-data. The Sense-datum Theory is not inventing factitious entities, it is merely drawing our attention to the immediate objects of sense which, from our ordinary preoccupation with common objects, we are in the habit of cold-shouldering out of conversation. If logical considerations seem to require that having a sensation shall not be on all fours with descrying hawks, or gazing at horse-races, so much the worse for those considerations, since having a visual sensation certainly is a non-inferential discerning of a particular sensible object.

Let us consider, then, the hackneyed instance of a person looking at a round plate tilted away from him, which he may therefore describe as looking elliptical; and let us see what, if anything, requires us to say that he is descrying a something which really is elliptical. It is agreed that the plate is not elliptical but round, and for the argument's sake we may concede that the spectator is veraciously reporting that it looks elliptical, (though round plates, however steeply tilted, do not usually look elliptical). The question is whether the truth of his report that the plate looks elliptical implies that he is really espying, or scanning, an object of sense which is elliptical, something which, not being the plate itself, can claim to be entitled "a look" or "a visual appearance of the plate." We may also grant that if we are bound to say that he has come across an object of sense which is really elliptical and is a visual appearance of the plate, then this elliptical object is a two-dimensional colour patch, momentary in existence and proprietary to one percipient, i.e. that it is a sense-datum and therefore that there are sense-data.

Now a person without a theory feels no qualms in saying that the round plate might look elliptical. Nor would he feel any qualms in saying that the round plate looks as if it were elliptical. But he would feel qualms in following the recommendation to say that he is seeing an elliptical look of a round plate. Though he talks easily enough in some contexts of the looks of things, and easily enough in other contexts of seeing things, he does not ordinarily talk of seeing or of scanning the looks of things, of gazing at views of races, of catching glimpses of glimpses of hawks, or of descrying the visual appearances of tree-tops. He would feel that, if he mixed his ingredients in these fashions, he would be talking the same sort of nonsense as he would if he moved from talking of eating biscuits and talking of taking nibbles of biscuits to talking of eating nibbles of biscuits. And he would be quite right. He cannot significantly speak of "eating nibbles," since "nibble" is already a noun of eating, and he cannot talk of "seeing looks," since "look" is already a noun of seeing.

When he says that the tilted plate has an elliptical look, or looks as if it were elliptical, he means that it looks as an elliptical but untilted plate would look. Tilted round things sometimes do look quite or exactly like untilted elliptical things; straight sticks half-immersed in water occasionally do look rather like unimmersed bent sticks; solid but distant mountains sometimes do look rather like flat mural decorations quite near to one's nose. In saying that the plate looks elliptical, he is not characterizing an extra object, namely "a look," as being elliptical, he is likening how the tilted round plate does look to how untilted elliptical plates do or would look. He is not saying "I am seeing a flat elliptical patch of White," but "I might be seeing an elliptical and untilted piece of white china." We may say that the nearer aeroplane looks faster than the distant aeroplane, but we could not say that it has "a faster look." "Looks faster" means "looks as if it is flying faster through the air." Talking about the apparent speeds of aeroplanes is not talking about the speeds of appearances of aeroplanes.

In other words, the grammatically unsophisticated sentence "the plate has an elliptical look" does not, as the theory assumes, express one of those basic relational truths which are so much venerated in theory and so seldom used in daily life. It expresses a fairly complex proposition of which one part is both general and hypothetical. It is applying to the actual look of the plate a rule or a recipe about the typical looks of untilted elliptical plates, no matter whether there exist such pieces of china or not. It is what I have elsewhere called a mongrel-categorical statement. It is analogous to saying of someone that he is behaving judicially, or talking like a pedagogue. The squinter, aware of his squint, who reports that it looks just as if there were two candles on the table, or that he might be seeing two candles, is describing how the single candle looks by referring to how pairs of candles regularly look to spectators who are not squinting; and if, not being aware of his squint he says that there are two candles on the table, he is, in this case, misapplying just the same general recipe. The expressions "it looks . . . ," "it looks as if . . . ," "it has the appearance of . . . ," "I might be seeing . . . " and plenty of others of the same family contain the force of a certain sort of open hypothetical prescription applied to a case in hand. When we say that someone has a pedantic appearance, we do not mean to suggest that there are two kinds of pedantic beings, namely some men and some appearances of men. We mean that he looks rather like some pedantic people look. Similarly there are not two kinds of elliptical objects, namely some platters and some looks; there are only some platters which are elliptical and others which look as if they were elliptical.

In ordinary life there are certain ways in which we are quite ready to speak of patches and splashes of colour. A housewife might say that her sitting-room needed a splash of crimson, without specifying crimson paper, crimson flowers, crimson rugs, or crimson curtains. She might ask her husband to go out and buy "an expanse of crimson . . . ," leaving it to him to fill in the lacuna with "geraniums," "distemper," "cretonne," or whatever else would meet her requirements. In a similar way an observer peering through a gap in a hedge might say that he saw an area of yellow . . . , but be unable to specify whether what he had seen were yellow daffodils, yellow charlock, yellow canvas, or any other specific kind of common object or material. To complete his sentence he could say only "I saw something yellow."

In contrast with this ordinary use of lacuna-expressions like "a patch of yellow . . ." and "a splash of crimson something or other," the Sense-datum Theory recommends another idiom in which we are to say "I see a patch of White" (and not "I see a patch of white . . .") or "he espied a two-dimensional, elliptical expanse of Blue (and not "a flat-looking, elliptical-looking blue something or other").

Now I am denying that having a visual sensation is a sort of observation describable as the sensing or intuiting of colour patches. But I am not denying that a woman can properly ask her husband to buy a splash of crimson . . . , or that a pedestrian can properly be said to espy an expanse of yellow something or other through a hole in the hedge. What the Sense-datum Theory has done is to try to skim an ethereal cream off such ordinary lacuna-descriptions of common objects; to talk as if it had found a new class of objects, where it has only misconstrued a familiar range of statements mentioning how otherwise unparticularised common objects are found to look.

Talking about looks, sounds, and smells, about expanses, shapes and colours, just as much as talking about perspectives, hazes, focuses, and twilights, is already talking about common objects, since it is applying learned perception recipes for the typical appearances of common objects to whatever one is trying to make out at the moment. To say that someone caught a glimpse, or heard a sound, is already to say more than would be involved in barely describing his visual and auditory sensations, for it is already to range what he is attending to under fairly general perception recipes.

This point may be illustrated by reference to the historic doctrine of Secondary Qualities. It was half-correctly observed that when a common object is described as green, bitter, chilly, pungent, or shrill, it is being characterized as looking, tasting, feeling, smelling, or sounding so and so to a sentient observer; it was correctly noticed, too, that conditions which affect his sensitivity make a difference in how the things look, taste, feel, smell, or sound to him. How loud a train sounds depends in part upon the distance of the observer from the train, upon his degree of hardness of hearing, upon the direction in which his head is turned, upon whether his ears are covered and so forth. Whether water of a certain thermometer-temperature feels chilly or cosy depends on the prior thermometer-temperature of his hands. From such facts the theoretical jump was made to the doctrine that to say that an object is green is to say something about the visual sensations of the particular observer who reports that it is green. It was supposed that "green," "bitter," "chilly," and the rest are adjectives which properly apply to sensations and are only improperly applied to common objects. And then, as it is obviously absurd to say that a sensation is a green thing, or an elliptical thing, or a chilly thing, it seemed necessary to allot to sensations their own peculiar objects, so that "green" might be suitably applied not to the having of a sensation but to a peculiar object internally nursed by that sensation. The ban on characterizing common objects of anyone's observation by Secondary Quality adjectives led to the invention of some counterpart, privy objects to carry those adjectives. Because Secondary Quality adjectives would not behave except as predicates in observation reports, sensations had to be construed as being themselves observations of special objects.

But when I describe a common object as green or bitter, I am not reporting a fact about my present sensation, though I am saying something about how it looks or tastes. I am saying that it would look or taste so and so to anyone who was in a condition and position to see or taste properly. Hence I do not contradict myself if I say that the field is green, though at the moment it looks greyish-blue to me; or that the fruit is really bitter, though it appears to me quite tasteless. And even when I say that the grass, though really green, looks greyish-blue to me, I am still describing my momentary sensation only by assimilating it to how common objects that are really greyish-blue normally look to anyone who can see properly. Secondary Quality adjectives are used and are used only for the reporting of publicly ascertainable facts about common objects; for it is a publicly ascertainable fact about a field that it is green, i.e. that it would look so and so to anyone in a position to see it properly. What else could the people who teach other people to talk, teach them about the use of these adjectives? It must be noticed that the formula "it would look so and so to anyone" cannot be paraphrased by "it would look *green* to anyone," for to say that something looks green is to say that it looks as it would if it were green and conditions were normal. We cannot say how something looks, or would look, except by mentioning the ascertainable properties of common objects, and then saying that this looks now as that can be expected to look.

12. THE ANALYSIS OF PROPOSITIONS ABOUT MATERIAL THINGS

G. E. MOORE

Moore here outlines one of the major problems facing any attempt to build a full theory of perception on the Sense-datum Analysis. Although later writers (Selections 10 and 11) regard that analysis as contrary to common sense, this passage is part of Moore's well-known "A Defence of Common Sense" which first appeared in Vol. II of *Contemporary British Philosophy,* edited by J. H. Muirhead (George Allen & Unwin, Ltd., London and the Macmillan Company, New York, 1925). This article is also included in G. E. Moore, *Philosophical Papers* (1959), published by the same firms.

I am not at all sceptical as to the *truth* of such propositions as "The earth has existed for many years past," "Many human bodies have each lived for many years upon it," i.e. propositions which assert the existence of material things: on the contrary, I hold that we all know, with certainty, many such propositions to be true. But I am very sceptical as to what, in certain respects, the correct *analysis* of such propositions is. And this is a matter as to which I think I differ from many philosophers. Many seem to hold that there is no doubt at all as to their *analysis,* nor, therefore, as to the analysis of the proposition "Material things have existed," in certain respects in which I hold that the analysis of the propositions in question is extremely doubtful; and some of them, as we have seen, while holding that there is no doubt as to their *analysis,* seem to have doubted whether any such propositions are *true.* I, on the other hand, while holding that there is no doubt whatever that many such propositions are wholly true, hold also that no philosopher, hitherto, has succeeded in suggesting an analysis of them, as regards certain important points, which comes anywhere near to being certainly true.

It seems to me quite evident that the question how propositions of the type I have just given are to be analysed, depends on the question how propositions of another and simpler type are to be analysed. I know, at present, that I am perceiving a human hand, a pen, a sheet of paper, etc.; and it seems to me that I cannot know how the proposition "Material things exist" is to be analysed, until I know how, in certain respects, these simpler propositions are to be analysed. But even these are not simple enough. It seems to me quite evident that my knowledge that I am now perceiving a human hand is a deduction from a pair of propositions simpler still—propositions which I can only express in the form "I am perceiving *this*" and "*This* is a human hand." It is the analysis of propositions of the latter kind which seems to me to present such great difficulties, while nevertheless the whole question as to the *nature* of material things obviously depends upon their analysis. It seems to me a surprising thing that so few philosophers, while saying a great deal as to what material things *are* and as to what it is to perceive them, have attempted to give a clear account as to what precisely they suppose themselves to *know* (or to *judge,* in case they have held that we don't *know* any such propositions to be true, or even that no such propositions *are* true) when they know or judge such things as "This is a hand," "That is the sun," "This is a dog," etc.

Two things only seem to me to be quite certain about the analysis of such propositions (and even with regard to these I am afraid some philosophers would differ from me) namely that whenever I know, or judge, such a proposition to be true, (1) there is always some *sense-datum* about which the proposition in question is a proposition—some sense-datum which is *a* subject (and, in a certain sense, the principal or ultimate subject) of the proposition in question, and (2) that, nevertheless, *what* I am knowing or judging to be true about this sense-datum is not (in general) that it is *itself* a hand, or a dog, or the sun, etc., as the case may be.

Some philosophers have I think doubted whether there are any such things as other philosophers have meant by "sense-data" or "sensa." And I think it is quite possible that some philosophers (including myself, in the past) have used these terms in senses such that it is really doubtful whether there are any such things. But there is no doubt at all that there are sense-data, in the sense in which I am now using that term. I am at present seeing a great number of them, and feeling others. And in order to point out to the reader what sort of things I mean by sense-data, I need only to ask him to look at his own right hand. If he does this he will be able to pick out something (and, unless he is seeing double, *only* one thing) with regard to which he will see that it is, at first sight, a natural view to take that that thing is identical, not, indeed, with his whole right hand, but with that part of its surface which he is actually seeing, but will also (on a little reflection) be able to see that it is doubtful whether it can be identical with the part of the surface of his hand in question. Things *of the sort* (in a certain respect) of which this thing is, which he sees in looking at his hand, and with regard to which he can understand how some philosophers should have supposed it to *be* the part of the surface of his hand which he is seeing, while others have supposed that it can't be, are what I mean by "sense-data." I therefore define the term in such a way that it is an open question whether the sense-datum which I now see in looking at my hand and which is a sense-datum of my hand is or is not identical with that part of its surface which I am now actually seeing.

That what I know, with regard to this sense-datum, when I know "This is a human hand," is not that it is *itself* a human hand, seems to me certain because I know that my hand has many parts (e.g. its other side, and the bones inside it), which are quite certainly *not* parts of this sense-datum.

I think it certain, therefore, that the analysis of the proposition "This is a human hand" is, roughly at least, of the form "There is a thing, and only one thing, of which it is true both that it is a human hand and that *this surface* is a part of its surface." In other words, to put my view in terms of the phrase "theory of representative perception," I hold it to be quite certain that I do not *directly* perceive *my hand*; and that when I am said (as I may be correctly said) to "perceive" it, that I "perceive" it means that I perceive (in a different and more fundamental sense) something which is (in a suitable sense) *representative* of it, namely a certain part of its surface.

This is all that I hold to be *certain* about the analysis of the proposition "This is a human hand." We have seen that it includes in its analysis a proposition of the form "This is part of the surface of a human hand" (where "This," of course, has a different meaning from that which it has in the original proposition which has now been analysed). But this proposition also is undoubtedly a proposition about the sense-datum, which I am seeing, which is a sense-datum *of* my hand. And hence the further question arises: *What,* when I know *"This is part of the surface of* a human hand," am I knowing about the sense-datum in question? Am I, in this case, really knowing about the sense-datum in question that it *itself* is part of the surface of a human hand? Or, just as we found in the case of "This is a human hand," that what I was knowing about the sense-datum was certainly not that it *itself* was a human hand, so, is it perhaps the case, with this new proposition, that even here I am not knowing, with regard to the sense-datum, that it is *itself* part of the surface of a hand? And, if so, what is it that I am knowing about the sense-datum itself?

This is the question to which, as it seems to me, no philosopher has hitherto suggested an answer which comes any where near to being *certainly* true.

There seem to me to be three, and only three, alternative types of answer possible; and to any answer yet suggested, of any of these types, there seem to me to be very grave objections.

(1) Of the first type, there is but one answer: namely, that in this case what I am knowing really is that the sense-datum *itself* is part of the surface of a human hand. In other words that, though I don't perceive *my hand* directly, I do *directly* perceive part of its surface; that the sense-datum itself *is* this part of its surface and not merely something which (in a sense yet to be determined) "represents" this part of its surface; and that hence the sense in which I "perceive" this part of the surface of my hand is not in its turn a sense which needs to

be defined by reference to yet a third more ultimate sense of
"perceive," which is the only one in which perception is
direct, namely that in which I perceive the sense-datum.

If this view is true (as I think it may just possibly be), it
seems to me certain that we must abandon a view which has
been held to be certainly true by most philosophers, namely
the view that our sense-data always really have the qualities
which they sensibly appear to us to have. For I know that if
another man were looking through a microscope at the same
surface which I am seeing with the naked eye, the sense-datum
which he saw would sensibly appear to him to have qualities
very different from and incompatible with those which my
sense-datum sensibly appears to me to have: and yet, if my
sense-datum is identical with the surface we are both of us
seeing, his must be identical with it also. My sense-datum
can, therefore, be identical with this surface only on condition that it is identical with his sense-datum; and since his
sense-datum sensibly appears to him to have qualities incompatible with those which mine sensibly appears to me to
have, his sense-datum can be identical with mine only on
condition that the sense-datum in question either has not got
the qualities which it sensibly appears to me to have, or has
not got those which it sensibly appears to him to have.

I do not, however, think that this is a fatal objection to
this first type of view. A far more serious objection seems to
me to be that, when we see a thing double (have what is
called "a double image" of it), we certainly have *two* sense-
data each of which is *of* the surface seen, and which cannot
therefore both be identical with it; and that yet it seems as if, if
any sense-datum is ever identical with the surface *of* which it
is a sense-datum, each of these so-called "images" must be
so. It looks, therefore as if every sense-datum is, after all, only
"representative" of the surface, *of* which it is a sense-datum.

(2) But, if so, what relation has it to the surface in question?

This second type of view is one which holds that when I
know "this is part of the surface of a human hand," what I
am knowing with regard to the sense-datum which is *of* that

surface, is, *not* that it is *itself* part of the surface of a human hand, but something of the following kind. There is, it says, *some* relation, *R,* such that what I am knowing with regard to the sense-datum is either "There is one thing and only one thing, of which it is true both that it is a part of the surface of a human hand, and that it has *R* to this sense-datum," or else "There are a set of things, of which it is true both that that set, taken collectively, *are* part of the surface of a human hand, and also that each member of the set has *R* to this sense-datum, and that nothing which is not a member of the set has *R* to it."

Obviously, in the case of this second type, many different views are possible, differing according to the view they take as to what the relation *R* is. But there is only one of them which seems to me to have any plausibility; namely that which holds that *R* is an ultimate and unanalysable relation, which might be expressed by saying that *xRy* means the same as *"y* is an appearance or manifestation of *x"*; i.e. the analysis which this answer would give of "This is part of the surface of a human hand" would be "There is one and only one thing of which it is true both that it is part of the surface of a human hand, and that this sense-datum is an appearance or manifestation of it."

To this view also there seem to me to be very grave objections, chiefly drawn from a consideration of the questions how we can possibly *know* with regard to any of our sense-data that there is one thing and one thing only which has to them such a supposed ultimate relation; and how, if we do, we can possibly *know* anything further about such things, e.g. of what size or shape they are.

(3) The third type of answer, which seems to me to be the only possible alternative if (1) and (2) are rejected, is the type of answer which J. S. Mill [Selection 22] seems to have been implying to be the true one when he said that material things are "permanent possibilities of sensation." He seems to have thought that when I know such a fact as "This is part of the surface of a human hand," what I am knowing with regard to the sense-datum which is the principal subject

of that fact, is not that it is itself part of the surface of a
human hand, nor yet, with regard to any relation, that *the*
thing which has to it that relation is part of the surface of a
human hand, but a whole set of hypothetical facts each of
which is a fact of the form "If *these* conditions had been fulfilled, I should have been perceiving a sense-datum intrinsically
related to *this* sense-datum in *this* way," "If *these* (other)
conditions had been fulfilled, I should have been perceiving
a sense-datum intrinsically related to *this* sense-datum in *this*
(other) way," etc.

With regard to this third type of view as to the analysis
of propositions of the kind we are considering, it seems to me,
again, just *possible* that it is a true one; but to hold (as Mill
himself and others seem to have held) that it is *certainly,* or
nearly certainly, true, seems to me as great a mistake, as to
hold with regard either to (1) or (2), that they are *certainly,*
or nearly certainly, true. There seem to me to be very grave
objections to it; in particular the three: (*a*) that though, in
general, when I know such a fact as "This is a hand," I certainly do know some hypothetical facts of the form "If *these*
conditions had been fulfilled, I should have been perceiving
a sense-datum of *this* kind, which would have been a sense-
datum of the same surface of which *this* is a sense-datum,"
it seems doubtful whether any conditions with regard to which
I know this are not themselves conditions of the form "If this
and that *material thing* had been in those positions and conditions . . ."; (*b*) that it seems again very doubtful whether
there is any intrinsic relation, such that my knowledge that
(under *these* conditions) I should have been perceiving a
sense-datum of *this* kind, which would have been a sense-
datum of the same surface of which *this* is a sense-datum, is
equivalent to a knowledge, with regard to that relation, that
I should, under those conditions, have been perceiving a
sense-datum related by it to *this* sense-datum; and (*c*) that,
if it were true, the sense in which a material surface is
"round" or "square," would necessarily be utterly different
from that in which our sense-data sensibly appear to us to be
"round" or "square."

13. AN ANALYSIS OF PERCEPTUAL CONSCIOUSNESS

H. H. PRICE

In this passage, pp. 139–150 of his *Perception* (Methuen, London, 1932), Price embarks on his positive account of *perceptual consciousness*, i.e. the mode of consciousness, additional to sensing, which is involved in perceiving or thinking one perceives a material thing. (Cp. note to Selection 7.)

We shall begin with a single act of perceptual consciousness taken in isolation. When we have several such acts suitably related, new forms of perceptual consciousness arise, which we must consider later: at present it is the simplest and primary form which concerns us. Suppose then, that I see a tree, in that sense of the word in which "to see" stands for a specific form of consciousness, distinct from but accompanying sensing, and does not merely convey that the tree is present to my senses, i.e. that I am sensing a sense-datum which does in fact belong to the tree.

Now in the first place it is clear that this perceptual consciousness is not a form of *knowing*. It is neither "knowledge by acquaintance" (as sensing is) nor is it "knowledge of facts about." For it may be mistaken. It may be that the thing is not a tree but something else. It may be not over there but somewhere else (I may have been deceived by a mirror image); it may not have the size or the shape I take it to have. Or perhaps I am even having a complete hallucination and there is no material object present to my senses at all.

Accordingly certain philosophers, notably Reid, have described perceptual consciousness as *belief*; and this seems a plausible suggestion. But unfortunately we here encounter a difficulty of terminology, since the word is sometimes used in a very wide sense and sometimes in a narrow one. It seems best to follow Cook Wilson in restricting the expression "to

166

believe that S is P" to that state of mind in which, being aware of certain facts, (1) we know that they are evidence of S's being P, (2) we know that they do *not* make it certain that S is P, (3) we have towards the problematic conception S-P a feeling of confidence capable of varying in strength.[1] Now if this be so, belief includes or at any rate is conditioned by a form of *inference*; for the apprehension that a set of premises ABC are evidence for (or make probable) a particular conclusion is no less to be called inference than the apprehension that a certain other set, say ABCDE, necessitate that conclusion. But as we have seen, the Causal Theory was obliged to admit that in perceptual consciousness as we have it now (whatever it may have been in our infancy) there is no trace of inference, though according to that theory only inference could justify it.

Further, it follows from this account of belief, that we cannot strictly be said to believe without evidence:[2] what is so described is not belief but something else. Moreover, since *ex hypothesi* we know that the evidence does not amount to proof, we cannot believe that S is P, without knowing that, after all, S may not be P. Belief even at its firmest is never wholly undoubting; we are still aware that, after all, we may be wrong. Or, if we cease to be aware of that, we have slipped out of belief into another state of mind.

Now perceptual consciousness is not like this. Let us grant for argument's sake that the existence of a sense-datum of such and such a sort, taken along with some further facts already known, does in fact make it probable (if not on causal grounds, then on some others) that there now exists a tree having such and such characteristics. Nevertheless, in my act of perceptual consciousness I am not *apprehending* that this conclusion is made probable; the notion of probability does not enter my head at all. There may be facts about my sense-datum which could be used by an external philosopher as evidence for the existence of the tree if he knew them. But I, the subject of the perceptual act, do not use them so. I am in a state of mind which is, so to speak, below the level of evidence-using.

This state of mind much more resembles what Cook Wilson calls *being under an impression that* than what he calls belief. In "being under an impression" we simply jump straight from the awareness of A to the thought of B, without any preliminary wondering or considering of evidence, indeed without any rational process whatever; for instance, we jump from hearing a knock on the door to the thought that our friend Jones has arrived.[3] And as there has been no consideration of evidence, so there is no consciousness that we may be wrong; one just has not raised the question whether one is liable to be wrong or not. We may also appeal once again to the time-honoured analogy of reading print. The reader does not say to himself "These words here are evidence that Caesar crossed the Rubicon; so on the whole I believe that he actually did." One simply passes straight from the written symbols to the propositions which they signify. Only in our case there is not even a passage. The two states of mind, the acquaintance with the sense-datum and the perceptual consciousness of the tree, just arise together. The sense-datum is presented to us, and the tree dawns on us, all in one moment. The two modes of "presence to the mind," utterly different though they are, can only be distinguished by subsequent analysis.

Agreeably with this, there is in an act of perceptual consciousness no element of doubt, no awareness of insufficiency or inconclusiveness, as there is in belief proper; and in this again it resembles both reading and "being under an impression that." True, it may have to be revised later, as when we correct an illusion or hallucination. We may say that *in fact* it is always provisional and liable to correction. But this provisionality is not present to the mind of the conscious subject himself: not because he has asked himself "Am I liable to be mistaken about this?" and decided that he is not, but because he simply has not raised the question at all. When he does raise the question and asks himself "But is this really a tree?," at once he slips out of the perceptual consciousness of the tree, not indeed into mere sensing, but into a less determinate consciousness whose object is "a material thing of some kind or other." And so long as he retains this doubt, it is possible for him to believe that on the whole the thing is a tree after all, but it is not possible for him to *see* it as a tree; on the other hand, he cannot hold this belief unless he still sees it as some body or other.

Accordingly it would be nearer the mark to describe perceptual consciousness (in this its simplest and primary form) not as belief, but as *absence of disbelief*:[4] or again as "the not doubting that." Perhaps, however, the best term is *acceptance* or *taking for granted*. And we shall in future call this primary form of perceptual consciousness *perceptual acceptance*.

What then is it that is taken for granted? That there exists a material thing: and not merely that there exists some material thing or other somewhere or other, but a material thing such that this sense-datum which I now sense belongs to it. Nor is this definite enough. The material thing, whose existence we take for granted, is still further specified as having a *front surface* of a certain sort, where "front" means nearer than its other surfaces to the point of view at which the perceptually-conscious subject is. (What the thing's back surface or sides or insides may be is not as yet specified. In the primary perceptual act we only take for granted that it has some sort of back surface or other: what sort, we leave it to subsequent acts to determine.)

But in what way exactly is the front surface thus specified? What nature it is taken to have obviously depends partly upon the nature of the present sense-datum; but partly also on our acquired dispositions. Thus if the thing is very familiar to us, we still attribute to it a front surface of a highly determinate kind even when the sense-datum is excessively faint and undifferentiated: as when I recognize a familiar house at a good distance off, or in a mist. Here, however, we shall neglect this effect of acquired dispositions in order to study the perceptual consciousness as far as possible in its most elementary form. And it is in any case necessary to go back to this form of it, if we can. For everything was once unfamiliar to us, and the acquired dispositions which we have now were only built up by the repetition of acts of a more elementary type in which no acquired dispositions were present. Thus in any case we come back in the end to the specification of the front surface by the sense-datum alone.

But in what manner the sense-datum specifies the front surface it is not easy to be sure. On the one hand we might be tempted to say that we take the sense-datum to *be* the front surface of the material thing,[5] or to be *coincident* therewith: (so that Naïve Realism would be perfectly right, provided we substituted "taking for granted" for "knowing"). This is plausible for touch and for vision at a fairly short range: thus it is plausible to say that I take the brown sense-datum which I sense at this moment to *be* the surface of the table at which I am writing. But when we turn to long-range vision we get into difficulty. Thus when two men are present to my senses, one five feet off and one a hundred yards off, I do not take for granted that the distant one is smaller than the other, or that he has a flat face; yet there can be no doubt that the sense-datum belonging to him is sensibly smaller than that belonging to the other man, and that it is flat.

Further, as Professor G. E. Moore has pointed out, the ordinary percipient when he sees something cannot be said to take for granted that his sense-datum is "in Physical Space," as it would have to be if it were, or were *coincident* with, the surface of a material thing: nor yet that it is not in Physical Space. At the level of perceptual consciousness the question simply is not raised. The truth is, I think, that perceptual consciousness (in this respect as in others) is, so to speak, more negative than positive. It is rather that we do not assert a difference between the sense-datum and the surface, than that we do assert their identity.

Now of course we may ask, what is *in fact* the spatial relation between the sense-datum and the surface of the material thing? And it is a plausible answer that one single sense-datum taken alone cannot be said to stand in any spatial relation with any material thing, i.e. to be anywhere in "Physical Space" at all: what has position in Physical Space being a certain sort of *group* of sense-data taken collectively. Now this might lead us into a second temptation. We might

be tempted to say: what we take for granted in perceptual
consciousness is that this present sense-datum is a member of
a group which taken as a whole is, or is coincident with, the
front surface of a material thing. But this, too, we must
resist, for it is an "over-rationalization" of the perceptual
state of mind; we should be making the plain man, or indeed
the plain animal, into a philosopher. If there really is the
material thing, and if it really has the surface which the
perceptual subject takes it to have (and of course the act
of perceptual acceptance is always liable to be erroneous)
then the sense-datum really was a member of such a group.
But it does not follow that the conscious subject himself
either takes it to be a member of such a group, or takes it
not to be: the question whether it is or isn't simply has not
occurred to him.

The most we can say is this: in perceptual consciousness,
we do not regard the single sense-datum as *completely*
specifying the shape, size, and situation of the front surface
of the material thing which we are taking to exist. We regard
it as *restricting the possibilities* to a greater or less extent; we
leave the complete specification of them to subsequent sense-
data. Thus if the present sense-datum is triangular I take it
that the thing's front surface is not circular or square,[6] but
I am by no means sure that it has not wavy edges, rounded
corners, and a different relation of height to base. The degree
in which the sense-datum is taken to restrict the possibilities
depends mainly on two factors: its degree of differentiation,
and in the case of sight its "stereoscopic" character. When the
sense-datum is flat, and uniform in colour and outline, we only
make a "rough shot" at the shape of the thing's front surface:
we take it to be "fairly large," "more or less round," or
"broader than it is high." When the sense-datum is full of
detail and completely stereoscopic, we are very much more
definite in our taking (though of course the resources of
language may fail us if we attempt to state it in words), e.g.
we take the front surface to be about seven feet by three, approximately rectangular in shape, and divided into panels.
But the back and side surfaces, though we take for granted

that there are some, still remain unspecified; we assume, too, that even the front surface could still be specified more, if we looked closer or used a magnifying glass, though only in relatively minor respects. Here we are less inclined to admit a non-identity of the sense-datum and the thing's surface, if we are asked. But still it would be false to say that we do positively take them to be identical.

To sum up this part of our discussion: What the perceptually conscious subject takes for granted when he senses a particular visual or tactual sense-datum is that there now exists a material thing to which this sense-datum belongs; and that this thing has a front surface of a certain general character, to be more exactly determined by subsequent perceptual acts. What general character the surface is taken to have, and how determinate that character is, does depend upon the nature of the present sense-datum. But it is not true that he takes the sense-datum to be identical with the surface, though (his state being an unreflective one) he does fail to distinguish them.

Next, we must be quite clear that the material thing whose existence we take for granted differs radically from any datum that we sense. All that they have in common is that both are particulars. That is, what we *mean* by the term "a material thing" is quite different from what we *mean* by "a sense-datum," whether there are actually any instances of material thinghood or not.

In the first place, a sense-datum is something *transitory*: it endures only for a few moments. But by a material thing we mean something which *persists* for a long period, both before the sense-datum existed and after it has existed.

Secondly, a sense-datum is *spatially incomplete,* having no back, top, bottom, or insides. Its goods, so to speak, are entirely in the shop-window. Hence it has been said to exist only from a place. By a material thing, on the other hand, we mean something *spatially complete,* a three-dimensional whole, with back, top, and bottom as well as front, and having an inside as well as an outside: something which does not exist from any special place.

Thirdly, a sense-datum, being somato-centric [i.e. either attributed to the body or of a series varying concomitantly with bodily data; Cp. *Perception,* p. 38], is *private* to the mind which senses it. But a material thing is conceived to be *public,* accessible to an indefinitely large number of minds.

Fourthly, there are *many kinds* of sense-data, e.g. colour-expanses, sounds, pressures, and these kinds are mutually exclusive. But the *same* material thing has sense-data of several different kinds "belonging to" it, usually of all the different kinds. It can be present to our senses in many different ways, and we can have perceptual consciousness of it in many different ways. (This characteristic is called by Dr. Broad "neutrality.")

Lastly, sense-data have no *causal* characteristics. They do indeed make a difference to the world; for if minds were not aware of them, minds could not voluntarily originate changes in matter; to be aware of something is, however, not the same as to be changed by that something, and consequently the relation between sense-data and the awareness of sense-data cannot be a causal relation. But by a material thing we *mean* something which has causal characteristics: and the different kinds of material things (as diamonds, cats, hydrochloric acid) are classified by their different causal characteristics— the power of cutting glass, or catching mice, or dissolving chalk. The most fundamental of these causal characteristics is "impenetrability," i.e. the power of keeping other things out of the space one is in. This no sense-datum displays.

Thus even if visual and tactual sense-data had been "physical" in the sense of being parts of the surfaces of material things, as Naïve Realism maintained, we still could not have said that they *were* material things; still less could the other kinds of sense-data have been so. At most they would only have been *constituents* of material things. And even if a material object had been nothing but a collection of sense-data, as the Selective Theory and some forms of Idealism think, still the collection as a whole would have had many characteristics which no single member of it has in isolation: so that even on that theory there would be a fundamental difference between a sense-datum and a material thing; the distinctive properties of matter would have been "emergent" characteristics characterizing the group as a whole, but not the individual members of it taken separately.

Thus not only is perceptual consciousness a radically different form of consciousness from the sensing which it accompanies, being a form of taking-for-granted, whereas that is a form of knowing; what we are conscious of is also radically different. And this is a point on which all theories of Perception are really agreed, whatever terms they use, and however much they may diverge in other ways, though it has not always been clearly stated.[7]

Now it does not follow from anything we have said, nor is it in fact true, that the material thing which we take to exist necessarily does exist. So far as we have yet shown, it may never in any instance exist, and perceptual consciousness may be nothing but an inevitable and continuing error.[8] Nor need the material thing have the kind of front surface which we take it to have. When we sense a sense-datum s and take for granted the existence of a material thing M, it is quite certain that the sense-datum exists at that moment, however short-lived it may be. But as yet, and so far as this single perceptual act goes, it is not in the least certain that there is any such thing as M at all: I may be having an hallucination. Or if there is such a material thing, it may not have exactly the sort of front surface that I take it to have; its shape, size, or situation may be other than I take them to be; I may be having an illusion. (Or equally I may be having neither.)

Thus although we cannot sense what is not there at the moment of sensing, we can be perceptually conscious of what is not there. (It must be remembered of course that we are only speaking of the single act of perceptual consciousness; when we have a series of such acts, other considerations arise.) This only sounds paradoxical so long as we confound the two forms of consciousness, or again because we confound perceptual consciousness with the having a material thing present to one's senses: which we the more readily do, because words like "see," "hear," "feel,"[9] "smell," and even the word "perceive," are commonly used for all these.

Let us consider once more the celebrated case of the delirious man who "sees a pink rat." The correct analysis seems to be this: (1) He is acquainted with a pink sense-datum; and about the existence of this ("wild" though it is) there is no doubt whatever. It may be a poor and fleeting entity, but still it is a real one. (2) He takes for granted the existence of a rat, and he takes for granted that this rat has a front surface of a certain general sort—what sort, and how specifically conceived by him, depends upon the particular nature of the sense-datum and of his acquired mental dispositions. This rat is not real. Still he really does have perceptual consciousness of it, in exactly that sense in which he has a simultaneous perceptual consciousness of his table or his boot. Thus three things are indubitably real: the sensing, the sense-datum, and the act of perceptual consciousness. Only one thing is not real—the material thing which is the object[10] of his perceptual consciousness.

We may notice another and less-discussed instance, the blue sky. When I look upwards on a cloudless day, I *sense* a blue expanse which certainly exists; but what I am perceptually conscious of is a vast and more or less bowl-shaped thing, the "vault of Heaven," and this is what I call the sky. Plainly I do not mean by "the sky" that huge mass of air particles, which (as we believe) is in fact the sense-datum's differential condition. Perhaps it is air that I *ought* to be conscious of, but as a matter of fact I am not; and moreover, people had perceptual consciousness of the blue sky long before they knew that air existed at such an altitude, or indeed before they know that it existed at all. On the other hand, I do not mean by "the blue sky" simply the blue sense-datum; for I mean something which persists whether I am sensing or not, and something public to an indefinite multitude of observers. That is what I *mean* and what I am perceptually conscious of; but in point of fact no such bowl exists. What exists are the various blue sense-data sensed by various observers, and the several perceptual acts of the observers.

We may sum up the situation by saying that the object of any one act of perceptual consciousness is as such *ostensible* only, and has, as it were, a *prima facie* character. It "claims" to be real and to have certain characteristics, and it may in the end turn out to have them; but equally it may not. Yet in spite of this it is no mere arbitrary fancy: it is forced upon me by the character of the sense-datum which I am sensing and no other ostensible but precisely this one could ostend itself to me here and now, the sense-datum being what it is.[11]

It follows from this that any single perceptual act is as such provisional and requires confirmation by subsequent acts. In this it is quite unlike sensing; which being a form of intuitive awareness, we could not even wish that it should be confirmed, for the very idea of confirmation is in its case absurd.

There is another difference between the two forms of consciousness, connected—as we shall see—with this last one. Perceptual consciousness admits of *degrees of definiteness* (and indefiniteness). But sensing cannot be called either definite or indefinite. It exists in full perfection or not at all; it is an immediate "confrontation" of mind and sense-data, and admits of no degrees. This is not because it is a form of knowing or apprehending. For that *can* be indefinite; thus we often know that A is larger than B without being able to say how much larger. Sensing admits of no degrees of definiteness because it is a *non-attributive* form of consciousness. Where a characteristic is attributed to something (or discerned in it), the attribution may be more or less definite; i.e. the characteristic attributed may be more specific, or less. But where there is no attribution but simply confrontation, there is no room for indefiniteness.

But perceptual consciousness may have all degrees of definiteness, ranging in the case of a single perceptual act from the mere consciousness of some material thing or other I can't say what, which is the lower limit, to the consciousness (for instance) of a rectangular thing seven feet by three with dark spots on it. And if we bring in acquired perceptual dispositions, still greater definiteness is possible. For these enable us in suitable cases to take for granted not merely the existence of a thing having such and such a specific sort of front surface, but such and such a specific sort of thing behaving in such and such a specific sort of way; for instance, of a short-eared owl flying at just above stalling-point: all this and more may be taken for granted in one single perceptual act. Nor is there any upper limit of definiteness; on the one hand there might be a more differentiated sense-datum than this one, on the other our perceptual dispositions (our "powers of observation"[12] as we call them) might become more delicate than they are.

The sense-datum, on the other hand, no more admits of degrees of definiteness than the sensing does. The notion of definite and indefinite do not apply to it at all. It is a particular existent having a perfectly specific nature (whether describable by us or not). It is of just exactly this shade of colour and has just this shape and no other. There is, however, some danger of confusion about this. For sense-data are sometimes said to be "dim" or "vague." Thus a landscape or view is said to be "dim," and novelists and other picturesque writers are too fond of speaking of "dim forms" and "vague shapes." But these adjectives properly belong not to the sense-datum, but to the perceptual act which it makes possible, and from which it derives its practical importance. A so-called vague sense-datum is really one which permits only of a vague or indefinite perceptual act: e.g. it enables us to take for granted the existence of some large body or other, but we cannot tell whether the thing is a horse or a haystack. Thus it is the perceptual act which is vague, not the sense-datum; the sense-datum is not vague but *ineffective*.

There are, however, certain characteristics which sense-data do have, and which because this ineffectiveness results from them are sometimes miscalled vagueness. Thus a sense-datum may be of *faint intensity,* very *uniform* in all its parts, and only *slightly different* from neighbouring sense-data. And these characteristics do vary in degree from one sense-datum to another. But the intensity of the sense-datum is always a perfectly determinate degree, be it great or small, and the same is true of the other characteristics. Thus terms like "vague," "definite," and "indefinite" can only be applied to our cognitive acts, and (as we have seen) not to all of them, for instance, not to sensing.

[Price then goes on to consider other important characteristics of the act of perceptual acceptance, e.g. that it (falsely) seems intuitive, and to distinguish it carefully from judging (with which the Idealists identified it). In a subsequent chapter (VII) he considers how several acts of perceptual acceptance may be combined to give a settled conviction or assurance of the existence and characteristics of a particular material thing.]

Author's Notes

[1] Cf. *Statement and Inference,* Part II, ch. 3. On "problematic conceptions," cf. the same work, Part III, ch. 5.

[2] Still less can we believe contrary to the evidence. The schoolboy who defined faith as "*believing* what you know ain't true" was guilty of a contradiction; and would still have been so, even if he had said only "believing what you know to be improbable."

[3] This is vulgarly called "jumping to conclusions"; which of course may happen to be true ones, and indeed are likely to be true more often than not, since our associative dispositions (to which such jumps are due) have been acquired through experience of often-repeated and therefore probably regular conjunctions.

[4] Cf. the description of the attitude of the reader of poetry or fiction as "a willing suspension of disbelief." Only in our case the suspension is neither willing nor unwilling; it is just automatic.

[5] Or as Professor H. A. Prichard has expressed it, "We straight off mistake a colour for a body" (where "colour" means "colour-expanse").

[6] Of course I might be wrong even in this, owing to some complicated optical conditions. But we are here discussing what I *take* to be the case, not what *is* the case. Nor are we yet asking how we know whether it is the case or not.

[7] The point was clearly seen, and clearly stated, by Hume, Reid, and Kant; by other philosophers both before and since, not so clearly.

[8] As Hume appears to think.

[9] As when we say in the dark, "I can feel a keyhole here." The verb "to touch" does not show this ambiguity. To touch A means "to have A present to one's senses by means of a tactual datum."

[10] I here mean by "object" only "object-of," i.e. that which is before the mind in a particular sort of consciousness. There is no reason why this should not be unreal—unless "consciousness" be equated with "knowing," which seems an unfortunate use of language. So also we speak of the object of hope or of desire; plainly, only that which is not real can be desired or hoped for.

[11] Perhaps we may compare these ostensibles which are the objects of the primary type of perceptual consciousness with the *prima facie duties* which Dr. W. D. Ross holds to be the objects of the primary type of moral consciousness. Cf. *The Right and the Good*, ch. 2.

[12] That is really, of perceptual recognition.

Part III
Types of Realism

14. IDEAS AND THEIR CAUSES

John Locke

Locke's *Essay Concerning Human Understanding* (published in 1690) is one of the classical sources of Representative Realism; he held that, in perceiving, the mind's immediate awareness is of "ideas" (i.e. approximately, sense-data) caused by and only in part resembling the qualities of external objects. In the first of the two passages given here (Book II, chapter 8, sec. 8 ff. of the *Essay*) he outlines the extent of this resemblance in his famous doctrine of Primary and Secondary Qualities; and in the second (Book IV, chapter 11) he faces—and, some would say, fails to see—the fatal objection to all such theories: how if we are aware only of ideas do we know of the existence of their external causes?

Ideas and Qualities

Whatsoever the mind perceives in itself, or is the immediate object of perception, thought, or understanding, that I call ideas; and the power to produce any ideas in our mind I call quality of the subject wherein that power is. Thus a snowball having the power to produce in us the ideas of white, cold, and round, the powers to produce those ideas in us, as they are in the snowball, I call qualities; and as they are sensations or perceptions in our understandings, I call them ideas; which ideas, if I speak of sometimes as in the things themselves, I would be understood to mean those qualities in the objects which produce them in us.

Qualities thus considered in bodies, are first, such as are utterly inseparable from the body, in what estate soever it be; such as in all the alterations and changes it suffers, all the force can be used upon it, it constantly keeps; and such as sense constantly finds in every particle of matter which has bulk enough to be perceived, and the mind finds inseparable from every particle of matter, though less than to make itself singly be perceived by our senses; e.g. take a grain of wheat, divide it into two parts, each part has still solidity, extension, figure, and mobility; divide it again, and it retains still the same qualities, and so divide it on till the parts become insensible, they must retain still each of them all those qualities: for division (which is all that a mill, or pestle, or any other body does upon another, in reducing it to insensible parts) can never take away either solidity, extension, figure, or mobility from any body, but only makes two or more distinct separate masses of matter of that which was but one before; all which distinct masses, reckoned as so many distinct bodies, after division make a certain number. These I call original or primary qualities of body, which I think we may observe to produce simple ideas in us, viz., solidity, extension, figure, motion or rest, and number.

Secondly, such qualities which in truth are nothing in the objects themselves, but powers to produce various sensations in us by their primary qualities, i.e. by the bulk, figure, texture, and motion of their insensible parts, as colour, sounds, tastes, etc. these I call secondary qualities. To these might be added a third sort, which are allowed to be barely powers, though they are as much real qualities in the subject as those which I, to comply with the common way of speaking, call qualities, but for distinction, secondary qualities. For the power in fire to produce a new colour, or consistency, in wax or clay, by its primary qualities, is as much a quality in fire as the power it has to produce in me a new idea or sensation of warmth or burning, which I felt not before, by the same primary qualities, viz. the bulk, texture, and motion of its insensible parts.

The next thing to be considered is, how bodies produce ideas, in us; and that is manifestly by impulse, the only way which we can conceive bodies to operate in.

If then external objects be not united to our minds, when they produce ideas therein, and yet we perceive these original qualities in such of them as singly fall under our senses, it is evident that some motion must be thence continued by our nerves or animal spirits, by some parts of our bodies, to the

JOHN LOCKE 185

brain, or the seat of sensation, there to produce in our minds the particular ideas we have of them. And since the extension, figure, number, and motion of bodies, of an observable bigness, may be perceived at a distance by the sight, it is evident some singly imperceptible bodies must come from them to the eyes, and thereby convey to the brain some motion, which produces these ideas which we have of them in us.

After the same manner that the ideas of these original qualities are produced in us, we may conceive that the ideas of secondary qualities are also produced, viz. by the operations of insensible particles on our senses. For it being manifest that there are bodies, and good store of bodies, each whereof are so small that we cannot, by any of our senses, discover either their bulk, figure, or motion, as is evident in the particles of the air and water, and others extremely smaller than those, perhaps as much smaller than the particles of air and water as the particles of air and water are smaller than peas or hail-stones: let us suppose at present, that the different motions and figures, bulk and number of such particles, affecting the several organs of our senses, produce in us those different sensations, which we have from the colours and smells of bodies; e.g. that a violet, by the impulses of such insensible particles of matter of peculiar figures and bulks, and in different degrees and modifications of their motions, causes the ideas of the blue colour and sweet scent of that flower to be produced in our minds, it being no more impossible to conceive that God should annex such ideas to such motions, with which they have no similitude, than that he should annex the idea of pain to the motion of a piece of steel dividing our flesh, with which that idea hath no resemblance.

What I have said concerning colours and smells may be understood also of tastes and sounds, and other the like sensible qualities; which, whatever reality we by mistake attribute to them, are in truth nothing in the objects themselves, but powers to produce various sensations in us, and depend on these primary qualities, viz. bulk, figure, texture, and motion of parts, as I have said.

From whence I think it easy to draw this observation, that

the ideas of primary qualities of bodies are resemblances of them, and their patterns do really exist in the bodies themselves; but the ideas produced in us by these secondary qualities have no resemblance of them at all. There is nothing like our ideas existing in the bodies themselves. They are in the bodies, we denominate from them, only a power to produce those sensations in us; and what is sweet, blue, or warm in ideas, is but the certain bulk, figure, and motion of the insensible parts in the bodies themselves, which we call so.

Flame is denominated hot and light; snow white and cold; and manna white and sweet, from the ideas they produce in us: which qualities are commonly thought to be the same in those bodies that those ideas are in us, the one the perfect resemblance of the other, as they are in a mirror; and it would by most men be judged very extravagant if one should say otherwise. And yet he that will consider that the same fire, that at one distance produces in us the sensation of warmth, does at a nearer approach produce in us the far different sensation of pain, ought to bethink himself what reason he has to say, that his idea of warmth, which was produced in him by the fire, is actually in the fire; and his ideas of pain, which the same fire produced in him the same way, is not in the fire. Why are whiteness and coldness in snow, and pain not, when it produces the one and the other idea in us, and can do neither but by the bulk, figure, number, and motion of its solid parts?

The particular bulk, number, figure, and motion of the parts of fire, or snow, are really in them, whether any one's senses perceive them or no; and therefore they may be called real qualities, because they really exist in those bodies: but light, heat, whiteness, or coldness, are no more really in them than sickness or pain is in manna. Take away the sensation of them; let not the eyes see light or colours, nor the ears hear sounds; let the palate not taste, nor the nose smell; and all colours, tastes, odours, and sounds, as they are such particular ideas, vanish and cease, and are reduced to their causes, i.e. bulk, figure, and motion of parts.

A piece of manna of a sensible bulk is able to produce in us
the ideas of a round or square figure, and, by being removed
from one place to another, the ideas of motion. This idea of
motion represents it as it really is in the manna moving: a
circle or square are the same, whether in ideas or existence,
in the mind or in the manna; and this both motion and figure
are really in the manna, whether we take notice of them or
no: this every body is ready to agree to. Besides, manna by
the bulk, figure, texture, and motion of its parts, has a power
to produce the sensations of sickness, and sometimes of acute
pains or gripings in us. That these ideas of sickness and pain
are not in the manna, but effects of its operations on us, and
are nowhere when we feel them not: this also every one
readily agrees to. And yet men are hardly to be brought to
think, that sweetness and whiteness are not really in manna;
which are but the effects of the operations of manna, by the
motion, size, and figure of its particles on the eyes and palate;
as the pain and sickness caused by manna are confessedly
nothing but the effects of its operations on the stomach and
guts, by the size, motion, and figure of its insensible parts.

Let us consider the red and white colours in porphyry:
hinder light from striking on it, and its colours vanish, it no
longer produces any such ideas in us; upon the return of light
it produces these appearances on us again. Can any one think
any real alterations are made in the porphyry by the presence
or absence of light; and that those ideas of whiteness and
redness are really in porphyry in the light, when it is plain
it has no colour in the dark? It has, indeed, such a configuration of particles, both night and day, as are apt, by the rays of
light rebounding from some parts of that hard stone, to
produce in us the idea of redness, and from others the idea
of whiteness; but whiteness or redness are not in it at any
time, but such a texture, that hath the power to produce such
a sensation in us.

Ideas being thus distinguished and understood, we may
be able to give an account how the same water, at the same
time, may produce ideas of cold by one hand, and of heat

by the other; whereas it is impossible that the same water, if those ideas were really in it, should at the same time be both hot and cold: for if we imagine warmth, as it is in our hands, to be nothing but a certain sort and degree of motion in the minute particles of our nerves or animal spirits, we may understand how it is possible that the same water may, at the same time, produce the sensations of heat in one hand, and cold in the other; which yet figure never does, that never producing the idea of a square by one hand, which has produced the ideas of a globe by another. But if the sensation of heat and cold be nothing by the increase or diminution of the motion of the minute parts of our bodies, caused by the corpuscles of any other body, it is easy to be understood, that if that motion be greater in one hand than in the other; if a body be applied to the two hands, which has in its minute particles a greater motion, than in those of one of the hands, and a less than in those of the other; it will increase the motion of the one hand, and lessen it in the other, and so cause the different sensations of heat and cold that depend thereon.

I have in what just goes before been engaged in physical inquiries a little farther than perhaps I intended. But it being necessary to make the nature of sensation a little understood, and to make the difference between the qualities in bodies, and the ideas produced by them in the mind, to be distinctly conceived, without which it were impossible to discourse intelligibly of them, I hope I shall be pardoned this little excursion into natural philosophy, it being necessary in our present inquiry to distinguish the primary and real qualities of bodies, which are always in them (viz. solidity, extension, figure, number, and motion, or rest; and are sometimes perceived by us, viz. when the bodies they are in are big enough singly to be discerned) from those secondary and imputed qualities, which are but the powers of several combinations of those primary ones, when they operate, without being distinctly discerned; whereby we may also come to know what ideas are, and what are not, resemblances of something really existing in the bodies we denominate from them.

Our Knowledge of the Existence of Other Things

The knowledge of our own being we have by intutition. The existence of a God reason clearly makes known to us. The knowledge of the existence of any other thing we can have only by sensation; for there being no necessary connexion of real existence with any idea a man hath in his memory, nor of any other existence but that of God, with the existence of any particular man; no particular man can know the existence of any other being, but only when by actual operating upon him it makes itself perceived by him. For the having the ideas of any thing in our mind no more proves the existence of that thing, than the picture of a man evidences his being in the world, or the visions of a dream make thereby a true history.

It is, therefore, the actual receiving of ideas from without, that gives us notice of the existence of other things, and makes us know that something doth exist at that time without us, which causes that idea in us, though perhaps we neither know nor consider how it does it: for it takes not from the certainty of our senses, and the ideas we receive by them, that we know not the manner wherein they are produced: e.g. whilst I write this, I have, by the paper affecting my eyes, that idea produced in my mind which, whatever object causes, I call white; by which I know that that quality or accident (i.e. whose appearance before my eyes always causes that idea) doth really exist, and hath a being without me. And of this, the greatest assurance I can possibly have, and to which my faculties can attain, is the testimony of my eyes, which are the proper and sole judges of this thing, whose testimony I have reason to rely on as so certain, that I can no more doubt, whilst I write this, that I see white and black, and that something really exists, that causes that sensation in me, than that I write or move my hand: which is a certainty as great as human nature is capable of, concerning the existence of any thing but a man's self alone and of God.

The notice we have by our senses of the existence of things

without us, though it be not altogether so certain as our intuitive knowledge, or the deductions of our reason, employed about the clear abstract ideas of our own minds; yet it is an assurance that deserves the name of knowledge. If we persuade ourselves that our faculties act and inform us right, concerning the existence of those objects that affect them, it cannot pass for an ill-grounded confidence: for I think nobody can, in earnest, be so sceptical as to be uncertain of the existence of those things which he sees and feels. At least, he that can doubt so far (whatever he may have with his own thoughts) will never have any controversy with me; since he can never be sure I say anything contrary to his own opinion. But besides the assurance we have from our senses themselves, that they do not err in the information they give us, of the existence of things without us, when they are affected by them, we are farther confirmed in this assurance by other concurrent reasons.

First, it is plain those perceptions are produced in us by exterior causes affecting our senses; because those that want the organs of any sense never can have the ideas belonging to that sense produced in their minds. This is too evident to be doubted: and therefore we cannot but be assured that they come in by the organs of that sense, and no other way. The organs themselves, it is plain, do not produce them; for then the eyes of a man in the dark would produce colours, and his nose smell roses in the winter: but we see nobody gets the relish of a pine-apple till he goes to the Indies, where it is, and tastes it.

Secondly, because sometimes I find that I cannot avoid the having those ideas produced in my mind. For though when my eyes are shut, or windows fast, I can at pleasure recall to my mind the ideas of light, or the sun, which former sensations had lodged in my memory; so I can at pleasure lay by that idea, and take into my view that of the smell of a rose, or taste of sugar. But, if I turn my eyes at noon towards the sun, I cannot avoid the ideas, which the light, or sun, then produces in me. So that there is a manifest difference between the ideas laid up in my memory (over which, if they were there only, I should have constantly the same power to dispose of them, and lay them by at pleasure) and those which force themselves upon me, and I cannot avoid having. And therefore it must needs be some exterior cause, and the brisk acting of some objects without me, whose efficacy I cannot resist, that produces those ideas in my mind, whether I will or not. Besides, there is nobody who doth not perceive the difference in himself between contemplating the sun, as he hath the ideas of it in his memory, and actually looking upon it; of which two his perception is so distinct, that few of his ideas are more distinguishable one from another. And therefore he hath certain knowledge, that they are not both memory, or the actions of his mind, and fancies only within him; but that actual seeing hath a cause without.

Thirdly, add to this, that many of those ideas are produced in us with pain, which afterwards we remember without the least offence. Thus the pain of heat or cold, when the idea of it is revived in our minds, gives us no disturbance; which when felt, was very troublesome, and is again, when actually repeated; which is occasioned by the disorder the external object causes in our bodies when applied to it.

Fourthly, our senses in many cases bear witness to the truth of each other's report, concerning the existence of sensible things without us. He that sees a fire may, if he doubt whether it be any thing more than a bare fancy, feel it too; and be convinced, by putting his hand in it: which certainly could never be put into such exquisite pain by a bare idea or phantom, unless that the pain be a fancy too; which yet he cannot, when the burn is well, by raising the idea of it, bring upon himself again.

Thus I see, whilst I write this, I can change the appearance of the paper; and by designing the letters tell beforehand what new idea it shall exhibit the very next moment, by barely drawing my pen over it: which will neither appear (let me fancy as much as I will) if my hands stand still; or though I move my pen, if my eyes be shut: nor, when those characters are once made on the paper, can I choose afterwards but see them as they are; that is, have the ideas of such letters as I have made. Whence it is manifest, that they are not merely the sport and play of my own imagination, when I find that the characters, that were made at the pleasure of my own thoughts, do not obey them; nor yet cease to be, whenever I shall fancy it; but continue to affect the senses constantly and regularly, according to the figures I made them. To which if we will add, that the sight of those shall, from another man, draw such sounds as I beforehand design they shall stand for; there will be little reason left to doubt that those words I write do really exist without me, when they cause a long series of of my imagination, nor could my memory retain them in that regular sounds to affect my ears, which could not be the effect order.

15. THE DUALIST THEORY OF SECONDARY QUALITIES

W. P. MONTAGUE

The well-known American philosopher William Pepperell Montague (1873–1953) was originally one of the New Realists who maintained a form of Direct or non-Dualist Realism, but his best-known epistemological work *Ways of Knowing* (George Allen & Unwin, Ltd., London; The Macmillan Company, New York, 1925) attempts to state the case for and against all the main views, and finally adopts an eclectic position. This passage (pp. 253–257 of that book) gives a later argument than Locke's for the distinction of Primary and Secondary Qualities.

The physical objects that figure in our experience possess two distinct kinds of qualities or properties, the quantitative and the nonquantitative. The quantitative qualities comprise number, position, size, shape, duration, mobility, and inertia or mass—in other words, all the forms of spatial, temporal, and spatio-temporal relations. The nonquantitative qualities comprise color, sound, smell, taste, and the various modes of tactual sensation (with the possible exception of the quality of resistance or force). Between these two sets of qualities there exist three important contrasts, which it is necessary to understand.

In the first place the quantitative qualities form a continuous and homogeneous series, any one of whose terms can be expressed as a function of any other. For example the number 10 can be expressed as $7 + 3$, as $\frac{20}{2}$, as the square root of 100, etc. And as with numbers, so with spatial and temporal relations: each quantity is capable of precise determination by comparison with other quantities of the same kind. The nonquantitative qualities, on the other hand, are discontinuous, heterogeneous, and incommensurable, and therefore no one of them can be expressed as a function of any other. To illustrate: if a child knew the meaning of 3 and of 7, and of the operation of addition, I could make him understand the meaning of 10 by explaining to him that it was 7 + 3; but if he knew only the colors of blue and yellow, I could never by a comparison of these colors, make him understand the nature of green. Or, again, a person might be perfectly familiar with the fact that heat qualities and light qualities give rise to one another, but he would not in the least be able to imagine how or why this transformation took place. But if instead of being concerned with heat and light qualities, he is concerned with long waves and short waves, he is easily able to understand how and why each system can be transformed into the other. In the second place, the quantitative qualities of an object are revealed through many different senses, but most clearly through those of sight and touch, while the nonquantitative qualities of a given kind are revealed only through a single sense. Thus number is revealed through all five of the senses; position through sight and touch, and to a slight extent through hearing and smell; shape and motion through sight and touch. But color is revealed only through sight; sound only through hearing; taste, smell, and hardness only through their respective sense organs of palate, nose, and skin. In the third place, the quantitative qualities of a given object, besides being directly observable, are also capable of being indirectly and experimentally proved to exist by their effect upon other objects; while the nonquantitative qualities are without ascertainable effects,[1] and their existence can be known only by direct observation.

The three contrasts just described between the two sets of qualities have had an interesting and important influence on the development of scientific methods. During the Middle Ages, when the Aristotelian conception of Nature was current, the nonquantitative qualities were regarded as more important than the quantitative. This was probably due to the fact that in our own conscious life they figure more prominently; and Nature's processes were then regarded as more or less analogous to conscious processes. But with the coming of Galileo, Descartes, and the other founders of modern physics, medieval anthropomorphism gave way to a view of nature which was mechanistic rather than teleological, and quantitative rather than qualitative. From this new standpoint the nature and behavior of physical objects were conceived as determined, not by internal powers, but by the external or spatial relations obtaining between bodies. Consequently the quantitative properties came to be regarded as all-important or "primary," while the nonquantitative properties were regarded as without effect upon the movements of bodies, and hence as "secondary." The principal justification for this change of attitude consists in the first of the three above-mentioned contrasts between the two kinds of qualities. It is enormously more useful to describe physical facts in terms of commensurable, continuous, and homogeneous quantity than to describe them in terms of the incommensurable, discontinuous, and heterogeneous qualities of the special senses. We have already spoken of the gain in intelligibility that results from a reduction of the change from heat qualities to light qualities to a change from long vibrations to short vibrations. And the same principle is involved in reducing the changes from solid to liquid and liquid to gas, to changes in the spatial structure of a molecular system. To reduce all differences of material condition to differences in mode of motion, or in spatial structure, is analogous to reducing fractions to a common denominator. What was hitherto incommensurable and heterogeneous has become commensurable and homogeneous. Or, to use another figure, we might compare the reduction of quality to quantity in the fields of matter and energy to the introduction of a monetary system in a community which had hitherto conducted the exchange of its goods by methods of direct barter. Various articles of merchandise, such as food, clothes, building materials, etc. become admirably commensurable if a price in currency is attached to each article. The value of each in terms of the others can then be easily ascertained and expressed. The quantitative relations, in terms of which modern science seems to describe all the facts of the physical world, thus fill the role of a common denominator or universal medium of exchange. With reference to the second of the differences between primary and secondary qualities, it is easy to see that those properties of a body which are capable of being observed and verified by several senses would furnish an instrument of description greatly superior to any that was based upon a single sense. And thirdly the possibility of discovering the quantitative properties of bodies indirectly by their effects upon other bodies, makes them definitely preferable, as an instrument of description, to the nonquantitative qualities, which, as we have seen, are without discoverable effects, except those directly produced upon the special sense organs of the observer.

And now, the reader may ask, admitting that these are three good and valid reasons for the scientist's insistence upon a purely quantitative description of his world, what bearing has all this upon the dualistic theory of knowledge? The answer may be given very simply. From the belief that the nonquantitative qualities of objects are ineffective and useless, it is but a short and tempting step to the belief that they are not really objective attributes at all, but merely subjective effects which are produced upon the mind of the observer, and which exist only therein. The dualistic theory makes this step possible, for, according to that theory, the objects presented in direct perception have their locus within the percipient, and are in no sense numerically identical with their extra-organic causes. Then, too, if the secondary or nonquantitative qualities have ceased to be welcome in the realm of physical causes, they have to be, out of mere decency, as it were, provided for in an asylum, and what more natural than to regard the mind itself as that refuge? Since the secondary qualities are restricted in their effects to the perceiver's own processes, it seems appropriate to think of them as essentially and exclusively mental in their nature, and hence as of interest to psychology rather than to physics.

(Consider as an illustration of this point the way in which we determine the temperature of a thing. I put my hand in a bowl of water and it feels hot. The hotness, of course, appears as an attribute of the water, but I have no way of expressing accurately the degree of its intensity. I may call it "a little hot," "pretty hot," "very hot," "unbearably hot," etc. The lack of precision is bad enough, but there is another defect in this direct method of measuring temperature which, from the point of view of science, is still worse. If I ask a friend to test the water, he will, as likely as not, give a different estimate of its degree of hotness. There is no way to tell which of us is "right." We cannot even be sure that our words mean the same thing; for the sensation which he might describe as "very hot," I might, if I experienced it, describe as "pretty hot," and as long as we consider the specific and non-quantitative quality of "hotness," we can do nothing to overcome these difficulties. But suppose that instead of attempting to test the heat of the water by its direct effect upon our sense organs, we recognize that inasmuch as the secondary quality of hotness can be correlated with, or reduced to, the primary quality of motion (on the part of the molecules of a substance), and thus measured by its effect upon other bodies, it would be both possible and desirable to ascertain the degree of heat by its effect upon the expansion of mercury; we then put a thermometer in the water and, noting the height at which the column of mercury stands, we secure a perfectly satisfactory measure of the water's temperature. This indirect method of measurement is satisfactory, first because it is quantitatively precise, and second, because it is objectively and experimentally verifiable in the sense of being independent of such variable factors as the sensitiveness of the skin of the observer. We are to bear in mind that these advantages are due entirely to the capacity of *the primary or quantitative properties of bodies to produce effects upon other bodies and not merely upon a particular sense organ.*)[2]

Thus it is that the theory of epistemological dualism comes to be acceptable to the student of natural science because it seems to accord better than either of the other epistemological theories with his well-grounded desire to reduce nature to a purely quantitative system of masses and motions.

[A reply to this type of argument may be found in Selection 16 (p. 206). Other arguments to show that colors have no objective physical existence are given in Selection 2 (pp. 44-45) and Selection 4 (pp. 73-74).]

Editor's Notes

[1] It may be objected that an object's color affects its radiation and absorption of heat. To which the reply might be that as color sensations are dependent on the type of light reflected, the color and heat phenomena are parallel effects of a common cause, viz. the reflective power of surface texture—a complex of primary qualities.

[2] In the original, this paragraph was a footnote.

16. PERSPECTIVE REALISM

E. B. McGilvary

Evander Bradley McGilvary (1864–1953), the distinguished American philosopher, attempted in his Perspective Realism to provide an alternative to the usual dualist
interpretation of the facts of illusion and perceptual relativity. Like Austin (Selection 10), he did not believe that
these phenomena show that we perceive sense-data and not
physical objects, but his analysis requires us to revise our
ordinary conception of the perceived qualities of such
objects and to regard them as primarily relational. This
selection is taken from his article "Perceptual and Memory
Perspectives" in *Journal of Philosophy,* Vol. XXX, 1933,
pp. 310 ff.

Of late there has been a well-recognized tendency to treat
certain phases of experiences as instances of perspectives. The
reader need only recall certain features of the philosophies
of Whitehead, George Herbert Mead, and Lord Russell, to
assure himself of the truth of this statement. It is my purpose
in this paper to fall in with this movement and if possible to
carry it still further. First let me touch briefly upon the logic
of perspectives with a view to seeing whether perceptual experiences may not adequately be treated as perspectives.

Among relational complexes there is an important kind of
which a group of brothers is a familiar instance. Here the
brotherhood relation is conditioned; i.e. it is derived from a
relation in which each of the terms, A,B,C, stands to F and
M, the common parents. The parents are not members of the
group of brothers, but it is by virtue of the sonship relation
in which each member of this group stands to F and M that
A, B, and C are brothers.

It should be observed that the condition of a conditioned
complex is not necessarily the cause of the physical existence
of the terms of the conditioned complex, although in special
cases it may be. Such a special case we have in the instance

of brothers, who owe their physical existence to their parents. But just at present I am dealing with the *logic* of relations, not with physics or physiology. To name a few relational complexes whose conditions are not the causes of the physical existence of the terms of the complexes, we have roommates, fellow townsmen, U.S. Senators, France's allies in the World War, and the satellites of Jupiter. It should also be repeated that the condition of a conditioned complex is not a term in *that* complex.

In projective geometry we have instances of conditioned complexes. Take any point O called the center of projection, and consider a group of other points in their respective relations of direction from O. Thus all points in any straight line segment OM are projectively (i.e., directionally) identical with respect to O. Let A and B be any two points on OM, and let C and D be any two points on another straight line segment ON. Consider the straight line segments AC and BD. Any point F on AC is projectively identical with some point G on BD, and the projective (i.e. angular) length of AC is equal to the projective length of BD, in the projection from O. By giving the plane determined by OM and ON a rotation of 180 degrees about the line OP that bisects the angle MON, we get two surfaces described by the rotation of AC and BD. Any point on either surface is projectively identical with some point on the other surface, and the projective areas of the two surfaces are equal.

When in the preceding paragraph it is said that certain lines are projectively equal in length, and that certain surfaces are projectively equal in area, it is meant that these mathematical elements *where they respectively are* are equal in the projection *from* O. More generally, *any spatial element in a projection has its projective characters where it is, this "where" being determined in the first instance by distance and direction from the center of projection.* Thus in any projection there are two places under consideration, the place *at* which and the place *from* which. The projection, while "transcending" either place, does not transcend *itself.* . . .

Let us now pass to an application of projective geometry

which all draughtsmen learn to make. I will describe it as simply as I can. Keeping one eye constantly closed, I place a cube on the table before me; and at right angles to the direction of the center of the cube from my open eye, I interpose a sheet of transparent material upon which pencil tracings can be made. Holding my head steady I look at the cube through the transparent sheet and trace on the sheet the projections of the seen edges of the cube. What I have thus done is to make a drawing of the outlines of the cube as seen from my position with respect to the cube. It is important to emphasize the thoroughly relational character of the situation involved in that performance. (1) There is the relation of distance and direction of the cube from the retinal focus of the pencil of light rays that came from the cube through my optic lens. (2) There is the perpendicular relation of the sheet to the direction between that focus and the cube. (3) There is the relation between (a) what under these conditions I have drawn and (b) what I saw when I was drawing it. It is this last relation that I wish to emphasize here; but in emphasizing it I must not ignore two other relational facts: (c) What I have drawn is called a linear perspective drawing of the cube in the plane of the sheet, and (d) what I saw (among other things) was the cube *in the visual perspective,* the mathematical characters of the cube being determined by its distance and direction from my retinal focus. The drawing is on the sheet; and when the drawing was made the cube was *beyond* the sheet. In (d), the visual perspective, the cube *where it was,* as determined by its distance and direction from my retinal focus, had, *from where that focus was,* the perspective shape I saw.

But we often express this fact elliptically. We say: "The cube had . . . this perspective shape . . . where my eye was." I have indicated by omission periods the respective places where four important words are left out namely, "where it was" and "from." We then are likely to erect a theory on these omissions and say that what we saw was *where the eye was*; and since the cube was *not* where the eye was, we are constrained to say what we saw was *not* the cube, but *some-*

thing else. Thus a literal interpretation of an idiom is made to distort the facts.

From the preceding account it appears that a linear perspective is a conditioned complex consisting of shapes and sizes of objects. The perspective spatial shapes of the objects are conditioned (among other things) by the directions from which rays of light from the respective parts of the objects arrive at the retinal focus; and the perspective sizes of the objects are conditioned by the distances and directions traveled by these respective rays to that focus. If a convex lens is interposed between the eye and an object, the rays arrive from more divergent directions, and therefore in the perspective thus conditiond the object is perspectively larger than it would be in the perspective conditioned by a "naked" eye. This "magnification" is not an illusion, unless incorrect inferences are actually or implictly made as to the size the object would have in some *other* perspective.

In what has gone before I have been at pains not to prejudge the question whether the cube used as an example was a "physical" thing. But now I insist that there is nothing to prove that it is not. It is *measurable* and thus meets the requirements made by mathematical physicists for recognition of anything as physical. The fact that in different perspectives it has different sizes and different shapes does not prejudice its physicality, since physicists use *angular* measurements with as much frequency as superpositional measurements, and have well-known transformations for passing from one kind of measurement to the other. It is just as much a *physical* fact that the moon's mean diameter as actually measured from the earth is 31'51.5, as that it is 2150.6 miles as hypothetically measured on the moon. In view of all this I assume as a *postulate* that, *unless* there is reason to the contrary in any *specific* case, *the seen spatial characters of objects in monocular perspectives are physical characters that belong to physical objects*: however, they thus belong *not absolutely, but with respect to the physical conditions under which the perspectives obtain*. If such a view is to have a distinctive name, I would suggest as the most appropriate name "perspective realism."

Before proceeding to consider other perspectives, it is desirable to enter upon a digression, on return from which we shall be the better able to go further. An obvious objection to my postulate is that after all the object *in itself* can not have all the shapes it is seen to have. But what is meant by an "object-in-itself?" Still dealing only with spatial characters, I think that the natural interpretation of "in" in the expression "object-in-itself" is a spatial interpretation. By an object-in-itself (*in eo ipso*), then, is meant—at least I mean—an object *where* it is. In view of what has already been said above, any spatial object-in-itself—i.e., any spatial object where it is as defined by its spatial relations to other objects—does there have the perspective characters we have been considering. But it does not have these characters *by itself* (*per se*), i.e. *apart from any relations* in which it stands. I should like to rescue the term "thing-in-itself" from the bad repute it has acquired as a result of the confusion prevailing between what a thing really is as part of a larger world and what a thing would be if it were all there is. In this world of ours I know of nothing that is *by itself; en revanche* I know of no reason for not saying that I know many spatial characters that spatial things have *in themselves,* i.e. *in the places where they are,* provided I qualify this assertion by saying that these characters belong to the things by virtue of their relations to something somewhere else.

Much confusion has arisen from not distinguishing between relations and relational characters. For instance, a log, and not the log's relation to something else, is heavy; but it is heavy in relation, say, to a twig. The heaviness is *in* the log *relatively* to the twig. The difficulty is accentuated when instead of using adjectives such as "long" and nouns such as "father," we use abstract nouns such as "length" and "fatherhood." Are these nouns names of relational characters or of relations? They are ambiguously used of both, and then the trouble begins. Thus when, in some exposition of the physical theory of relativity, we are told that length is a relation and not a character belonging to some long thing, we immediately demur because we have actually seen noses that have in themselves inordinate length. On the other hand, when it is said that long human noses have their excessive lengths *in* themselves, we interpret this as meaning that apart from their relations to anything else they have their excessive lengths; then, recalling elephants' trunks, we are tempted to say that any such excessive length is a relation in which human noses stand to elephant's trunks. Thus we are driven from pillar to post. But the difficulty is obviated when we distinguish between characters which things have in virtue of their relations, and the relations in virtue of which they have these characters.

(It may be remarked, by the way, that the recognition of this distinction between relational characters and relations removes one difficulty involved in the question much discussed as to the proper way to categorize "beauty." A painting or a face is beautiful: it has the quality of beauty, and it has this quality where it is itself; but it has this quality only in relation to some percipient. Now some claim that beauty is "objective," and seem to mean thereby that it belongs to the beautiful object *apart from any relation in which it stands*. Correctly finding that beauty is a character of the object, they proceed incorrectly to deny that it is a *relational* character. On the other hand, their opponents, finding correctly that there is a relation involved, incorrectly proceed to say that beauty *is* the relation involved.)

Let us now return from this long digression. What has been said of spatial qualities must also be said of temporal qualities. But when we come to these, we are faced with a linguistic inadequacy. In classical projective geometry time is ignored as it is more generally ignored in elementary textbooks of classical Euclidean geometry. But in applied projective geometry, i.e., in spatial perspectives, we may not properly ignore them, for here the projections used are the lines of the propagation of light from object to eye. This propagation takes time. Thus we find ourselves dealing with four dimensions, inseparably related. Since not all parts of an object "foreshortened" in a perspective are at exactly equal distances from the eye, what is shown in a perspective drawing is not a picture of what is *physically* simultaneous. Of course in the case of objects in the immediate neighborhood of the eye, this deviation from the physically simultaneous is negligible. But when a projective drawing is made of sun and moon during an eclipse, the sun as shown is physically earlier by some eight minutes, and the moon is physically earlier by a second and a third, than the shown "station-point" or center of projection on the earth. Such a drawing is of a four-dimensional state of affairs, represented in only two of its dimensions: the third spatial dimension and the time dimension are left out of the picture. Dealing now with time only in its physical meaning, we have in such a projective drawing, not only a there-from-here picture, but also a picture of then-from-now. If a prominence on the sun is shown, it is a prominence of eight minutes earlier than the station-point shown. And if a "displaced" star is shown, this represents a "displacement" of a star years earlier than the sun shown. There may thus be many different *thens-theres* from the one *here-now,* and at the various *thens-theres* there were various *characters* as from *here-now.* . . .

We now pass on to such "secondary" characters as colors. Once grant, as our theory assumes, that the *spatial* characters of a seen physical apple are perspective characters of the physical apple not where the apple is, but not from where the seeing organism is, it is but a step to assuming that the color of the apple is also a perspective character of the physical apple where the apple is—i.e. of the apple-in-itself. While of course, it is always hazardous to insist on taking literally the words of one's mother tongue, there is no harm in cautiously *trying out* literal interpretations and adopting such as fit into the framework of a general theory and also seem fitly to describe what one finds in experience. I therefore try out the availability for this purpose of what is known as "aerial perspective" in the language of artists. Just as draughtsmen endeavor to do justice to linear perspective, so painters strive for aerial perspective on their canvas. Ignoring as irrelevant to my purpose what is called idealization in painting, I assume that a still-life canvas of a dish of fruit with an apple among them may be recognized as being a realistic picture of what is painted. In such a case it is an accurate representation of the apple that is present in my field of vision; and in such a case that *apple* out there where I see it is red with varying shades on differing parts of its surface. Were I to choose a different station-point the shades would be different. But whatever the station-point, the *apple's* surface has those respective shades of color in the perspective from that physiological station-point. Were I color-blind, I am told that I should see colors that are different; but then there would be something different conditioning the perspective, namely, a different physiological condition in my nervous system. Were a glass of a certain chemical constitution interposed between my eyes and the apple, I should see still another color in the apple. Which, then, of all these colors is the color of the apple? Why not say that they are all colors of the apple, but that each color is the color of the apple in the perspective within which the apple has that color? Why, if the apple is to be colored, should it have only *one* color? If we assume that every color ever seen in any apple is the color of *that* apple in the perspective of the organism which thus sees it, its color may vary with the organism, with the varying conditions of light, with the varying distances and varying particles floating in the air, etc.; but whatever color there is, it is the color of the *apple* in the perspective determined by all the pertinent factors. . . .

If, then, the *apple* is a *physical* apple, its redness is a perspective quality of the physical apple. But is the redness a *physical* quality of the apple? The answer is that, with the meaning now generally given by mathematical physicists to "physical," the redness is not physical, any more than the redness of a red square figure is a *mathematical* quality of that figure, although its squareness is a mathematical quality. The *quality* of the redness does not yield directly to the metrical treatment of the experimental physicist. But while discussing this subject it is well to point out that without colors—which I here use to include brightnesses as well—we should have practically no science of physics, since accurate measurement would be impossible. For instance, the displacement of spectrum lines would never have been discovered by touch or smell or taste; ordinary thermometers and clocks could not be read with any precision without discerned color differences; and galvanometers reveal their physical secrets only to the physicist who can see differences in the colors shown by needle and background. Some physical instruments could, of course, be read tactually, but with what sacrifice of nicety! A blind man can learn theoretical physics from books printed in Braille; but if the only physical observations were made by blind men, there would be no important books on physics printed in Braille. Without much exaggeration one can say that everything that physicists directly measure is either spatial or temporal distance between *colored* outlines, and this is done by use of standard distances between *colored* outlines. If everything that is needed as part of the apparatus of physics is physical, colors are indispensably physical; but the physicist calls "physical" only what he as physicist is interested in ascertaining. In this sense colors are *not* physical; they are instrumentalities used by him for a purpose, just as dynamometers and interferometers are instrumentalities. Nature supplies the colors, he has to construct the other instruments named. (But nature also supplies sun, planets, and stars, which are physical chronometers.) Each science has its own specific problems, and the solutions of these problems are what are "scientific" for that science; all else is either instrumental or irrelevant. But irrelevance of a character to a problem in hand does not prove its irrelevance to the *whole* nature of the thing that is under investigation with reference to *selected* characters.

What, then, is a "thing"? It is the integrity, i.e., the entireness, of all its relational characters, and it is all that just where it is and when it is (this "where" and "when" being also relational), but it is that only with all the respectiveness implied in all its relational characters. This may remind the malicious reader of the trite story of the Scilly(?) islanders who live by taking in each other's washing. Of course the point of the joke is its limitation to the single activity of *washing*. Let washing be only an example of men's multi-farious economic and financial activities which are all collectively called "washing," and then the whole economic and financial life of the world consists in each person's taking in others' washings. In the larger world we call the universe, everything lives by taking in some other things' washings. A joke ceases to be a joke when it is on everybody.

17. THE CAUSAL THEORY OF PERCEPTION

BERTRAND RUSSELL

In this passage from *The Analysis of Matter* (Dover Publications, Inc., New York and George Allen & Unwin, Ltd., London, 1927), pp. 200–217, Russell abandons the phenomenalism of his earlier works (cp. Selection 8), and though he still makes use of a phenomenalist "construction" out of sense-data (here referred to as percepts), he is now convinced that our perceptions have external causes. He here argues that this is the most plausible explanation of the sequences and patterns of our sense-data; his first step is to show that examination of these data requires us to reject solipsism. There is another treatment of the same problem in Selection 18; Russell's "Causal Theory" is in fact a form of "Physical Realism."

What grounds have we for inferring that our percepts and what we recollect do not constitute the entire universe? I believe that at bottom our main ground is the desire to believe in simple causal laws. But proximately there are other arguments. When we speak to people, they behave more or less as we should if we heard such words, not as we do when we speak them. When I say that they behave in a similar manner, I mean that our perceptions of their bodies change in the same sort of way as our perceptions of our own bodies would in correlative circumstances. When an officer who has risen from the ranks gives the word of command, he sees his men doing what he used to do when he heard the same sounds as a private; it is therefore natural to suppose that they have heard the word of command. One may see a crowd of jackdaws in a newly-ploughed field all fly away at the moment when one hears a shot; again it is natural to suppose that the jackdaws heard the shot. Again, reading a book is a very different experience from composing one; yet, if I were a solipsist, I should have to suppose that I had composed the works of Shakespeare and Newton and Einstein, since they have entered into my experience. Seeing how much better they are than my own books, and how much less labour they have cost me, I have been foolish to spend so much time composing with the pen rather than with the eye. All this, however, would perhaps be the better for being set forth formally.

First, there is a preliminary labour of regularizing our own percepts. I spoke of seeing others do what we should do in similar circumstances; but the similarity is obvious only as a result of interpretation. We cannot see our face (except the nose, by squinting) or our head or our back; but tactually they are continuous with what we can see, so that we easily imagine what a movement of an invisible part of our body ought to look like. When we see another person frowning, we can imitate him; and I do not think the habit of seeing ourselves in the glass is indispensable for this. But probably this is explained by imitative impulses—i.e. when we see a bodily action, we tend to perform the same action, in virtue of a physiological mechanism. This of course is most noticeable in children. Thus we first do what someone else has done, and then realize that what we have done is what he did. However, this complication need not be pursued. What I am concerned with is the passage, by experience, from "apparent" shapes and motions to "real" shapes and motions. This process lies within the perceptual world: it is a process of becoming acquainted with congruent groups—i.e. to speak crudely, with groups of visual sensations which correspond to similar tactual sensations. All this has to be done before the analogy between the acts of others and our own acts becomes obvious. But as it lies within the perceptual world, we may take it for granted. The whole of it belongs to early infancy. As soon as it is completed, there is no difficulty in interpreting the analogy between what we perceive of others and what we perceive of ourselves.

The analogy is of two kinds. The simpler kind is when others do practically the same thing as we are doing—for instance, applaud when the curtain goes down, or say "Oh" when a rocket bursts. In such cases, we have a sharp stimulus, followed by a very definite act, and our perception of our own act is closely similar to a number of other perceptions which we have at the same time. These, moreover, are all associated with perceptions very like those which we call perceptions of our own bodies. We infer that all the other people have had perceptions analogous to that of the stimulus to our own act. The analogy is very good; the only question is: Why should not the very same event which was the cause of our own act have been the cause of the acts of the others? Why should we suppose that there had to be a separate seeing of the fall of the curtain for each spectator, and not only one seeing which caused all the appearances of bodies to appear to applaud? It may be said that this view is far-fetched. But I doubt if it would be unreasonable but for the second kind of analogy, which is incapable of a similar explanation.

In the second kind of analogy, we see others acting as we should act in response to a certain kind of stimulus which, however, we are not experiencing at the moment. Suppose, for example, that you are a rather short person in a crowd watching election returns being exhibited on a screen. You hear a burst of cheering, but can see nothing. By great efforts, you manage to perceive a very notable result which you could not perceive a few moments earlier. It is natural to suppose that the others cheered because they saw this result. In this case, their perceptions, if they occurred, were certainly not *identical* with yours, since they occurred earlier; hence, if the stimulus to their cheering was a perception analogous to your subsequent perception, they had perceptions which you could not perceive. I have chosen a rather extreme example, but the same kind of thing occurs constantly; someone says "There's Jones," and you look round and see Jones. It would seem odd to suppose that the words you heard were not caused by a perception analogous to what you had when you looked round. Or your friend says "Listen," and after he has said it you hear distant thunder. Such experiences lead irresistibly to the conclusion that the percepts you call other people are associated with percepts which you do not have, but which are like those you would have if you were in their place. The same principle is involved in the assumption that the words you hear express "thoughts."

The argument in favour of the view that there are percepts, connected with other people, which are not among our own percepts, is presupposed in the acceptance of testimony, and comes first in logical order when we are trying to establish the existence of things other than our own percepts, both because of its inherent strength, and because of the usefulness of testimony in the further stages. The argument for other people's percepts seems to common sense so obvious and compelling that it is difficult to make oneself examine it with the necessary detachment. Nevertheless it is important to do so. As we have seen, there are three stages. The first does not take us outside our own percepts, but consists merely in the arrangement of them in groups. One group consists of all the percepts which common sense believes to be those of an identical object by different senses and from different points of view. When we eliminate reference to an object, a group must be constituted by correlations, partly between one percept and another (touch and sight when an object is held in the hand), partly between one percept and the changes in another (bodily movement and changes of visual and tactual perceptions while we move). In assuming that these correlations will hold in untested cases, we are of course using induction; otherwise, the whole process is straightforward. The process enables us to speak of a "physical object" as a group of percepts, and to explain what we mean by saying that a near object and a distant object are "really" of the same size and shape. Also we can explain what we mean by saying that a physical object does not "really" change as we walk away from it (i.e. as we have the percepts which make us say we are walking). This is the first stage in the argument.

In the second stage, we note the likeness of the physical objects called other people's bodies to each other and to our own body; we also note the likeness of their behaviour to our behaviour. In the case of our own behaviour, we can observe a number of correlations between stimulus and reaction (both being percepts). For example, we feel hunger or thirst, and then we eat or drink; we hear a loud noise, and we jump; we see Jones, and we say "Hullo, Jones." The behaviour of the percepts we call other people's bodies is similar to that of our own body in response to this or that stimulus; sometimes we experience the stimulus, and behave just as others do, which is the second stage; sometimes we do not experience the stimulus, but suppose, from their behaviour, that other people have experienced it, which is the third stage. This is a particularly plausible supposition if we ourselves experience the stimulus in question very shortly after we have observed the behaviour which led us to infer it. The third stage is the more important, since in the second we *might* attribute the behaviour of others to the stimulus which we perceive, and thus escape inferring unperceived existents, while in the third stage this alternative is not open to us. It will be seen that, in the third stage, the argument is the usual causal-inductive type of argument upon which all empirical laws are based. We perceive A and B conjoined in a number of cases, and we then infer A and B in a case in which we do not know by perception whether A is present or not. Moreover, the argument for other people's perceptions is the same in form and cogency as the argument for the future truth of laws of correlation among our own percepts. We have exactly as good reason for believing that others perceive what we do not as we have for believing that we shall have a perception of touch if we stretch out our hand to an object which looks as if it were within reach.

The argument is not demonstrative, either in the one case or in the other. A conjuror might make a waxwork man with a gramophone inside, and arrange a series of little mishaps of which the gramophone would give the audience warning. In dreams, people give evidence of being alive which is similar in kind to that which they give when we are awake; yet the people we see in dreams are supposed to have no external existence. Descartes' malicious demon is a logical possibility. For these reasons, we may be mistaken in any given instance. But it seems highly improbable that we are always mistaken. From the observed correlation of A and B we may argue, as regards cases in which B is observed but we do not know whether A exists or not, either: (1) A is always present, or (2) A is generally present, or (3) A is sometimes present. Dreams suffice to show that we cannot assert (1). But dreams could be distinguished from waking life by a solipsist, unless his dreams were unusually rational and coherent. We may therefore exclude them before beginning our induction. Even then, it would be very rash to assert (1). But (2) is more probable, and (3) seems extremely probable. Now (3) is enough to allow us to infer a proposition of great philosophic importance, namely: there are existents which I do not perceive. This proposition, therefore, if induction is valid at all, may be taken as reasonably certain. And, if so, it increases the probability of other propositions which infer the existence of this or that unperceived existent. The argument, though not demonstrative, is as good as any of the fundamental inductions of science.

We have been considering hitherto, not the external world in general, but the percepts of other people. We might say that we have been trying to prove that other people are alive, and not mere phantoms like the people in dreams. The exact thing we have been trying to prove is this: Given an observed correlation among our own percepts, in which the second term is what one would naturally call a percept of our own bodily behaviour, and given a percept of similar behaviour in a physical object not our own body but similar to it, we infer that this behaviour was preceded by an event analogous to the earlier term in the observed correlation among our percepts. This inference assumes nothing as to the distinction of mind and body or as to the nature of either.

In virtue of the above argument, I shall now assume that we may enlarge our own experience by testimony—i.e. that the noises we hear when it seems to us that other people are talking do in fact express something analogous to what we should be expressing if we made similar noises. This is a particular case of the principle contained in the preceding paragraph. I think the evidence for other people's percepts is the strongest we have for anything that we do not perceive ourselves; therefore it seems right to establish this, so far as we can, before proceeding to consider our evidence for "matter" —i.e. for existents satisfying the equations of physics. This must be our next task; but it will be well to begin with common-sense material "things" conceived as the causes of perceptions.

Having now admitted the percepts of other people, we can greatly enlarge the group constituting one "physical object." Within the solipsistic world, we found means of collecting groups of percepts and calling the group one physical object; but we can now enrich our group enormously. A number of people sitting near each other can all draw what they see, and can compare the resulting pictures; there will be similarities and differences. A number of stenographers listening to a lecture can all take notes of it, and compare results. A number of people can be brought successively into a room full of hidden roses, and asked "What do you smell?" In this way it appears that the world of each person is partly private and partly common. In the part which is common, there is found to be not identity, but only a greater or less degree of similarity, between the percepts of different people. It is the absence of identity which makes us reject the naïve realism of common sense; it is the similarity which makes us accept the theory of a common origin for similar simultaneous perceptions.

The argument here is, I think, not so good as the argument for other people's percepts. In that case, we were inferring something very similar to what we know in our own experience, whereas in this case we are inferring something which can never be experienced, and of whose nature we can know no more than the inference warrants. Nevertheless, the common-sense arguments for an external cause of perception are strong.

To begin with, we can without assuming anything that no one perceives, establish a common space and time in which we all live. (Our discussion is necessarily confined to people on the surface of the earth, since other people, if they exist, have not succeeded in communicating with us; consequently the complications of relativity do not yet arise.) The usual methods of determining latitude and longitude can be applied, without assuming that the readings of clock and sextant have the physical meaning usually assigned to them. Altitudes, also, can be measured by the usual methods. By these means, observers can be arranged in a three-dimensional order. Of course the resulting space will not be a continuum, since it will contain only so many "points" as there are observers. But the motion of an observer can be sensibly continuous, so that we can construct "ideal" points of view with defined mathematical properties, and thus build up, for mathematical purposes, a continuous space. We can thus arrive at the laws of perspective, taken in a generalized sense; that is to say, we can correlate the differences between correlated perceptions with differences in the situations of the percipients. And in the space derived from "points of view" we can place physical objects. For, let A and B be two observers, a and b their correlated visual percepts, which, being correlated, are described as percepts of one physical object O. If the angular dimensions of a are larger than those of b, we shall say (as a definition) that A is nearer to O than B is. We can thus construct a number of routes converging on O. We shall construct our geometry so that they intersect, and shall define their intersection as the place where O is. If O happens to be a human body, we shall find that the place of O, so defined, is identical with the place of O as an observer in the space of points of view.[1]

The correlation of the times of different percipients offers no difficulty, since, as before observed, our percipients are all on the earth. The usual method of light-signals can be employed. But here we come upon one of the arguments for the causal theory of perception, as against both common sense and phenomenalism. (We may define phenomenalism, at least for the moment, as the view that there are only percepts.) Suppose a gun on a hilltop is fired every day at twelve o'clock: many people both see and hear it fired, but the further they are from it the longer is the interval between seeing and hearing. This makes it very difficult to accept a naïvely realistic view as to the hearing, since, if that view were correct, there would have to be a fixed interval of time (presumably zero) between the sight and the sound. It also makes it natural to adopt a causal view of sound, since the retardation of the sound depends upon the distance, not upon the number of intermediate percipients. But hitherto our space was purely "ideal" except where there were percipients; it seems odd, therefore, that it should have an actual influence. It is much more natural to suppose that the sound travels over the intervening space, in which case something must be happening even in places where there is no one with ears to hear. The argument is perhaps not very strong, but we cannot deny that it has *some* force.

Much stronger arguments, however, are derivable from other sources. Suppose a room arranged with a man concealed behind a curtain, and also a camera and dictaphone. Suppose two men came into the room, converse, dine, and smoke. If the record of the dictaphone and the camera agrees with that of the man behind the curtain, it is impossible to resist the conclusion that something happened where they were which bore an intimate relation to what the hidden man perceived. For that matter, one might have two cameras and two dictaphones, and compare their records. Such correspondences, which are only more extreme forms of those with which primitive common sense is familiar, make it inconceivably complicated and unplausible to suppose that nothing happens where there is no percipient. If the dictaphone and the hidden man give the same report of the conversation, one must suppose some causal connection, since otherwise the coincidence is in the highest degree improbable. But the causal connection is found to depend upon the position of the dictaphone at the time of the conversation, not upon the person who hears its record. This seems very strange, if its record does not exist until it is heard, as we shall have to suppose if we confine the world to percepts. I will not emphasize the more obvious oddities of such a world, as e.g., the one once brought forward by Dr. G. E. Moore, that a railway train would only have wheels when it is not going, since, while it is going, the passengers cannot see them.

Before accepting such arguments, however, we must see what could be said against them by a phenomenalist. Let us, therefore, proceed to state the case for phenomenalism. . . .

We have, in the first place, real percepts, collected into groups each of which is defined by the characteristic that common sense would call all its members percepts of one physical object. These real percepts, as we saw, vary from one percipient to another in such a way as to allow us to construct a space of percipients, and to locate physical objects in this space. Let us, for the moment, adopt the view that nothing exists except percepts, our own and other people's. We shall then observe that the percepts forming a given group can always be arranged about a centre in the space of percipients, and we can fill out the group by interpolating "ideal" ["possible" is the more usual term—Ed.] percepts, continuous in quality with actual percepts, in regions where there are no actual percipients. (A region of space which is "ideal" at one moment may be actual at another owing to motion of a percipient. The successive positions of an observer watching Cleopatra's Needle from a passing tram form a sensibly continuous series.) If a number of people hear a gun fired, there are differences in the loudness and the time of their percepts; we can fill out the actual percepts by "ideal" noises varying continuously from one actual one to another. The same can be done with correlated visual percepts; also with smells. We will call a group thus extended by interpolation and extrapolation a "full" group: its members are partly real, partly ideal. Each group has a centre in the space of percipients; this centre is real if occupied by a percipient, while otherwise it is ideal. (Our space is not assumed to be a smooth geometrical space, and the centre may be a finite volume.) As a rule, even when the centre is occupied by a percipient, it nevertheless contains no member of the group, not even an ideal member: "the eye sees not itself." A group, that is to say, is hollow: when we get sufficiently near to its centre it ceases to have members. This is a purely empirical observation.

A full group which contains any real members will be

called a "real" group; a group whose members are all ideal will be called "ideal." It remains to show how we are to define an ideal group.

In addition to the laws correlating percepts forming one group—which may be called, in an extended sense, laws of perspective—there are also laws as to the manner in which percepts succeed one another. These are causal laws in the ordinary sense; they are included in the usual laws of physics. When we know a certain number of members of a full group, we can infer the others by the laws of perspective; it is found that some exist and some do not, but all that do exist are members of the calculated full group. In like manner, when we are given a sufficient number of full groups, we can calculate other full groups at other times. It is found that some of the calculated full groups are real, some ideal, but that all real groups are included among those calculated. (I am assuming an impossible perfection of physics.) Two groups belonging to different times may, in virtue of causal relations which we shall explain when we come to discuss substance, be connected in the way which makes us regard them as successive states of one "thing" or "body." (The time of a full group, by the way, is not exactly the time at which its members occur, but slightly earlier than the earliest real member—or much earlier, in the case of a star. The time of a full group is the time at which physics places the occurrence supposed to be perceived.) The whole series of groups belonging to a given "thing" is called a "biography." The causal laws are such as to allow us sometimes to infer "things." A thing is "real" when its biography contains at least one group which is "real," i.e. contains at least one percept; otherwise a thing is "ideal." This construction is closely analogous to that of "ideal" points, lines, and planes in descriptive geometry. We have to ask ourselves whether there are any reasons for or against it.

The above construction preserves the whole of physics, at least formally; and it gives an interpretation, in terms of percepts and their laws, to every proposition of physics which there is any empirical reason to believe. "Ideal" percepts, groups, and things, in this theory, are really a shorthand for stating the laws of actual percepts, and all empirical evidence has to do with actual percepts. The above account, therefore, preserves the truth of physics with the bare minimum of hypothesis. Of course there should be also rules for determining when a calculated percept is real and when it is ideal; but this is difficult, since such rules would have to contain a science of human actions. It may be known that you will see certain things if you look through a telescope, but it is difficult to know whether you will look through it. This completion of our science is therefore not possible at present; but that is no argument against the truth of our science so far as it goes. It is obvious that the method might be extended so as to make all perceptions except one's own "ideal"; we should then have a completely solipsistic interpretation of physics. I shall, however, ignore this extension, and consider only that form of the theory in which all percepts are admitted.

The metaphysic which we have been developing is essentially Berkeley's: whatever is, is perceived. But our reasons are somewhat different from his. We do not suggest that there is any impossibility about unperceived existents, but only that no strong ground exists for believing in them. Berkeley believed that the grounds against them were conclusive; we only suggest that the grounds in their favour are inconclusive. I am not asserting this: I am proposing it as a view to be considered.

The great difficulty in the above theory of "ideal" elements is that it is hard to see how anything merely imaginary can be essential to the statement of a causal law. We have to explain the dictaphone which repeats the conversation. We will suppose that it was seen in place before and after the conversation, but not during it. Consequently, on the view we are examining, it did not exist at all during the conversation. Causal laws, stated without fictitious elements will thus involve action at a distance in time and space. Moreover, our percepts are not sufficient to determine the course of nature; we derive causal laws from close observation, and preserve them in other cases by inventing "ideal" things. This would not be necessary if percepts sufficed for the causal determination of future percepts. Thus the view we are examining is incompatible with physical determinism, in fact though not in form. We could multiply difficulties of this kind indefinitely. No one of them is conclusive, but in the aggregate they suffice to account for the fact that it is almost impossible to compel oneself to believe such a theory. Perhaps continuity (not in a strict mathematical sense) is one of the strongest objections. We experience sensible continuity when we move our own body, and when we fixedly observe some object which does not explode. But if we repeatedly open and shut our eyes we experience visual discontinuity, which we find it impossible to attribute to the physical objects which we alternately see and do not see, the more so as, to another spectator, they remain unchanged all the time. Causation at a distance in time, though not logically impossible, is also repugnant to our notions of the physical world. Therefore, although it is logically possible to interpret the physical world in terms of ideal elements, I conclude that this interpretation is unplausible, and that it has no positive grounds in its favour.

Nevertheless the above construction remains valid and important, as a method of separating perceptual and non-perceptual elements of physics, and of showing how much can be achieved by the former alone. As such, I shall continue to utilize it in the sequel. The only thing rejected is the view that "ideal" elements are unreal.[2]

The matter would, of course, be otherwise in this last respect if we could accept the argument for idealism, whether of the Berkeleyan or the German variety. These arguments profess to prove that what exists *must* have a mental character, and therefore compel us to interpret physics accordingly. I reject such *a priori* argumentation, whatever conclusion it may be designed to prove. There is no difficulty in interpreting physics idealistically, but there is also, I should say, no necessity for such an interpretation. "Matter" is known only as regards certain very abstract characteristics, which might quite well belong to a manifold of mental events, but might also belong to a different manifold. In fact, the only manifolds known for certain to possess the mathematical properties of the physical world are built up out of numbers and belong to pure mathematics. Our reason for not regarding "matter" as actually being an arithmetical structure derived from the finite integers is the connection of "matter" with perception; that is why our present discussion is necessary. But this connection tells us extremely little about the character of the unperceived events in the physical world. Unlike idealists and materialists, I do not believe that there is any other source of knowledge from which this meagre result can be supplemented. Like other people, I allow myself to speculate: but this is an exercise of imagination, not a process of demonstrative reasoning.

I shall assume henceforth not only that there are percepts which I do not perceive, connected with other people's bodies, but also that there are events causally connected with percepts, as to which we do not know whether they are perceived or not. I shall assume, e.g., that if I am alone in a room and I shut my eyes, the objects in it which I no longer see (i.e. the causes of my visual percepts) continue to exist, and do not suddenly become resurrected when I re-open my eyes. This must be taken in conjunction with what was said earlier about perspective in a generalized sense, and about the common space in which we locate the physical objects which, for common sense, are perceived by several people at once. We collect correlated percepts into a group, and we suppose that there are other members of the group, corresponding to places where there is no percipient—or, to speak more guardedly, where there is not known to be a percipient. But we no longer assume, as when we were constructing "ideal" elements, that what is at such places is what we should perceive if we went to them. We think, e.g., that light consists of waves of a certain kind, but becomes transformed, on contact with the eye, into a different physical process. Therefore what occurs before the light reaches an eye is presumably different from what occurs afterwards, and therefore different from a visual percept. But it is supposed to be causally continuous with the visual percept; and it is largely for the sake of this causal continuity that a certain reinterpretation of the physical world seems desirable.

In some ways, the language of causation is perhaps not the best for expressing what is intended. What is intended may be expressed as follows. Confining ourselves, to begin with, to the percepts of various observers, we can form groups of percepts connected approximately, though not exactly, by laws which may be called laws of "perspective." By means of these laws, together with the changes in our other percepts which are connected with the perception of bodily movement, we can form the conception of a space in which percipients are situated, and we find that in this space all the percepts belonging to one group (i.e. of the same physical object, from the standpoint of common sense) can be ordered about a centre, which we take to be the place where the physical object in question is. (For us, this is a *definition* of the place of a physical object.) The centre is not to be conceived as a point, but as a volume, which may be as small as an electron or as large as a star. The essential assumption for what is commonly called the causal theory is that the group of percepts can be enlarged by the addition of other events, ranged in the same space about the same centre, and connected both with each other and with the group of percepts by laws which include the laws of perspective. The essential points are (1) the arrangement about a centre, (2) the continuity between percepts and correlated events in other parts of the space derived from percepts and locomotion. The first is a matter of observation; the second is a hypothesis designed to secure simplicity and continuity in the laws of correlation suggested by the grouping of percepts. It cannot be demonstrated, but its merits are of the same kind as those of any other scientific theory.

Author's Notes

[1] On this subject, cf. my *Our Knowledge of the External World*.
[2] The character of the "ideal" elements, also, will be less similar to that of percepts than in the above construction, or at least cannot be known to be so similar.

18. THE JUSTIFICATION OF REALISM

A. O. Lovejoy

Like Selection 1 this comes from Professor Lovejoy's *The Revolt Against Dualism* (Open Court, 1929). It consists in pp. 266–270 and 298–302, the intervening pages being a discussion of contemporary physicists' pronouncements. Compare this selection with Selection 17 (Russell).

It seems worth while to consider afresh what reasons—other than "instincts," to which some realists seem to me to appeal too simply—can be given for believing that there is a world of existing particulars which are nobody's "ideas"—which, in other words, are independent of awareness—and to ask how much, or what sort, of knowledge of that world it is permissible to suppose that we can attain. . . .

The case for physical realism should not, I think, be made to rest primarily or wholly—as it is by Russell in his later period—upon the assumed necessity of postulating external causal objects to account for our percepts—objects about which we can infer no more than that there are differences of some kind in them, corresponding numerically, but not necessarily or probably in their qualities, to the differences between percepts. It is true that if there *are* external objects, and if they cannot be identical with our data, we must be able to infer so much, at least, about them, if we are to base any judgments whatever concerning them upon perception. And it is also true that our disposition to assume that our experiences have causes is somewhat too disparagingly described when it is called mere "animal faith." It is a faith, indeed, but—in the form represented in the phase of Mr. Russell's philosophy to which I have referred—it is a highly critical and extremely attenuated faith. And it is a part of the general faith that reality has a greater degree of orderliness, of interconnection of parts, and therefore of intelligibility, than is manifested in the confused phantasmagoria of unsupplemented sensation. But it is not the primary form of that faith; it is derivative from something more fundamental. For there is no obvious gain in the coherency and intelligibility of the world if you merely take an isolated momentary bit of perceptual content and assert concerning it: this must have had a cause external in some sense to itself.

The more fundamental postulate to which I refer—and the better reason for accepting realism—will begin to appear if we consider what the "independence" which might be ascribed to physical reals, and would constitute the first essential of their physicality, would be. It would have to do primarily with the *time* of their existence. Consciousness in general and the consciousness of this or that sensible object in particular, is fluctuating and intermittent. For you an object now exists and now does not exist; when you are in deep sleep or a swoon the whole world is nonexistent. The primary function of "real objects," the way in which the belief in them helps us to regard the universe as more coherent than sense-experience, consists in their filling the temporal gaps between actual perceptions. The "independence" of a thing means, concretely, its continued existence, or the continuance of a connected series of events of which it is a member, at times when it is not being attended to by me, nor necessarily by any one like me. The starting point of the argument for physical realism, I suggest, is the plain man's normal and reasonable belief that the processes of nature do not stop when he stops noticing them. It is not the "outerness" of the object perceived, *when* it is perceived, but the *persistence of something which is in some manner connected* with what is perceived, during the interperceptual intervals, that is the primary natural postulate out of which the belief in an external world, in objects which exist though they are not given in experience, arises. How irrepressible this belief is may be judged from the emphatic affirmation of it even by phenomenalists who ostensibly refuse to admit any metempirical realities. Thus Petzoldt, after declaring that "there is no scientific meaning in the assumption that there exists behind experience something-or-other as its bearer or

generator," forthwith proceeds to castigate those who will not
believe in "a perdurance of objects which is independent of
us"—who fail to regard the fact that "things always turn up
again quite independently of whether I have had my eyes
open or not, at the place they previously had, or at some
place wholly independent of my thought." Petzoldt, in short,
apparently finds it superfluous to suppose that there are any
common and independent realities behind our experiences,
but impossible to conceive that there are none between our
experiences.

The belief in the continuance of things or processes between perceptions is not a blank act of faith, as would be the
postulation of an external causal object for a single momentary
percept; it may be said to be—not, indeed, rigorously verified
—but strengthened by one of the most familiar of empirical
facts, namely, that the same uniform causal sequences of
natural events which may be observed within experience
appear to go on in the same manner when not experienced.
You built a fire in your grate of a certain quantity of coal,
of a certain chemical composition. Whenever you remain in
the room there occurs a typical succession of sensible phenomena according to an approximately regular schedule of
clock-time; in, say, a half-hour the coal is half-consumed; at
the end of the hour the grate contains only ashes. If you build
a fire of the same quantity of the same material under the
same conditions, leave the room, and return after any given
time has elapsed, you get approximately the same sense-
experiences as you would have had at the corresponding
moment if you had remained in the room. You infer, therefore, that the fire has been burning as usual during your
absence, and that being perceived is not a condition necessary for the occurrence of the process. But a consistent
idealist or phenomenalist cannot say this. He is committed
to the proposition either that the fire has not been or, at all
events, cannot legitimately be assumed to have been, burning when no one was perceiving it; his doctrine amounts to a
gratuitous assumption of the universal jumpiness or temporal
discontinuity of causal sequences. The most that he can admit

—and he cannot admit less—is that fires and other natural processes behave *as if* they went on when unobserved; if he desires to make this seem more intelligible, he may invoke some preestablished harmony, or resort to a species of occasionalism—assuming that when you return to the room after an hour God (as Descartes would have said) deceives you by putting into your mind a percept of a grate full of ashes, though *these* ashes are not the effects of any fire.[1] But such "explanations" of the facts are plainly arbitrary and far-fetched; they multiply types of causal agency beyond necessity. And to be content with a mere *Philosophie des Als-Ob* in such a case—to say that, although nothing at all that was like a fire or would have caused you to perceive a fire, if you had remained in the room, was really happening while you were absent, nevertheless all goes on as though the fire had been burning during that interval—this, surely, is a singularly strained and artificial notion, wholly foreign to the normal propensities of our intelligence.

Naïve realism, however, infers more from this type of fact than is warranted;[2] it supposes that while you were not in the room *exactly the same* phenomena were going on as you would have experienced had you been there—the play of color in the flames, the qualities experienced by you in thermal sensation, and so on. To suppose this is to assume that certain of the factors in the case—namely, your presence in the room and your psychophysical constitution—make no difference in the content of your experience. This positive assumption of the complete irrelevance of certain actual antecedents or concomitants of a given effect is not only gratuitous and improbable, but is in conflict with familiar empirical evidences of the concomitant variation of sense-data with differences in the perceptible natures or states of percipients. What is reasonably inferable is that some process capable of causing an organism, constituted as you are, to have the perceptual experience of a burning fire, has been continuously going on while you were not in such relations to it as actually to perceive any fire. The causal theory of perception is thus derivative from, not logically prior to, the postulate of the continuance of the orderly sequences of nature during inter-perceptual intervals. The world of external causal entities or events is the world that you are obliged to assume when you accept the evidence for such continuance, while recognizing the probability that your own makeup, as a body or a mind or both, plays some part in determining the qualitative char-acter of your percepts. The specific qualities characteristic of the potentially unperceived, that is, interperceptual, process, remain, so far as these considerations go, undetermined; you cannot, thus far, tell how much of what you experience is due to external events, how much to the nature of "that which is acted upon" by these events. But this does not weaken the reasons for believing that there *are* such tem-porally persistent and therefore independent events. Matter, or the physical order, still remains, not only as, in Mill's phrase, "a permanent possibility of sensation," but as a con-tinuing existent capable of causing sensations under certain circumstances. . . .

We shall take three conclusions as already established: (a) there is an order of existences or events which persists when unperceived; (b) this is causally related to our sensa; (c) the particulars belonging to it cannot be identical with our sensa. Our problem, then, is whether, given these premises and the common facts of every-day experience, we can reach any further probable propositions concerning the extra-perceptual, neutral, causal order. One such proposition, manifestly, is that we have power to act upon this order. Processes which apparently go on unperceived can be initiated by percipient beings. And the unobserved interperceptual causal processes will vary (as their subsequently observed effect will show) with variations in the specific characters of our sense-data while we are initiating those processes; e.g., if I build my fire of wood instead of coal, the time required for it to burn out will be shorter and the ashes which I find on returning to the room will be of a different quality. It is equally a fact of everyday experience that certain percepts or images do not initiate (or are not correlated with) processes capable of continuing during interperceptual intervals and producing observable terminal effects identical with those observable when the entire sequence of intermediate stages has been attended to. If I merely imagine or dream of a fire in the grate, I do not—after ceasing so to dream or imagine— experience the visual and tactual content called ashes. Purely visual content is not found by us to be sufficient to start fires (or to give sensible evidence of the physical equivalent of a fire having started in the extra-perceptual world), or to be correlated with the initiation by us of any physical process. The same fact is illustrated by the comparative sterility of pink rats. If I am able to initiate a physical process, my action (if experienced at all by myself) is experienced in the form of tactual and kinesthetic as well as (in some cases) visual sense-data; it is, in short, one of the primary dis- coveries of experience that tactual and kinesthetic sensations have a different and more constant relation to the physical causal order than do visual percepts or images. The former are the phases of our experience in which we as percipients appear to have causal contact with that order. And it is reasonable to suppose that this fact throws some light upon the nature of the external causal world.

Furthermore, if, like everyone else, we assume that there are many percipients, and that they can through language convey some information to one another about the char- acteristics of their respective sense-data, we find that each of them is able to act upon the other percipients, that is, to determine in some degree what experiences they shall have; and that this action upon them is usually, and probably always, conditional upon initiating (in the sense and in the manner already indicated) physical processes. If I light a fire, other men as well as myself will feel the heat; they may, in consequence of my action, observe a sensible fire con- tinuously while I do not; while if I imagine or dream of a fire, their experience remains unaffected. One of the two principal reasons why we do not regard dream-fires as indica- tions of the occurrence of events (at least the kind of events ordinarily connected with sensible fires) in the persistent and therefore independent world is that they do not cause others to have sensations of warmth or to find perceptible ashes in their perceptible grates. Purely private percepts are called illusory, not merely because they happen to be private, but because they do not causally interact directly, or in the manner in which other qualitatively similar percepts do, with the world which is the medium of communication and interaction between us.

Now what observably happens when I thus act upon the external world and through it affect other men's experience and my own subsequent experiences, is usually that with my perceptible body I push and pull other perceptible objects about in my perceptual space. And with the movements which I thus determine as data of my own perception there may be—under conditions empirically definable—correlated perceptions of movement in the experience of others. They report to me that they see what they call my body moving, and other objects moving in ways uniformly connected with my bodily movements. That their percepts of what they call my body are not my body itself is true; and it is also true that the perceptual objects which they see moving in consequence of my bodily movements are not existentially nor qualitatively identical with those which I see, nor yet with any entity in the neutral causal order. The question may nevertheless be asked: Are the causal processes in the external world which are initiated by motions (i.e. by those which I perceive) and which terminate in motions (i.e. those which other men perceive) also of the nature of motions? The idealist answers definitely in the negative; the phenomenalist and the all-but agnostic physicist answer that we have, at any rate, no reason whatever for thinking so. But there are, I think, certain considerations which, though not demonstrative, make an affirmative answer to the question the more plausible.

(a) In the first place, it is at least not *impossible* that the processes which cause and link together the percepts of different times and different persons are of the same general sort as the causal sequences which empirically occur within our perceptual experience. No fact of experience, obviously, can prove the contrary.

(b) It is a simpler assumption about the unperceived causal processes that they are of the same sort as those perceived, rather than of some wholly different sort. In making such an assumption we still follow the rule of continuity in our conjectures about that which we cannot directly experience. We do not postulate differences in the nature of things beyond necessity. If I suppose that, when I have the experience of moving my body and pushing and pulling something about, thereby producing effects in the neutral causal order, I *am* pushing or pulling something about, and that this *is* a way in which effects in that order are produced, I am enabled to conceive of the external world with which I am in relation in action as fundamentally homogeneous with the perceptual world; and though it may not be so, it appears to me more sensible to proceed upon the hypothesis that it is, so long as there is no good evidence to the contrary.

(c) The spaces in which our perceptible effective bodily movements take place, whether or not they are literally parts of a single Space, are at all events congruent; they fit together in a remarkable way. For example, a hundred men from as many different places are summoned to attend an international conference in Geneva. They thereupon consult maps, time-tables, Baedekers, to find the routes to take in order to reach that city. These useful works were prepared by yet other men. They do not, however, purport to be descriptions of the arrangement of things in private perceptual spaces of their authors; they profess to represent a set of spatial relations which will hold good in the perceptual experience of any inhabitant of the earth. The routes which they describe are not routes to a hundred private Genevas, but to a single Geneva conceived to have a determinate position in some common or public spatial order. And by a series of movements of their own legs, assisted by motions of trains and steamships, which follow spatial directions symbolized in the maps and guidebooks, the delegates to the conference presently find themselves having similar (though not identical) visual and tactual percepts, for example, percepts of the Quai Mont Blanc, and in a position in which they can sit down in the same room and talk to one another. The result may be that the construction of battleships in certain other places will be discontinued. The idealistic or phenomenalistic account of this affair is that there is no common space which is represented by the maps, and that no motion of what could strictly be called the body of any delegate took place. What happened was merely that their minds—which were throughout in no place at all—after first having private percepts of maps and then having visual and other sensations of motion, resulting, perhaps, in sensations of seasickness, subsequently experienced certain resemblant sense-percepts which they mistakenly called by the single name "Geneva," and others which they called the bodies and voices of their fellow delegates. In reality, therefore the delegates never met. Their private sequences of sense-data, for no known or conjecturable reason, happen eventually to coincide in part; at approximately the time when one of them has the kinesthetic sensations of opening his mouth and using his vocal organs, the others had correspondent visual sensations and also certain sound sensations of (more or less) intelligible words; but they were no nearer one another when this occurred than at the beginning. Now this is, no doubt, conceivable, in the sense that is not formally self-contradictory; but it seems to me incredibly farfetched, and I cannot avoid the suspicion that the human species (including physicists and even idealistic philosophers) is constitutionally incapable of really believing it—of thinking in this fashion of this kind of experience. Men have always believed, and will, doubtless, continue to believe, that the way to arrive at a place is to go there; and they will always be recalcitrant to a view which requires them to hold, or to regard it as probable, that (for example) the ill-fated passengers of the *Titanic* were not really in the same ship or even in the same space. So long as the experienced bodily movements of a number of separate percipients thus fit into a single spatial pattern; so long as, in consequence of motions in convergent directions in that pattern (and not otherwise), the percipients find themselves face to face; so long as (to vary the illustration) through such bodily movements (and not otherwise) they are enabled not only to destroy the bodies of other men but also to bring all *their* perceiving to an end, by firing bullets in the direction in which the other men's bodies are perceived—so long men will naturally conceive of the processes in the common world through which their respective sense-data are caused as occurring in a single common spatial or spatio-temporal order and as consisting of motions therein. That this conceived common space is literally identical with their perceived spaces they may find reason to doubt; that the bodies which effectively move in it have all the properties of the bodies sensibly perceived, or are particulars existentially identical with them, they will find good reasons for denying. But the fact that their apprehension of bodies must be recognized by them to be mediate or representational and to contain "psychic additions" and distortions need not, and pretty certainly will not, prevent them from thinking that they have bodies—unique bodies, that is, each of which belongs to one percipient, and is not merely the multitudinous aggregate of the percepts of it— bodies which are therefore assignable to the public spatial system, which have positions relative to other bodies which can change these positions, and in doing so cause changes in other bodies and modify thereby the sense-content, or even bring to an end the existence, of other percipient beings.

Such, then, is a brief and incomplete indication of the normal genesis of this prejudice. It gains further strength from a hundred other characteristics of ordinary perceptual experience, which there is no time to recall.[3] It is, I venture to suggest, a prejudice to which the plain man and even the philosopher may continue to yield without the fear of imminent confutation—and one which even the physicist will find it useful to take (as he usually does) as the starting point of his further analyses and of his extension of our understanding of the world we live in.

NOTES

[1] The phenomenalists would be more likely to say that the permanent possibility of the sensation of fire continued, that if you

had returned to the room at any time you would have had fire-like sense-data (Ss.22 and 23). But why does the possibility continue, why would you get these data—and how does the phenomenalist know it?—unless there is a fire actually there?—ED.

2 Compare Hume, S.21.—ED.

3 Cp. certain considerations mentioned by Bertrand Russell, *Analysis of Matter,* p. 209 [= S.17 pp. 216-217]—LOVEJOY

19. THE AIM OF CRITICAL REALISM

R. W. SELLARS

A leading exponent of American Critical Realism (as was A. O. Lovejoy), Roy Wood Sellars (1880–   ) here explains how the movement sought to provide a new analysis of the concepts of perception and knowledge which would preserve the benefits of the general Realist position and yet avoid the clear defects of Naïve and Representative Realism. This selection is taken from the first half of his article "A Statement of Critical Realism" which appeared in *Revue Internationale de Philosophie,* I, 1938–39.

The aim of the critical realists was to keep the intention of perception, its direct concern with physical things, while recognizing that sensory appearances could not be considered, as naïve realism supposed, the very surface of external things. In other words, the critical realists saw in the act of perception something more than mere apprehension or acquaintance. They believed that it contained something akin to judgment or belief. In short, they began to distinguish between what is given in perception—usually spoken of as the datum—and *the more inclusive operation* of perceptual reference, intent or affirmation joined with a characterization of the object, so affirmed, in terms of properties founded on what has been discriminated in the sensory appearance. In other words, the opinion was being entertained that perceiving is a complex operation which uses sensory appearances as a guide but is concerned with what it regards as things. Contrary to Locke, then, ideas are not the primary objects of perceptual cognition, but, instead, physical things are. It follows, of course, that an object of knowledge is that with which the act of cognition is concerned and that the act of cognition can be concerned with something other than sensations and images.

This realistic movement sought, then, to do justice to the apparent directness of meaning and belief in natural realism while recognizing the part played by sensory appearances.

It saw that it was necessary—even at the level of sense-perception—to distinguish between intuition and something akin to judgment. Do we not regard ourselves as aware of public things in perception? Public things which we can characterize and compare and relate to one another? And yet reflection forces us to admit that such awareness is guided and mediated by sensory appearances. It was, quite clearly, the job of critical epistemology to analyze the perceptual experience in such a way as to bring out the beliefs and categories and conceptions operating in sense-perception as well as the sensory material. Perceiving involves more than sensing or, as the modern psychologist might put it, a percept contains more than sensory qualities as such. There is belief, construction and interpretation, all this leading to what is taken to be the awareness of things.

Now this approach could be characterized as phenomenological or descriptive. Naïve realism was to be taken, not as a fact, but as a description of sense-perception, a starting-point for analysis. It is true that in perceiving we regard ourselves as in some fashion meaning and characterizing independent public things. May not this claim and belief be valid even though we must relinquish its more naïve interpretation which identifies the sensory appearance with the thing meant and believed in? In that case we should need to distinguish between the intuition of the sensory appearance, which alone is given, and the denotative selection of[1] a thing-object which is believed in and characterized. Denotative selection would be guided by the intuited sensory appearance but would not itself involve the entrance of the object into consciousness in a literal, intuitive way. By contrast with the sensory appearance the thing-object would be regarded as *transcendent*, as something to be affirmed and believed in and not given. I would myself suggest that transcendence is a contrast-meaning growing up in the human mind as this situation is realized. Private and public, immanent and transcendent are distinctions of an essentially correlative sort. They are products of reflection, of analysis. . . .

The task which faced the critical realist was set by the

history of thought itself. It may be formulated thus: Could a realistic position be worked out which avoided both the difficulties confronting naïve realism and those which, associated with Locke's too dominantly causal approach, led to the weaknesses of representative perception? It had long seemed that realistic philosophy was impaled on the horns of a dilemma. On the one hand, naïve realism was open to serious objections; and yet it seemed to be the only position which emphasized direct awareness of public things. On the other hand, Berkeley and Hume had succeeded in convincing thinkers that representationalism was equally precarious since it postulated a shadowy double of what is apparently perceived. It must not be forgotten that there went with this latter development the rejection of abstract ideas and the adoption of atomic sensationalism. It is likely that this psychology led to blindness to the actual complexity of the perceptual experience. Modern psychology, whether Gestaltist or eclectic, recognizes the large amount of interpretation that enters into perception.

Critical realism is, then, in essentials, an attempt to escape between the horns of the traditional dilemma by reanalyzing the perceptual experience. It seeks to make explicit what is more or less implicit there. It is its thesis that, in perception, we regard ourselves as apparently aware of public things and that, in such sense-perception, we look, hear, and feel *through* sensory factors at objects. The belief in enduring, public things to which we must adjust ourselves *dominates the perceptual experience.* It is for this reason that we tend to mistake our sensations for these things. It is *as though* they were the appearances of public things, even the very surface of them. The category of thinghood—whose basis I shall examine later—exercises this control over sensory data by giving them a setting and meaning. We believe that there is more to a thing than its temporary appearance to us, that it is the seat of active controls of all sorts, that it is executive. In short, all sorts of facts about the thing perceived are funded and influence our perceptual experience. . . .

It is by eliciting the distinctions implicit in the perceptual experience that critical realism avoids the fallacy of representative perception. In perception we do not infer physical objects and take them to be similar to our percepts. Rather is the perceptual experience an interpreted complex in which the sensory field is contrasted with more subjective attitudes and activities, and becoming the complement of these, is regarded as something to behave towards, something as real as the self, something public and independent. Memories and expectations and funded facts enter into the picture. It is in this general fashion that the categories of selfhood and thinghood develop; and, as they develop, the sensory data of the field become regarded as the surface of these things, as their appearances, as signs of them. A patch of color seems the very contour of a public thing; a tactual sensation is taken to be the rough surface of a handled thing.

So much in the way of preliminary suggestions. The intention of the approach can, I hope, now be made clear. It is an attempt to elicit the full nature of the perceptual experience and show that there is in it the belief in public objects which are somehow manifested in sensory appearances. Attitudes, expectations, memories, accepted facts, all operate interpretatively to make us regard ourselves as somehow aware of public, independent things. Sensory appearances are regarded as having a background of a substantial, executive sort. We tend to think of ourselves as aware of these things *through* the sensory appearances. We do not so much infer public objects as act toward them and characterize them in terms of properties founded on intuited colors and shapes. In all this you have an animal activity which the psychologist is studying. There is, if you will, stimulus *and complex interpretative response.*

In his discussion of perceiving the critical realist made much use of such terms as reference, intent, affirmation. He talked of referring to things, making things objects of a perceptual act. I can speak only of myself as regards the interpretation of these terms. There is for me nothing mystical or esoteric about their meaning. They simply call attention to the fact that the perceptual experience is a complex, developed, relational experience and is not to be reduced to such factors as colored fields or tactual sensations. I take it that in visual perception, for example, we are aware of a contrast between our attitude as a percipient and the object which we are perceiving. A patch of color, for instance, is interpreted as the surface of a thing. It is out there away from us. We can, if we will, walk toward it. In this it has contrast-meaning for us. It is set over against those feelings and sensations which we identify with our body. There is parity and contrast in the perceptual experience. Objective reference is no more than localization and selection of the things around us in terms of sensory factors, such as colors and pressures, regarded as the surfaces of things or as forces coming from things. There is context, relational contrast, categorical meaning. *In no sense is there any mystical transcendence of some literal kind in which a supposed substantial mind gets out of itself and makes a leap to external physical things.* It should always be remembered that the critical realist is simply seeking to do justice to the distinctions within the field of the individual's perceptual experience. A conceptual framework is operating.

It is in this quite empirical manner that I would account for the distinction made by critical realism between the intuition of sensory data and the belief in observed things. As a matter of fact, the normal, everyday, perceptual experience resembles that which naïve realism emphasizes, an apparent awareness of things, rather than an intuition of sensory data recognized as such. The perceptual experience is thick and shot full of meanings and relationships. Nevertheless, analysis shows that the only literally intuited object is the sensory datum but that, in perceiving as such, it is given a context which makes the percipient regard it as an appearing thing. It is to this identification or interpretation that belief, implicit or explicit, attaches. It is *as though* we were directly aware of a thing. Perceiving is not inferential but an affair of largely automatic interpretation. It has been the thesis of the critical realists that felt attitudes have much to do with the polarity of subject and object in the perceptual experience. But this is deepened with the recognition of individual things and classes of things, on the one hand, and with a growth of self-consciousness on the other. Increasingly the concept of continuance and the concept of causal executiveness penetrate the field of experience. The percipient regards himself as one among a number of things equally real with himself.

All this, so far as I can see, is the purest empiricism. All the categories operating in experience should be capable of verbalization and recognition. Selective intent, objective reference, and affirmation are terms used by critical realists as expressive of polarity and conscious attention at the perceptual level when I regard myself as observing things. So much for the descriptive, or phenomenological, side of the question.

But what has been achieved by this analysis of the perceptual experience? It is clear that there can be no return to naïve realism for the very terms of the analysis preclude it. Moreover, the critical realist accepts the relevance and weight of the traditional arguments against naïve realism, that is, the assumption that the denotative affirmation of things and their characterization constitutes a literal intuition of them. In his opinion the operation of the sensory factor in this process easily misleads. Because it is intuited, it is assumed that the thing we are dealing with is intuited. The sensory datum tends to be identified with the thing believed in, which, of course, is quite natural until reflection intervenes.

What, then is the task of reflection? It is to make explicit what is involved in perception. If psychology, physiology, and the main tradition in modern philosophy are right in their theory that sensory data are private and to be correlated with brain-events, then we must cease literally to identify them with the surface of things. Instead, we must speak of intuiting them and of denoting and characterizing the thing-objects which we regard ourselves as dealing with in perception. In making this distinction we become aware of the difference between immanence and transcendence. What is immanent can be intuited. What cannot be intuited but only believed in and denoted is transcendent. These I take to be empirical meanings, the products of reflection. The way is prepared for them by beliefs characteristic, as we have seen, of the perceptual experience and embodied in naïve realism.

The critical realist has been willing to listen to the results of psychological investigation and has rejected any atomistic, or mosaic, account of the perceptual experience at either the subjective or the objective pole of the field of consciousness. It has become clear that central, or cortical, processes are tremendously important for the content of perception or, as the psychologist calls it, the percept. The color or shade of brightness we see depends upon factors of organic balance or trend. There is a correlation between stimulus and sensory factor, but not the simple one-to-one correspondence which was at one time assumed. The Lockian passive-effect theory must be relinquished. Moreover the critical realist does not reduce the percept to the sensory factor as such. There is much spontaneous supplementation involving images and concepts. It is for this reason that I seem to myself at present to be perceiving a tree over there so many feet away from me. The verbalization of a perceptual experience into statements brings this interpretative complexity to the surface. What I regard myself as perceiving is set over against my awareness of my bodily self. That is, I take my organic sensations and feelings as connected with what I see or feel of my body, as one with my body, very much as I take a colored patch to be an external thing. In both cases I am concerned with enduring things and not with sensory factors as such. Beliefs and categories operate in perception. . . .

The flaw in the traditional causal theory of perception was that it did not work within such a prior, experimental analysis of the actual claims, meanings, and distinctions of status in perception. Instead, it postulated an external world of material things and treated brain-events as simple effects of external stimulation, effects represented in consciousness by sense impressions. The critical realists laid decisive stress upon the fact that the perceptual experience was far more complex than this atomistic and purely causal perspective suggested. They pointed out the supplementary role played by

conceptual interpretation and attitude. Interpretation, expectation, recognition, and conceptualization enter to make perceiving a higher-level operation than sensing. There is much
that suggests that sensations are *discriminata* within a perceptual field. Now while I believe the whole perceptual field
is of the nature of a patterned event in the brain, I would
emphasize the point that such a location is not intuited along
with the perceptual experience. It is of the nature of an ontological theory. Experientially we seem to our empirical selves
to be aware of sensible things outside our sensible and felt
bodies. The principle I wish to make is that, while the causal
conditioning of sensory data is quite compatible with the fact
that these data are given an interpretative setting which presents them as the appearances of things—it would be a
pleonasm to speak of external things—in epistemology we
must work from this interpretative setting and not from the
ontological theory of the locus of sensory data. In other words,
the theory of the mechanism of perceiving should not conflict with epistemology but must not be substituted for it. That
was the mistake that Locke made under the influence of the
dominant transmission theory of the mechanism of perception.
It induced him to substitute for the clues in the perceptual
experience *a reduction of perception to a mere awareness of
sensory impressions.*

I presume that it is fairly obvious by now how the critical
realist would reply to Berkeley. He would first of all, raise the
question of fact: did Berkeley do justice to the quasi-beliefs,
attitudes and conceptualizations discoverable in the perceptual
experience? The answer, of course, is an emphatic negative.
He admitted that it was a belief strangely prevailing among
men that they saw independent, material things. But he was
convinced that such a belief could not be given a significant
interpretation since, following Locke, he had reduced perceiving to an intuition of ideas. Hence it was an illusion to be
put under the label of abstract ideas. What an unempirical
position! Having reduced perceiving to sensing, that is, having
eliminated the category of thinghood and the beliefs which
went with it, Berkeley proceeds to show that there is nothing

about a sensation as such which would enable us to infer a material thing as its cause. And if a sensation be taken as an isolate or abstraction I would agree. The critical realist takes the object of perception as something believed in and *denoted through* the sensory appearance which is taken to be one with it. In his language it is affirmed in this fashion and not inferred. What dominates the perceptual experience is this concern with things in interplay with the body in which we feel ourselves in some fashion to be. This peculiar status of the body at the level of perception has not been enough emphasized. . . .

A few words with respect to Hume seem necessary. Hume, it may be recalled, went beyond Berkeley in trying to explain the fact that people do believe that they are perceiving independent, continuing things. He emphasizes the part played by constancy and coherence. "This influence from the constancy of our perceptions, like the precedent from their coherence, gives rise to the opinion of the continued existence of body, which is prior to that of its distinct existence, and produces the latter principle." Now I do not think that Hume's psychology is adequate, for he does not realize the role played by the body. The body is always with us, and we find that we experience its attitudes and our attempted control over other things.

Now Hume is ready to relinquish these acknowledged common-sense beliefs in independence and continuity by reason of his identification of perception with sensing. In fact, he calls sense impressions perceptions. These are, he says, our only objects. The only alternative he considers is representative perceptionism or the doubling of sense impressions, a view which he rightly rejects as untenable. But the alternative which the critical realist suggests is the recognition that the perceptual experience involves thing-meanings, beliefs, and attitudes and that the primary object is not a sense impression, as such, but sense impressions, if you will, ordered and interpreted in the service of such denotations and beliefs. The embodied self takes attitudes toward the not-self. Such an attitude, guided by a sensory appearance, is the basis of denotative reference. We point and say: "That thing over there." That thing is something I, as an embodied self, am concerned with. I can move toward it. I can have expectations about it and memories.

Is it not clear that the turning-point in epistemology must be an adequate analysis of the perceptual experience? Critical realism is not so much an epistemological dualism in any Lockian sense as clarification of the factors of perception, a correlation of intuition with sensory data and of denotation with objects.

EDITOR'S NOTE

1 "Reference to" would be the more usual expression. Note also that Sellars uses the term "intuition" for what the other authors represented here usually refer to as "direct awareness" or "acquaintance."

Part IV
Radical Theories

20. IDEALISM

BERKELEY

George Berkeley (1685–1753), Bishop of Cloyne in
Ireland, achieved fame by denying the existence of matter
—only minds (or spirits) exist, he claimed, and what we
take to be real material things are but collections of ideas
in the mind. Perhaps the main importance of his arguments
lies in the way they expose the weakness of the Representative Theory, both explicitly in trenchant criticism and
implicitly in the startling conclusions which are drawn from
the presuppositions (e.g. that all perception is of ideas)
which he shares with it. Also interesting are his anticipations of modern phenomenalism (e.g. pp. 248 and 260).
This selection is from the systematic statement of his philosophy in his *Principles of Human Knowledge* and comprises Sections 1–5, 8–11, 14–15, 18–20, 23–30, 33–34,
36, 42–45, 48, 58, with a few minor omissions.

It is evident to any one who takes a survey of the *objects*
of human knowledge, that they are either ideas actually imprinted on the senses; or else such as are perceived by attending to the passions and operations of the mind; or lastly,
ideas formed by help of memory and imagination—either
compounding, dividing, or barely representing those originally
perceived in the aforesaid ways. By sight I have the ideas of
light and colours, with their several degrees and variations.
By touch I perceive hard and soft, heat and cold, motion and
resistance, and of all these more and less either as to quantity
or degree. Smelling furnishes me with odours; and palate with
tastes; and hearing conveys sounds to the mind in all their
variety of tone and composition. And as several of these are
observed to accompany each other, they come to be marked
by one name, and so to be reputed as one thing. Thus, for
example, a certain colour, taste, smell, figure, and consistence
having been observed to go together, are accounted one
distinct thing, signified by the name *apple*; other collections

of ideas constitute a stone, a tree, a book, and the like sensible things—which as they are pleasing or disagreeable excite the passions of love, hatred, joy, grief, and so forth.

But, besides all that endless variety of ideas or objects of knowledge, there is likewise something which knows or perceives them, and exercises divers operations, as willing, imagining, remembering, about them. This perceiving, active being is what I call *mind, spirit, soul,* or *myself.* By which words I do not denote any one of my ideas, but a thing entirely distinct from them, wherein they exist, or, which is the same thing, whereby they are perceived—for the existence of an idea consists in being perceived.

That neither our thoughts, nor passions, nor ideas formed by the imagination, exist without the mind, is what everybody will allow. And to me it is no less evident that the various sensations or ideas imprinted on the sense, however blended or combined together (that is, whatever objects they compose), cannot exist otherwise than in a mind perceiving them. I think an intuitive knowledge may be obtained of this by any one that shall attend to what is meant by the term *exist* when applied to sensible things. The table I write on I say exists, that is, I see and feel it; and if I were out of my study I should say it existed—meaning thereby that if I was in my study I might perceive it, or that some other spirit actually does perceive it. There was an odour, that is, it was smelt; there was a sound, that is, it was heard; a colour or figure, and it was perceived by sight or touch. This is all that I can understand by these and the like expressions, for as to what is said of the absolute existence of unthinking things without any relation to their being perceived, that is to me perfectly unintelligible. Their *esse* is *percipi,* nor is it possible they should have any existence out of the minds or thinking things which perceive them.

It is indeed an opinion strangely prevailing amongst men, that houses, mountains, rivers, and in a word all sensible objects, have an existence, natural or real, distinct from their being perceived by the understanding. But, with how great an assurance and acquiescence soever this principle may be

entertained in the world, yet whoever shall find in his heart
to call it in question may, if I mistake not, perceive it to
involve a manifest contradiction. For, what are the fore-
mentioned objects but the things we perceive by sense? and
what do we perceive besides our own ideas or sensations? and
is it not plainly repugnant that any one of these, or any
combination of them, should exist unperceived?

If we thoroughly examine this tenet it will, perhaps, be
found at bottom to depend on the doctrine of *abstract ideas*.
For can there be a nicer strain of abstraction than to distinguish the existence of sensible objects from their being
perceived, so as to conceive them existing unperceived? Light
and colours, heat and cold, extension and figures—in a word
the things we see and feel—what are they but so many sensations, notions, ideas, or impressions on the sense? and is it
possible to separate, even in thought, any of these from perception? For my part, I might as easily divide a thing from
itself. I may, indeed, divide in my thoughts, or conceive apart
from each other, those things which, perhaps, I never perceived by sense so divided. Thus, I imagine the trunk of a
human body without the limbs, or conceive the smell of a
rose without thinking on the rose itself. So far, I will not
deny, I can abstract—if that may properly be called *abstraction* which extends only to the conceiving separately such
objects as it is possible may really exist or be actually perceived asunder. But my conceiving or imagining power does
not extend beyond the possibility of real existence or perception. Hence, as it is impossible for me to see or feel anything without an actual sensation of that thing, so is it
impossible for me to conceive in my thoughts any sensible
thing or object distinct from the sensation or perception of it.

But, say you, though the ideas themselves do not exist
without the mind, yet there may be things like them, whereof
they are copies or resemblances, which things exist without
the mind in an unthinking substance. I answer, an idea can
be like nothing but an idea; a colour or figure can be like
nothing but another colour or figure. If we look but never
so little into our thoughts, we shall find it impossible for us

to conceive a likeness except only between our ideas. Again, I ask whether those supposed originals or external things, of which our ideas are the pictures or representations, be themselves perceivable or no? If they are, then they are ideas and we have gained our point; but if you say they are not, I appeal to any one whether it be sense to assert a colour is like something which is invisible; hard or soft, like something which is intangible; and so of the rest.

Some there are who make a distinction betwixt *primary* and *secondary* qualities. By the former they mean extension, figure, motion, rest, solidity or impenetrability, and number; by the latter they denote all other sensible qualities, as colours, sounds, tastes, and so forth. The ideas we have of these they acknowledge not to be the resemblances of anything existing without the mind, or unperceived, but they will have our ideas of the primary qualities to be patterns or images of things which exist without the mind, in an unthinking substance which they call Matter. By Matter, therefore, we are to understand an inert, senseless substance, in which extension, figure, and motion do actually subsist. But it is evident, from what we have already shewn, that extension, figure, and motion are only ideas existing in the mind, and that an idea can be like nothing but another idea, and that consequently neither they nor their archetypes can exist in an unperceived substance. Hence, it is plain that the very notion of what is called *Matter,* or *corporeal substance,* involves a contradiction in it.

They who assert that figure, motion, and the rest of the primary or original qualities do exist without the mind in unthinking substances, do at the same time acknowledge that colours, sounds, heat, cold, and suchlike secondary qualities, do not—which they tell us are sensations existing in the mind alone, that depend on and are occasioned by the different size, texture, and motion of the minute particles of matter. This they take for an undoubted truth, which they can demonstrate beyond all exception. Now, if it be certain that those original qualities are inseparably united with the other sensible qualities, and not, even in thought, capable of being

abstracted from them, it plainly follows that they exist only
in the mind. But I desire any one to reflect and try whether
he can, by any abstraction of thought, conceive the extension
and motion of a body without all other sensible qualities.
For my own part, I see evidently that it is not in my power
to frame an idea of a body extended and moving, but I
must withal give it some colour or other sensible quality
which is acknowledged to exist only in the mind. In short,
extension, figure, and motion, abstracted from all other qualities, are inconceivable. Where therefore the other sensible
qualities are, there must these be also, to wit, in the mind
and nowhere else.

Again, *great* and *small, swift* and *slow,* are allowed to
exist nowhere without the mind, being entirely relative, and
changing as the frame or position of the organs of sense
varies. The extension therefore which exists without the
mind is neither great nor small, the motion neither swift nor
slow, that is, they are nothing at all. But say you, they are
extension in general, and motion in general: thus we see
how much the tenet of extended moveable substances existing
without the mind depends on that strange doctrine of *abstract
ideas.* And here I cannot but remark how nearly the vague
and indeterminate description of Matter or corporeal substance, which the modern philosophers are run into by
their own principles, resembles that antiquated and so much
ridiculed notion of *materia prima,* to be met with in Aristotle
and his followers. Without extension solidity cannot be conceived; since therefore it has been shewn that extension
exists not in an unthinking substance, the same must also be
true of solidity.

I shall farther add, that, after the same manner as modern
philosophers prove certain sensible qualities to have no existence in Matter, or without the mind, the same thing may
be likewise proved of all other sensible qualities whatsoever.
Thus, for instance, it is said that heat and cold are affections
only of the mind, and not at all patterns of real beings, existing in the corporeal substances which excite them, for that
the same body which appears cold to one hand seems warm

to another. Now, why may we not as well argue that figure and extension are not patterns or resemblances of qualities existing in Matter, because to the same eye at different stations, or eyes of a different texture at the same station, they appear various, and cannot therefore be the images of anything settled and determinate without the mind? Again, it is proved that sweetness is not really in the sapid thing, because the thing remaining unaltered the sweetness is changed into bitter, as in case of a fever or otherwise vitiated palate. Is it not as reasonable to say that motion is not without the mind, since if the succession of ideas in the mind become swifter the motion, it is acknowledged, shall appear slower without any alteration in any external object?

In short, let any one consider those arguments which are thought manifestly to prove that colours and tastes exist only in the mind, and he shall find they may with equal force be brought to prove the same thing of extension, figure, and motion. Though it must be confessed this method of arguing does not so much prove that there is no extension or colour in an outward object, as that we do not know by sense which is the true extension or colour of the object. But the arguments foregoing plainly shew it to be impossible that any colour or extension at all, or other sensible quality whatsoever, should exist in an unthinking subject without the mind, or in truth, that there should be any such thing as an outward object.

But though it were possible that solid, figured, moveable substances may exist without the mind, corresponding to the ideas we have of bodies, yet how is it possible for us to know this? Either we must know it by sense or by reason. As for our senses, by them we have the knowledge only of our sensations, ideas, or those things that are immediately perceived by sense, call them what you will: but they do not inform us that things exist without the mind, or unperceived, like to those which are perceived. This the materialists themselves acknowledge. It remains therefore that if we have any knowledge at all of external things, it must be by reason, inferring their existence from what is immediately perceived by sense. But (I do not see) what reason can induce us to believe the existence of bodies without the mind, from what we perceive, since the very patrons of Matter themselves do not pretend there is any necessary connexion betwixt them and our ideas? I say it is granted on all hands (and what happens in dreams, frenzies, and the like, puts it beyond dispute) that it is possible we might be affected with all the ideas we have now, though there were no bodies existing without resembling them. Hence, it is evident the supposition of external bodies is not necessary for the production of our ideas; since it is granted they are produced sometimes, and might possibly be produced always, in the same order we see them in at present, without their concurrence.

But, though we might possibly have all our sensations without them, yet perhaps it may be thought easier to conceive and explain the manner of their production, by supposing external bodies in their likeness rather than otherwise; and so it might be at least probable there are such things as bodies that excite their ideas in our minds. But neither can this be said; for, though we give the materialists their external bodies, they by their own confession are never the nearer knowing how our ideas are produced; since they own themselves unable to comprehend in what manner body can act upon spirit, or how it is possible it should imprint any idea in the mind. Hence it is evident the production of ideas or sensations in our minds, can be no reason why we should suppose Matter or corporeal substances, since that is acknowledged to remain equally inexplicable with or without this supposition. If therefore it were possible for bodies to exist without the mind, yet to hold they do so must needs be a very precarious opinion; since it is to suppose, without any reason at all, that God has created innumerable beings that are entirely useless, and serve to no manner of purpose.

In short, if there were external bodies, it is impossible we should even come to know it; and if there were not, we might have the very same reasons to think there were that we have now. Suppose—what no one can deny possible—an intelligence without the help of external bodies, to be affected

with the same train of sensations or ideas that you are, imprinted in the same order and with like vividness in his mind.
I ask whether that intelligence hath not all the reason to believe the existence of corporeal substances, represented by
his ideas, and exciting them in his mind, that you can possibly
have for believing the same thing? Of this there can be no
question—which one consideration were enough to make
any reasonable person suspect the strength of whatever arguments he may think himself to have, for the existence of
bodies without the mind.

But, say you, surely there is nothing easier than for me to
imagine trees, for instance, in a park, or books existing in a
closet, and nobody by to perceive them. I answer, you may
so, there is no difficulty in it; but what is all this, I beseech
you, more than framing in your mind certain ideas which
you call books and trees, and at the same time omitting to
frame the idea of any one that may perceive them? But do
not you yourselves perceive or think of them all the while?
This therefore is nothing to the purpose: it only shews you
have the power of imagining or forming ideas in your mind;
but it does not shew that you can conceive it possible the
objects of your thought may exist without the mind. To
make out this, it is necessary that you conceive them existing
unconceived or unthought of, which is a manifest repugnancy.
When we do our utmost to conceive the existence of external bodies, we are all the while only contemplating our
own ideas. But the mind taking no notice of itself, is deluded
to think it can and does conceive bodies existing unthought of
or without the mind, though at the same time they are apprehended by or exist in itself. A little attention will discover
to any one the truth and evidence of what is here said, and
make it unnecessary to insist on any other proof against the
existence of *material substance*.

Could men but forbear to amuse themselves with words,
we should, I believe, soon come to an agreement in this
point. It is very obvious, upon the least inquiry into our own
thoughts, to know whether it be possible for us to understand
what is meant by the *absolute existence of sensible objects in*

themselves, or without the mind. To me it is evident those words make out either a direct contradiction, or else nothing at all. And to convince others of this, I know no readier or fairer way than to entreat they would calmly attend to their own thoughts; and if by this attention the emptiness or repugnancy of those expressions does appear, surely nothing more is requisite for their conviction.

All our ideas, sensations, notions, or the things which we perceive, by whatsoever names they may be distinguished, are visibly inactive—there is nothing of power or agency included in them. So that one idea or object of thought cannot produce or make any alteration in another. To be satisfied of the truth of this, there is nothing else requisite but a bare observation of our ideas. For, since they and every part of them exist only in the mind, it follows that there is nothing in them but what is perceived: but whoever shall attend to his idea, whether of sense or reflection, will not perceive in them any power or activity; there is, therefore, no such thing contained in them. A little attention will discover to us that the very being of an idea implies passiveness and inertness in it, insomuch that it is impossible for an idea to do anything, or, strictly speaking, to be the cause of anything: neither can it be the resemblance or pattern of any active being. Whence it plainly follows that extension, figure, and motion cannot be the cause of our sensations. To say, therefore, that these are the effects of powers resulting from the configuration, number, motion, and size of corpuscles, must certainly be false.

We perceive a continual succession of ideas, some are anew excited, others are changed or totally disappear. There is therefore some cause of these ideas, whereon they depend, and which produces and changes them. That this cause cannot be any quality or idea or combination of ideas, is clear from the preceding section. It must therefore be a substance; but it has been shewn that there is no corporeal or material substance: it remains therefore that the cause of ideas is an incorporeal active substance or Spirit.

A Spirit is one simple, undivided, active being—as it perceives ideas it is called the *understanding,* and as it produces or otherwise operates about them it is called the *will.* Hence there can be no *idea* formed of a soul or spirit; for all ideas whatever, being passive and inert, they cannot represent unto us, by way of image or likeness, that which acts. A little attention will make it plain to any one that to have an idea which shall be like that active principle of motion and change of ideas is absolutely impossible. Such is the nature of *spirit,* or that which acts, that it cannot be of itself perceived, but only by the effects which it produceth.

I find I can excite ideas in my mind at pleasure, and vary and shift the scene as oft as I think fit. It is no more than willing, and straightway this or that idea arises in my fancy; and by the same power it is obliterated and makes way for another. But whatever power I may have over my own thoughts, I find the ideas actually perceived by sense have not a like dependence on my will. Wnen in broad daylight I open my eyes, it is not in my power to choose whether I shall see or no, or to determine what particular objects shall present themselves to my view; and so likewise as to the hearing and other senses, the ideas imprinted on them are not creatures of my will. There is therefore some *other* Will or Spirit that produces them.

The ideas of sense are more strong, lively, and distinct than those of the imagination; they have likewise a steadiness, order, and coherence, and are not excited at random, as those which are the effects of human wills often are, but in a regular train or series—the admirable connexion whereof sufficiently testifies the wisdom and benevolence of its Author. Now the set rules or established methods wherein the Mind we depend on excites in us the ideas of sense, are called the *laws of nature*; and these we learn by experience, which teaches us that such and such ideas are attended with such and such other ideas, in the ordinary course of things.

The ideas imprinted on the senses by the Author of nature are called *real things*: and those excited in the imagination being less regular, vivid, and constant, are more properly termed *ideas,* or *images of things,* which they copy and represent. But then our sensations, be they never so vivid and distinct, are nevertheless, ideas, that is, they exist in the mind, or are perceived in it, as truly as the ideas of its own framing. The ideas of sense are allowed to have more reality in them, that is, to be more strong, orderly, and coherent than the creatures of the mind; but this is no argument that they exist without the mind. They are also less dependent on the spirit, or thinking substance which perceives them, in that they are excited by the will of another and more powerful Spirit: yet still they are ideas, and certainly no idea, whether faint or strong, can exist otherwise than in a mind perceiving it.

Objections

(1) It will be objected that by the foregoing principles all that is real and substantial in nature is banished out of the world, and instead thereof a chimerical scheme of ideas takes place. All things that exist exist only in the mind, that is, they are purely notional. What therefore becomes of the sun, moon, and stars? What must we think of houses, rivers, mountains, trees, stones; nay, even of our own bodies? Are all these but so many chimeras and illusions on the fancy? To all which, and whatever else of the same sort may be objected, I answer, that by the principles premised we are not deprived of any one thing in nature. Whatever we see, feel, hear, or any wise conceive or understand, remains as secure as ever, and is as real as ever. There is a *rerum natura,* and the distinction between realities and chimeras retains its full force. We have shewn what is meant by *real things,* in opposition to *chimeras* or ideas of our own framing; but they both equally exist in the mind, and in the sense are alike *ideas*.

If any man thinks this detracts from the existence or reality of things, he is very far from understanding what hath been premised in the plainest terms I could think of. Take here an abstract of what has been said—There are spiritual substances, minds, or human souls, which will or excite ideas in themselves at pleasure; but these are faint, weak, and unsteady in respect of others they perceive by sense—which, being impressed upon them according to certain rules or laws of nature, speak themselves the effects of a Mind more powerful and wise than human spirits. These latter are said to have more *reality* in them than the former— by which is meant that they are more affecting, orderly, and distinct, and that they are not fictions of the mind perceiving them. And in this sense the sun that I see by day is the real sun, and that which I imagine by night is the idea of the former. In the sense here given of *reality,* it is evident that every vegetable, star, mineral, and in general each part of the mundane system, is as much a *real being* by our principles as by any other. Whether others mean anything by the term *reality* different from what I do, I entreat them to look into their own thoughts and see.

(2) It will be objected that we see things actually without or at a distance from us, and which consequently do not exist in the mind, it being absurd that those things which are seen at the distance of several miles, should be as near to us as our own thoughts. In answer to this, I desire it may be considered, that in a dream we do oft perceive things as existing at a great distance off, and yet for all that, those things are acknowledged to have their existence only in the mind.

But for the fuller clearing of this point, it may be worth while to consider, how it is that we perceive distance and things placed at a distance by sight. For that we should in truth see external space, and bodies actually existing in it, some nearer, others further off, seems to carry with it some opposition to what hath been said, of their existing nowhere without the mind. The consideration of this difficulty it was that gave birth to my *Essay Towards a New Theory of Vision,* which was published not long since. Wherein it is shown (i) that *distance* or outness is *neither immediately* of itself *perceived* by sight, nor yet apprehended or judged of by lines and angles, or any thing that hath a necessary connexion with it: but (ii) that it is *only suggested* to our thoughts by certain visible ideas and sensations attending vision, which in their own nature have no manner of similitude or relation, either with distance, or things placed at a distance. But by a connexion taught us by experience, they come to signify and suggest them to us, after the same manner that words of any language suggest the ideas they are made to stand for. Insomuch that a man born blind, and afterwards made to see, would not, at first sight, think the things he saw to be without his mind, or at any distance from him.

The ideas of sight and touch make two species, entirely distinct and heterogeneous. The former are marks and prognostics of the latter. . . . So that in strict truth the ideas of sight, when we apprehend by them distance and things placed at a distance, do not suggest or mark out to us things *actually* existing at a distance, but only admonish us what ideas of touch will be imprinted in our minds at such and such distances of time, and in consequence of such or such actions. It is, I say, evident that visible ideas are language whereby the governing Spirit, on whom we depend, informs us what tangible ideas he is about to imprint upon us, in case we excite this or that motion in our own bodies.

(3) It will be objected, that from the foregoing principles it follows, things are every moment annihilated and created anew. The objects of sense exist only when they are perceived: the trees therefore are in the garden, or the chairs in the parlour, no longer than while there is somebody by to perceive them. Upon shutting my eyes, all the furniture in the room is reduced to nothing, and barely upon opening them it is again created. In answer to all which, I refer the reader to what has been said and desire he will consider whether he means anything by the actual existence of an idea, distinct from its being perceived. For my part, after the nicest inquiry I could make, I am not able to discover that anything else is meant by those words. And I once more entreat the reader to sound his own thoughts, and not suffer himself to be imposed on by words. . . .

If we consider it, this objection will not be found reasonably charged on the principles we have premised, so as in truth to make any objection at all against our notions. For though we hold, indeed, the objects of sense to be nothing else but ideas which cannot exist unperceived, yet we may not hence conclude they have no existence, except only while they are perceived by *us*, since *there may be some other spirit that perceives them, though we do not*. Wherever bodies are said to have no existence without the mind, I would not be understood to mean this or that particular mind, but *all minds whatsoever*. It does not therefore follow from the foregoing principles, that bodies are annihilated and created every moment, or exist not at all during the intervals between our perception in them.

(4) It will be objected, that the notions we advance are inconsistent with several sound truths in philosophy and mathematics. For example, the motion of the earth is now universally admitted by astronomers, as a truth grounded on the clearest and most convincing reasons; but on the foregoing principles, there can be no such thing. For motion being only an idea, it follows that if it be not perceived, it exists not; but the motion of the earth is not perceived by sense. I answer, that tenet, if rightly understood, will be found to agree with the principles we have premised; for the question, whether the earth moves or no, amounts in reality to no more than this, to wit, whether we have reason to conclude from what hath been observed by astronomers, that if we were placed in such and such circumstances, and such or such a position and distance, both from the earth and sun, we should perceive the former to move among the choir of the planets, and appearing in all respects like one of them: and this, by the established rules of nature, which we have no reason to mistrust, is reasonably collected from the phenomena.

21. THE ROLE OF THE IMAGINATION IN PERCEPTION

HUME

David Hume (1711–1776) advanced a view of perception more radical even than Berkeley's, holding that, though for practical purposes we are forced to assume the existence of an external world, there is in fact no rational ground for believing that anything exists except the (fragmentary) series of resembling sense impressions of which alone we are directly aware. To maintain this he had to dispose of (1) the Representative Theory (which he does by arguments similar to Berkeley's) and (2) the common-sense assumption that the "objects of perception" have an independent external existence whether we perceive them or not. In this passage from his *Treatise of Human Nature,* Volume I, Part IV, Section 2, Hume attacks the latter view, seeking to show that it is the work of the imagination. The term "objects of perception" must be understood neutrally; whether these "objects" are "bodies" (i.e. external material things) or "impressions" (i.e. sense-data) is the question at issue.

The subject of our present enquiry is concerning the *causes* which induce us to believe in the existence of body: and my reasonings on this head I shall begin with a distinction. . . . We ought to examine apart those two questions, which are commonly confounded together, *viz.* Why we attribute a *continued* existence to objects, even when they are not present to the senses, and why we suppose them to have an existence *distinct* from the mind and perception. Under this last head I comprehend their situation as well as relations, their *external* position as well as the *independence* of their existence and operation. These two questions concerning the continued and distinct existence of body are intimately connected together. For if the objects of our senses continue to exist, even when they are not perceived, their existence is of course independent of and distinct from the perception;

and *vice versa*, if their existence be independent of the perception and distinct from it, they must continue to exist, even though they be not perceived. But though the decision of the one question decides the other; yet that we may the more easily discover the principles of human nature, from whence the decision arises, we shall carry along with us this distinction, and shall consider, whether it be the *senses, reason*, or the *imagination*, that produces the opinion of a *continued* or of a *distinct* existence. These are the only questions, that are intelligible on the present subject. For as to the notion of external existence, when taken for something specially different from our perceptions, we have already shown its absurdity.[1]

To begin with the *senses*, it is evident these faculties are incapable of giving rise to the notion of the *continued* existence of their objects, after they no longer appear to the senses. For that is a contradiction in terms, and supposes that the senses continue to operate, even after they have ceased all manner of operation. These faculties, therefore, if they have any influence in the present case, must produce the opinion of a distinct, not of a continued existence; and in order to, that, must present their impressions either as images and representations, or as these very distinct and external existences.

That our senses offer not their impressions as the images of something *distinct*, or *independent*, and *external*, is evident; because they convey to us nothing but a single perception, and never give us the least intimation of any thing beyond. A single perception can never produce the idea of a double existence, but by some inference either of the reason or imagination. When the mind looks farther than what immediately appears to it, its conclusions can never be put to the account of the senses; and it certainly looks farther, when from a single perception it infers a double existence, and supposes the relations of resemblance and causation betwixt them.

If our senses, therefore, suggest any idea of distinct existence, they must convey the impressions as those very existences, by a kind of fallacy and illusion. Upon this head we may observe that all sensations are felt by the mind, such as they really are, and that when we doubt whether they present themselves as distinct objects or as mere impressions, the difficulty is not concerning their nature, but concerning their relations and situation. Now if the senses presented our impressions as external to, and independent of ourselves, both the objects and ourselves must be obvious to our senses, otherwise they could not be compared by these faculties. The difficulty, then, is how far we are *ourselves* the objects of our senses.

It is certain there is no question in philosophy more abstruse than that concerning identity, and the nature of the uniting principle, which constitutes a person. So far from being able by our senses merely to determine this question, we must have recourse to the most profound metaphysics to give a satisfactory answer to it; and in common life it is evident these ideas of self and person are never very fixed nor determinate. It is absurd, therefore, to imagine the senses can ever distinguish betwixt ourselves and external objects.

Add to this, that every impression, external and internal, passions, affections, sensations, pains and pleasures are originally on the same footing; and that whatever other differences we may observe among them, they appear, all of them, in their true colours, as impressions or perceptions. And indeed, if we consider the matter aright, it is scarce possible it should be otherwise, nor is it conceivable that our senses should be more capable of deceiving us in the situation and relations, than in the nature of our impressions. For since all actions and sensations of the mind are known to us by consciousness, they must necessarily appear in every particular what they are, and be what they appear. Every thing that enters the mind, being in *reality* a perception, it is impossible anything should to *feeling* appear different. This were to suppose, that even where we are most intimately conscious, we might be mistaken.

But not to lose time in examining, whether it is possible for our senses to deceive us, and represent our perceptions as distinct from ourselves, that is as *external* to and *independent* of us; let us consider whether they really do so, and whether this error proceeds from an immediate sensation, or from some other causes.

To begin with the questions concerning *external* existence, it may perhaps be said, that setting aside the metaphysical question of the identity of a thinking substance, our own body evidently belongs to us; and as several impressions appear exterior to the body, we suppose them also exterior to ourselves. The paper, on which I write at present, is beyond my hand. The table is beyond the paper. The walls of the chamber beyond the table. And in casting my eye towards the window, I perceive a great extent of fields and buildings beyond my chamber. From all this it may be inferred that no other faculty is required, beside the senses, to convince us of the external existence of body. But to prevent this inference, we need only weigh the three following considerations. *First,* that, properly speaking it is not our body we perceive, when we regard our limbs and members, but certain impressions, which enter by the senses; so that the ascribing a real and corporeal existence to these impressions, or to their objects, is an act of the mind as difficult to explain, as that which we examine at present. *Secondly*, sounds, and tastes, and smells, tho' commonly regarded by the mind as continued independent qualities, appear not to have any existence in extension, and consequently cannot appear to the senses as situated externally to the body. *Thirdly*, even our sight informs us not of distance or outness (so to speak) immediately and without a certain reasoning and experience, as is acknowledged by the most rational philosophers.

As to the *independency* of our perceptions on ourselves, this can never be an object of the senses; but any opinion we form concerning it, must be derived from experience and observation: and we shall see afterwards,[2] that our conclusions from experience are far from being favourable to the doctrine of the independency of our perceptions. Meanwhile we may observe that when we talk of real distinct existences, we have commonly more in our eye their independency than external situation in place, and think an object has sufficient reality, when its being is uninterrupted, and independent of the incessant revolutions, which we are conscious of in ourselves.

Thus to resume what I have said concerning the senses; they give us no notion of continued existence, because they cannot operate beyond the extent, in which they really operate. They as little produce the opinion of a distinct existence, because they neither can offer it to the mind as represented, nor as original. To offer it as represented, they must present both an object and an image. To make it appear as original, they must convey a falsehood; and this falsehood must lie in the relations and situation: in order to which they must be able to compare the object with ourselves; and even in that case they do not, nor is it possible they should, deceive us. We may, therefore, conclude with certainty, that the opinion of a continued and of a distinct existence never arises from the senses.

To confirm this we may observe, that there are three different kinds of impressions conveyed by the senses. The first are those of the figure, bulk, motion and solidity of bodies. The second those of colours, tastes, smells, sounds, heat and cold. The third are the pains and pleasures, that arise from the application of objects to our bodies, as by the cutting of our flesh with steel, and such like. Both philosophers and the vulgar suppose the first of these to have a distinct continued existence. The vulgar only regard the second as on the same footing. Both philosophers and the vulgar, again, esteem the third to be merely perceptions; and consequently interrupted and dependent beings.

Now it is evident, that, whatever may be our philosophical opinion, colours, sounds, heat, and cold, as far as appears to the senses, exist after the same manner with motion and solidity and that the difference we make betwixt them in this respect arises not from the mere perception. So strong is the prejudice for the distinct continued existence of the former qualities, that when the contrary opinion is advanced by modern philosophers, people imagine they can almost refute it from their feeling and experience, and that their very senses contradict this philosophy. It is also evident, that colours, sounds, etc. are originally on the same footing with the pain that arises from steel, and pleasure that proceeds from a fire; and that the difference betwixt them is founded neither on perception nor reason, but on the imagination. For as they are confessed to be, both of them, nothing but perceptions arising from the particular configurations and motions of the parts of body, wherein possibly can their difference consist? Upon the whole, then, we may conclude, that as far as the senses are judges, all perceptions are the same in the manner of their existence.

We may also observe in this instance of sounds and colours, that we can attribute a distinct continued existence to objects without ever consulting *reason,* or weighing our opinions by any philosophical principles. And indeed, whatever convincing arguments philosophers may fancy they can produce to establish the belief of objects independent of the mind, it is obvious these arguments are known but to very few, and that it is not by them, that children, peasants, and the greatest part of mankind are induced to attribute objects to some impressions, and deny them to others. Accordingly we find that all the conclusions, which the vulgar form on this head, are directly contrary to those, which are confirmed by philosophy. For philosophy informs us, that every thing, which appears to the mind, is nothing but a perception, and is interrupted, and dependent on the mind; whereas the vulgar confound perceptions and objects, and attribute a distinct continued existence to the very things they feel or see. This sentiment, then, as it is entirely unreasonable, must proceed from some other faculty than the understanding. To which we may add, that as long as we take our perceptions and objects to be the same, we can never infer the existence of the one from that of the other, nor form any argument from the relation of cause and effect; which is the only one that can assure us of matter of fact. Even after we distinguish our perceptions from our objects, it will appear presently, that we are still incapable of reasoning from the existence of one to that of the other: so that upon the whole our reason neither does, nor is it possible it ever should, upon any supposition, give us an assurance of the continued and distinct existence of body. That opinion must be entirely owing to the *imagination*: which must now be the subject of our enquiry.

Since all impressions are internal and perishing existences, and appear as such, the notion of their distinct and continued existence must arise from a concurrence of some of their qualities with the qualities of the imagination, and since this notion does not extend to all of them, it must arise from certain qualities peculiar to some impressions. It will therefore be easy for us to discover these qualities by a comparison of the impressions, to which we attribute a distinct and continued existence, with those, which we regard as internal and perishing.

We may observe, then, that it is neither upon account of the involuntariness of certain impressions, as is commonly supposed, nor of their superior force and violence, that we attribute to them a reality, and continued existence, which we refuse to others, that are voluntary or feeble. For it is evident our pains and pleasures, our passions and affections, which we never suppose to have any existence beyond our perception, operate with greater violence, and are equally involuntary, as the impressions of figure and extension, colour and sound, which we suppose to be permanent beings. The heat of a fire, when moderate, is supposed to exist in the fire; but the pain, which it causes upon a near approach, is not taken to have any being except in the perception.

These vulgar opinions, then, being rejected, we must search for some other hypothesis, by which we may discover those peculiar qualities in our impressions, which make us attribute to them a distinct and continued existence.

After a little examination, we shall find, that all those objects, to which we attribute a continued existence, have a peculiar *constancy*, which distinguishes them from the impressions, whose existence depends upon our perception. Those mountains, and houses, and trees, which lie at present under my eye, have always appeared to me in the same order; and when I lose sight of them by shutting my eyes or turning my head, I soon after find them return upon me without the least alteration. My bed and table, my books and papers present themselves in the same uniform manner, and change not upon account of any interruption in my seeing or perceiving them. This is the case with all the impressions, whose objects are supposed to have an external existence; and is the case with no other impressions, whether gentle or violent, voluntary or involuntary.

This constancy, however, is not so perfect as not to admit of very considerable exceptions. Bodies often change their position and qualities, and after a little absence or interruption may become hardly knowable. But here it is observable, that even in these changes they preserve a *coherence,* and have a regular dependence on each other; which is the foundation of a kind of reasoning from causation, and produces the opinion of their continued existence. When I return to my chamber after an hour's absence, I find not my fire in the same situation, in which I left it: but then I am accustomed in other instances to see a like alteration produced in a like time, whether I am present or absent, near or remote. This coherence, therefore, in their changes is one of the characteristics of external objects, as well as their constancy.

Having found that the opinion of the continued existence of body depends on the *coherence* and *constancy* of certain impressions, I now proceed to examine after what manner these qualities give rise to so extraordinary an opinion.[3] To begin with the coherence; we may observe, that though those internal impressions, which we regard as fleeting and perishing, have also a certain coherence or regularity in their appearances, yet it is of somewhat a different nature, from that which we discover in bodies. Our passions are found by experience to have a mutual connexion with and dependence on each other; but on no occasion is it necessary to suppose, that they have existed and operated, when they were not perceived, in order to preserve the same dependence and connexion, of which we have had experience. The case is not the same with relation to external objects. Those require a continued existence, or otherwise lose, in a great

measure, the regularity of their operation. I am here seated
in my chamber with my face to the fire; and all the objects,
that strike my senses, are contained in a few yards around
me. My memory, indeed, informs me of the existence of many
objects; but then this information extends not beyond their
past existence, nor do either my senses or memory give any
testimony to the continuance of their being. When therefore
I am thus seated, and revolve over these thoughts, I hear on
a sudden a noise as of a door turning upon its hinges; and a
little after see a porter, who advances towards me. This
gives occasion to many new reflections and reasonings. First,
I never have observed, that this noise could proceed from
anything but the motion of a door; and therefore conclude,
that the present phenomenon is a contradiction to all past
experience, unless the door, which I remember on the other
side of the chamber, be still in being. Again, I have always
found, that a human body was possessed of a quality, which
I call gravity, and which hinders it from mounting in the air,
as this porter must have done to arrive at my chamber, unless
the stairs I remember be not annihilated by my absence. But
this is not all. I receive a letter, which upon opening it I
perceive by the hand-writing and subscription to have come
from a friend, who says he is two hundred leagues distant.
It is evident I can never account for this phenomenon, con-
formable to my experience in other instances, without spread-
ing out in my mind the whole sea and continent between us,
and supposing the effects and continued existence of posts
and ferries, according to my memory and observation. To
consider these phenomena of the porter and letter in a certain
light, they are contradictions to common experience, and may
be regarded as objections to those maxims, which we form
concerning the connexions of causes and effects. I am accustomed to hear such a sound, and see such an object in
motion at the same time. I have not received in this particular
instance both these perceptions. These observations are contrary, unless I suppose that the door still remains, and that it
was opened without my perceiving it: and this supposition,
which was at first entirely arbitrary and hypothetical, acquires

a force and evidence by its being the only one, upon which I can reconcile these contradictions. There is scarce a moment of my life, wherein there is not a similar instance presented to me, and I have not occasion to suppose the continued existence of objects, in order to connect their past and present appearances, and give them such a union with each other, as I have found by experience to be suitable to their particular natures and circumstances. Here then I am naturally led to regard the world, as something real and durable, and as preserving its existence, even when it is no longer present to my perception.

But though this conclusion from the coherence of appearances may seem to be of the same nature with our reasonings concerning causes and effects; as being derived from custom, and regulated by past experience; we shall find upon examination, that they are at the bottom considerably different from each other, and that this inference arises from the understanding, and from custom in an indirect and oblique manner. For it will readily be allowed, that since nothing is ever really present to the mind, besides its own perceptions, it is not only impossible that any habit should ever be acquired otherwise than by the regular succession of these perceptions, but also that any habit should ever exceed that degree of regularity. Any degree therefore, of regularity in our perceptions, can never be a foundation for us to infer a greater degree of regularity in some objects, which are not perceived; since this supposes a contradiction, viz. a habit acquired by what was never present to the mind. But it is evident, that whenever we infer the continued existence of the objects of sense from their coherence, and the frequency of their union, it is in order to bestow on the objects a greater regularity than what is observed in our mere perceptions. We remark a connexion betwixt two kinds of objects in their past appearance to the senses, but are not able to observe this connexion to be perfectly constant, since the turning about of our head or the shutting of our eyes is able to break it. What then do we suppose in this case, but that these objects still continue their usual connexion, notwithstanding their apparent interruption, and that the irregular appearances are joined by something, of which we are insensible? But as all reasoning concerning matters of fact arises only from custom, and custom can only be the effect of repeated perceptions, the extending of custom and reasoning beyond the perceptions can never be the direct and natural effect of the constant repetition and connexion, but must arise from the cooperation of some other principles.

I have already observed,[4] in examining the foundation of mathematics, that the imagination, when set into any train of thinking, is apt to continue, even when its object fails it, and like a galley put in motion by the oars, carries on its course without any new impulse. This I have assigned for the reason, why, after considering several loose standards of equality, and correcting them by each other, we proceed to imagine so correct and exact a standard of that relation, as is not liable to the least error or variation. The same principle makes us easily entertain this opinion of the continued existence of body. Objects have a certain coherence even as they appear to our senses; but this coherence is much greater and more uniform, if we suppose the objects to have a continued existence; and as the mind is once in the train of observing an uniformity among objects, it naturally continues, till it renders the uniformity as complete as possible. The simple supposition of their continued existence suffices for this purpose, and gives us a notion of much greater regularity among objects, than what they have when we look no farther than our senses.

But whatever force we may ascribe to this principle, I am afraid it is too weak to support alone so vast an edifice, as is that of the continued existence of all external bodies; and that we must join the *constancy* of their appearance to the *coherence,* in order to give a satisfactory account of that opinion. As the explication of this will lead me into a considerable compass of very profound reasoning; I think it proper, in order to avoid confusion, to give a short sketch or abridgement of my system, and afterwards draw out all its parts in their full compass. This inference from the constancy of our perceptions, like the precedent from their coherence, gives rise to the opinion of the *continued* existence of body, which is prior to that of its *distinct* existence, and produces that latter principle.

When we have been accustomed to observe a constancy in certain impressions, and have found, that the perception of the sun or ocean, for instance, returns upon us after an absence or annihilation with like parts and in a like order, as at its first appearance, we are not apt to regard these interrupted perceptions as different, (which they really are) but on the contrary consider them as individually the same, upon account of their resemblance. But as this interruption of their existence is contrary to their perfect identity, and makes us regard the first impression as annihilated, and the second as newly created, we find ourselves somewhat at a loss, and are involved in a kind of contradiction. In order to free ourselves from this difficulty, we disguise, as much as possible, the interruption, or rather remove it entirely, by supposing that these interrupted perceptions are connected by a real existence, of which we are insensible. This supposition, or idea of continued existence, acquires a force and vivacity from the memory of these broken impressions, and from that propensity, which they give us, to suppose them the same; and according to the precedent reasoning, the very essence of belief consists in the force and vivacity of the conception.

NOTES

¹ Part II, Sect. 6.—HUME

² *Treatise,* ed. Selby-Bigge, p. 210, Everyman ed., p. 203, where Hume claims: "When we compare experiments, and reason a little upon them, we quickly perceive, that the doctrine of the independent existence of our sensible perceptions is contrary to the plainest experience. . . . When we press one eye with a finger, we immediately perceive all the objects to become double, and one half of them to be removed from their common and natural position. But as we do not attribute a continued existence to both these perceptions, and as they are both of the same nature, we clearly perceive, that all our perceptions are dependent on our organs, and the disposition of our nerves and animal spirits. This opinion is confirmed by the seeming increase and diminution of objects, according to

their distance; by the apparent alterations in their figure; by the changes in their colour and other qualities from our sickness and distempers; and by an infinite number of other experiments of the same kind; from all which we learn, that our sensible perceptions are not possessed of any distinct or independent existence."—ED.

³ Compare Lovejoy, S.18, p. 227—ED.

⁴ Part II, Sect. 4.—HUME

22. PERMANENT POSSIBILITIES OF SENSATION

J. S. MILL

The influential British philosopher John Stuart Mill (1806–1873) is chiefly known for his ethical and political writings and for his Logic. But he also developed an interesting theory of perception, which he called "The Psychological Theory of the Belief in an External World" but which nowadays would be termed Phenomenalism. There is however a difference of emphasis in that Mill was concerned, somewhat as Hume was, to show that our belief in a continuing external world can be explained by the operation of our mental processes on the sequences of sensations we experience, rather than like modern phenomenalists to analyse material-object statements in terms of sense-data. Nevertheless he has some anticipations of this modern trend, e.g. on pp. 277 and 282. This selection comprises the bulk of Chapter XI of Mill's *Examination of Sir William Hamilton's Philosophy* (London, 1865).

I proceed to state the case of those who hold that the belief in the external world is not intuitive, but an acquired product.

This theory postulates the following psychological truths, all of which are proved by experience:

First, that the human mind is capable of Expectation. In other words, that after having had actual sensations, we are capable of forming the conception of Possible sensations; sensations which we are not feeling at the present moment, but which we might feel, and should feel if certain conditions were present, the nature of which conditions we have in many cases learnt by experience.

Secondly, the laws of the Association of Ideas. So far as we are here concerned, these laws are the following: 1st, Similar phenomena tend to be thought of together. 2nd, Phenomena which have either been experienced or conceived in close contiguity to one another, tend to be thought of together. The contiguity is of two kinds; simultaneity, and immediate succession. Facts which have been experienced or thought of simultaneously recall the thought of one another. Of facts which have been experienced or thought of in immediate succession, the antecedent, or the thought of it, recalls the thought of the consequent, but not conversely. 3rd, Associations produced by continuity become more certain and rapid by repetition. When two phenomena have been very often experienced in conjunction, and have not, in any single instance, occurred separately either in experience or in thought, there is produced between them what has been called Inseparable, or less correctly, Indissoluble Association: by which is not meant that the association must inevitably last to the end of life—that no subsequent experience or process of thought can possibly avail to dissolve it; but only that as long as no such experience or process of thought has taken place, the association is irresistible; it is impossible for us to think the one thing disjoined from the other. 4th, When an association has acquired this character of inseparability— when the bond between the two ideas has been thus firmly riveted, not only does the idea called up by association become, in our consciousness, inseparable from the ideas which suggested it, but the facts of phenomena answering to those ideas come at last to seem inseparable in existence: things which we are unable to conceive apart, appear incapable of existing apart; and the belief we have in their co-existence, though really a product of experience, seems intuitive. Innumerable examples might be given to this law. One of the most familiar, as well as the most striking, is that of our acquired perceptions of sight. Even those who consider the perception of distance by the eye as not acquired, but intuitive, admit that there are many perceptions of sight which, though instantaneous and unhesitating, are not intuitive. What we see is a very minute fragment of what we think we see. We see artificially that one thing is hard, another soft. We see artificially that one thing is hot, another cold. We see artificially that what we see is a book, or a stone, each of these being not merely an inference, but a heap of inferences, from the signs which we see, to things not visible. We see, and cannot help seeing, what we have learnt to infer, even when we know that the inference is erroneous, and that the apparent perception is deceptive. We cannot help seeing the moon larger when near the horizon, though we know that she is of precisely her usual size. We cannot help seeing a mountain as nearer to us and of less height, when we see it through a more than ordinarily transparent atmosphere.

Setting out from these premises, the Psychological Theory maintains, that there are associations naturally and even necessarily generated by the order of our sensations and of our reminiscences of sensation, which, supposing no intuition of an external world to have existed in consciousness, would inevitably generate the belief, and would cause it to be regarded as an intuition.

What is it we mean, or what is it which leads us to say, that the objects we perceive are external to us, and not a part of our own thoughts? We mean that there is concerned in our perceptions something which exists when we are not thinking of it; which existed before we had ever thought of it, and would exist if we were annihilated; and further, that there exist things which we never saw, touched, or otherwise perceived, and things which never have been perceived by man. The idea of something which is distinguished from our fleeting impressions by what, in Kantian language, is called Perdurability; something which is fixed and the same, while our impressions vary; something which exists whether we are aware of it or not, and which is always square (or of some other given figure) whether it appears to us square or round— constitutes altogether our idea of external substance. Whoever can assign an origin to this complex conception, has accounted for what we mean by the belief in matter. Now all this, according to the Psychological Theory, is but the form impressed by the known laws of association, upon the conceptions or notions, obtained by experience, of Contingent Sensations; by which are meant, sensations that are not in our present consciousness, and individually never were in our

consciousness at all, but which in virtue of the laws to which
we have learnt by experience that our sensations are subject,
we know that we should have felt under given supposable
circumstances, and under these same circumstances might
still feel.

I see a piece of white paper on a table. I go into another
room. If the phenomenon always followed me, or if, when it
did not follow me, I believed it to disappear *e rerum natura,* I
should not believe it to be an external object. I should consider it as a phantom—a mere affection of my senses: I
should not believe that there had been any Body there. But,
though I have ceased to see it, I am persuaded that the paper
is still there. I no longer have the sensations which it gave
me; but I believe that when I again place myself in the circumstances in which I had those sensations, that is, when I
go again into the room, I shall again have them; and further,
that there has been no intervening moment at which this
would not have been the case. Owing to this property of my
mind, my conception of the world at any given instant consists, in only a small proportion, of present sensations. Of
these I may at the time have none at all, and they are in
any case a most insignificant portion of the whole which I
apprehend. The conception I form of the world existing at
any moment, comprises, along with the sensations I am feeling, a countless variety of possibilities of sensation; namely,
the whole of these which past observation tells me that I
could, under any supposable circumstances, experience at this
moment, together with an indefinite and illimitable multitude
of others which though I do not know that I could, yet it is
possible that I might, experience in circumstances not known
to me. These various possibilities are the important thing to
me in the world. My present sensations are generally of little
importance, and are moreover fugitive: the possibilities, on
the contrary, are permanent, which is the character that
mainly distinguishes our idea of Substance or Matter from
our notion of sensation. These possibilities, which are conditional certainties, need a special name to distinguish them
from mere vague possibilities, which experience gives no

warrant for reckoning upon. Now, as soon as a distinguishing name is given, though it be only to the same thing regarded in a different aspect, one of the most familiar experiences of our mental nature teaches us, that the different name comes to be considered as the name of a different thing.

There is another important peculiarity of these certified or guaranteed possibilities of sensation; namely, that they have reference, not to single sensations, but to sensations joined together in groups. When we think of anything as a material substance, or body, we either have had, or we think that on some given supposition we should have, not some *one* sensation, but a great and even an indefinite number and variety of sensations, generally belonging to different senses, but so linked together, that the presence of one announces the possible presence at the very same instant of any or all of the rest. In our mind, therefore, not only is this particular Possibility of sensation invested with the quality of permanence when we are not actually feeling any of the sensations at all; but when we are feeling some of them, the remaining sensations of the group are conceived by us in the form of Present Possibilities, which might be realized at the very moment. And as this happens in turn to all of them, the group as a whole presents itself to the mind as permanent, in contrast not solely with the temporariness of my bodily presence, but also with the temporary character of each of the sensations composing the group; in other words, as a kind of permanent substratum, under a set of passing experiences or manifestations: which is another leading character of our idea of substance or matter, as distinguished from sensation.

Let us now take into consideration another of the general characters of our experience, namely, that in addition to fixed groups, we also recognize a fixed order in our sensations; an Order of succession which, when ascertained by observation, gives rise to the ideas of Cause and Effect, according to what I hold to be the true theory of that relation, and is on any theory the source of all our knowledge of what causes produce what effects. Now, of what nature is this fixed order among our sensations? It is a constancy of antecedence and sequence. But the constant antecedence and sequence do not generally exist between one actual sensation and another. Very few such sequences are presented to us by experience. In almost all the constant sequences which occur in Nature, the antecedence and consequence do not obtain between sensations, but between the groups we have been speaking about, of which a very small portion is actual sensation, the greater part being permanent possibilities of sensation, evidenced to us by a small and variable number of sensations actually present. Hence, our ideas of causation, power, activity, do not become connected in thought with our sensations as *actual* at all, save in the few physiological cases where these figure by themselves as the antecedents in some uniform sequence. Those ideas become connected, not with sensations, but with groups of possibilities of sensation. The sensations conceived do not, to our habitual thoughts, present themselves as sensations actually experienced, inasmuch as not only any one or any number of them may be supposed absent, but none of them need be present. We find that the modifications which are taking place more or less regularly in our possibilities of sensation, are mostly quite independent of our consciousness, and of our presence or absence. Whether we are asleep or awake the fire goes out, and puts an end to one particular possibility of warmth and light. Whether we are present or absent the corn ripens, and brings a new possibility of food. Hence we speedily learn to think of Nature as made up solely of these groups of possibilities, and the active force in Nature as manifested in the modification of some of these by others. The sensations, though the original foundation of the whole, come to be looked upon as a sort of accident depending on us, and the possibilities as much more real than the actual sensations, nay, as the very realities of which these are only the representations, appearances, or effects. When this state of mind has been arrived at, then, and from that time forward, we are never conscious of a present sensation without instantaneously referring it to some one of the groups of possibilities into which a sensation of that particular description enters; and if we do not yet know to what group to refer it, we at least feel an irresistible conviction that it must belong to some group or other; i.e. that its presence proves the existence, here and now, of a great number and variety of possibilities of sensation, without which it would not have been. The whole set of sensations as possible, form a permanent background to any one or more of them that are, at a given moment, actual; and the possibilities are conceived as standing to the actual sensations in the relation of a cause to its effects, or of canvas to the figures painted on it, or of a root to the trunk, leaves, and flowers, or of a substratum to that which is spread over it, or, in transcendental language, of Matter to Form.

When this point has been reached, the Permanent Possibilities in question have assumed such unlikeness of aspect, and such difference of apparent relation to us, from any sensations, that it would be contrary to all we know of the constitution of human nature that they should not be conceived as, and believed to be, at least as different from sensations as sensations are from one another. Their groundwork in sensation is forgotten, and they are supposed to be something intrinsically distinct from it. We can withdraw ourselves from any of our (external) sensations, or we can be withdrawn from them by some other agency. But though the sensations cease, the possibilities remain in existence; they are independent of our will, our presence, and everything which belongs to us. We find, too, that they belong as much to other human or sentient beings as to ourselves. We find other people grounding their expectations and conduct upon the same permanent possibilities on which we ground ours. But we do not find them experiencing the same actual sensations. Other people do not have our sensations exactly when and as we have them: but they have our possibilities of sensation; whatever indicates a present possibility of sensations to ourselves, indicates a present possibility of similar sensations to them, except so far as their organs of sensation may vary from the type of ours. This puts the final seal to our conception of the groups of possibilities as the fundamental reality in Nature. The permanent possibilities are common to us and to our

fellow-creatures; the actual sensations are not. That which
other people become aware of when, and on the same grounds,
as I do, seems more real to me than that which they do not
know of unless I tell them. The world of Possible Sensations
succeeding one another according to laws, is as much in
other beings as it is in me; and has therefore an existence
outside me; it is an External World.

Matter, then, may be defined, a Permanent Possibility of
sensation. If I am asked, whether I believe in matter, I ask
whether the questioner accepts this definition of it. If he does,
I believe in matter: and so do all Berkeleians. In any other
sense than this, I do not. But I affirm with confidence that
this conception of Matter includes the whole meaning attached to it by the common world, apart from philosophical,
and sometimes from theological, theories. The reliance of
mankind on the real existence of visible and tangible objects,
means reliance on the reality and permanence of Possibilities
of visual and tactual sensations, when no such sensations are
actually experienced. We are warranted in believing that this
is the meaning of Matter in the minds of many of its most
esteemed metaphysical champions, though they themselves
would not admit as much: for example, of Reid, Stewart, and
Brown. For these three philosophers alleged that all mankind,
including Berkeley and Hume, really believed in Matter, inasmuch as unless they did, they would not have turned aside to
save themselves from running against a post. Now all which
this manoeuvre really proved is that they believed in Permanent Possibilities of Sensation. We have therefore the un-
intentional sanction of these three eminent defenders of the
existence of matter, for affirming, that to believe in Permanent
Possibilities of Sensation is believing in Matter. It is hardly
necessary, after such authorities to mention Dr. Johnson, or
any one else who resorts to the *argumentum baculinum* of
knocking a stick against the ground. . . .

The belief in such permanent possibilities seems to me to
include all that is essential or characteristic in the belief in
substance. I believe that Calcutta exists, though I do not perceive it, and that it would still exist if every percipient in-

habitant were suddenly to leave the place, or be struck dead. But when I analyse the belief, all I find in it is, that were these events to take place, the Permanent Possibility of Sensation which I call Calcutta would still remain; that if I were suddenly transported to the banks of the Hoogly, I should still have the sensations which, if now present, would lead me to affirm that Calcutta exists here and now. We may infer, therefore, that both philosophers and the world at large, when they think of matter, conceive it really as a Permanent Possibility of Sensation. . . .

It may perhaps be said, that the preceding theory gives, indeed, some account of the idea of Permanent Existence which forms part of our conception of Matter, but gives no explanation of our believing these permanent objects to be external, or out of ourselves. I apprehend, on the contrary, that the very idea of anything out of ourselves is derived solely from the knowledge experience gives us of the Permanent Possibilities. Our sensations we carry with us whenever we go, and they never exist where we are not; but when we change our place we do not carry away with us the Permanent Possibilities of Sensation: they remain until we return, or arise and cease under conditions with which our presence has in general nothing to do. And more than all— they are, and will be after we have ceased to feel, Permanent Possibilities of sensation to other beings than ourselves. Thus our actual sensations and the permanent possibilities of sensation, stand out in obtrusive contrast to one another: and when the idea of Cause has been acquired, and extended by generalization from the parts of our experience to its aggregate whole, nothing can be more natural than that the Permanent Possibilities should be classed by us as existences generically distinct from our sensations, but of which our sensations are the effect.

23. PHENOMENALISM

A. J. AYER

Phenomenalism is here defended by one of its foremost modern exponents. The Selection is taken from pp. 166 ff. (Sections I–IV and VII) of Professor Ayer's paper, entitled "Phenomenalism," published in the *Proceedings of the Aristotelian Society,* Vol. XLVII, 1946–47. The paper is also reprinted in Ayer's *Philosophical Essays* (London, Macmillan and Company, 1954).

. . . All the same[1] it is not very hard to see what Price and other philosophers who talk about sense-data are getting at. For suppose that I am having an experience which it would be natural for me to describe by saying that I was holding a match-box in my hand and looking at it. In that case, assuming the experience to be veridical there is a familiar sense of the words "see" and "touch" in which what I am now seeing and touching is simply "this match-box." And there is also a familiar sense of the words "see" and "touch" in which what I am now seeing and touching is not the whole match-box but only a part of its surface. Now, in both these senses, if it should happen that the match-box does not exist, if I am dreaming or having an illusion, then either I am seeing something, or a part of something, other than a match-box, something that I mistake for a match-box, or, in the case of a total hallucination, I am not seeing or touching anything. But it is also possible to use the words "see" and "touch" in such a way that even if I am dreaming or having a complete hallucination, so that there is no physical object there, it can still be said that there is some object that I am seeing or touching, and further, that this object really has the characteristics that the physical object, which I mistakenly think that I am seeing or touching, in the other senses of the words "see" and "touch," appears to me to have. And what I am seeing in *this* sense may perhaps be a certain patch of colour, "standing out from a background of other colour patches and having a certain visual depth," though I am inclined on psychological grounds to doubt whether this would be an accurate description of any normal visual experience. Let us then call the whole of what everyone sees in this sense at any given moment his "visual sense-field." Then a visual sense-datum may be defined as anything that is the constituent of a visual sense-field. And, in general, a sense-datum may be defined as anything that is the constituent of a sense-field.

At this point it may be objected that I have not got away from the act-object analysis of sensation. For I have explained the use of the word "sense-datum" in terms of a special use of words like "touch" and "see" and these are transitive verbs. But the answer is that there is no need to assume that such words as "seeing" and "touching," in this usage, are names for mental acts. If the word "sensing" be used to designate the experience of which seeing, touching, and the rest, in this usage, are the various modes, then to say of something that it is sensed need be taken to imply no more than that it is sensibly present, or, in other words, that it appears: and to specify that it is seen or touched is merely to indicate what manner of appearance is in question. We might therefore say that to be seen is to appear visually, that to be touched is to appear tactually, and so on, though we should still have to distinguish different senses of "appear" as correlates of the different senses of "touch" and "see." Thus what we obtain by introducing the term "sense-datum" is a means of referring to appearances without prejudging the questions what it is, if anything, that they are appearances *of*, and what it is, if anything, that they appear *to*. And here it may be advisable to make the familiar point that the use of this term "sense-datum" is not intended to carry any factual implications about the character of these appearances. It is not designed, for example, to beg the question in favour of an atomic as opposed to a *Gestalt* theory of sensation. Thus, when philosophers like Professor Stout make it an objection to "the sense-datum theory," and so to phenomenalism, that what is sensibly "given" is something more substantial than a mere sense-datum, their argument is beside the mark. It is an empirical question whether the contents, say, of a visual field are more accurately to be described as patches of colour or coloured "objects." But even if it is decided, on empirical grounds, that what is seen is, in some sense, a coloured "object," it will still be a sense-datum, according to our usage.

Now if the word "sense-datum" is understood in this way, then if it is ever true that a physical object is being perceived, it must also be true that some sense-datum is being sensed. If, for example, it is a fact that I am seeing a match-box, in the appropriate sense of the word "see," then it *follows* that, in the appropriately different sense of the word "see," I am seeing some sense-datum. But the converse does not hold. I believe that I am now perceiving a match-box and this belief is directly based on the evidence of my senses. But from the fact that I am sensing the sense-data that I am now sensing it does not *follow* that I am perceiving a match-box. For if we disregard all the other evidence available to me, including the evidence of my memories, my having the sense-experiences that I am now having is compatible with there being no such match-box there; it is compatible with my being the victim of an illusion. Thus, when I say, truly as it happens, that I am now perceiving a match-box, part of what I am saying is that I am sensing sense-data of a certain kind; but only part. I am saying that and something more. But what more? That is our problem. And the phenomenalists' answer to it is that the more that I am saying is that further sense-data of the appropriate sort would, in the appropriate conditions, be obtainable.

If this answer is correct, then it seems to follow that the statement that I am perceiving this match-box, or whatever other physical object may be taken as an example, must be equivalent to some set of statements about sense-data. And since to say that I am perceiving a match-box entails saying that the match-box exists, the statement that this match-box exists must also, in that case, be equivalent to some set of statements about sense-data. And to say, as phenomenalists do, that physical objects are logical constructions out of sense-data is merely another way of expressing this. It does not mean that physical objects are literally composed of sense-data, or that physical objects are fictions and only sense-data real. It means simply that statements about physical objects are somehow reducible to statements about sense-data, or, as it is sometimes put, that to say anything about a physical object is to say something, though not necessarily the same thing, about sense-data. This, then, is the claim that we have to discuss.

II. The first point to be made is that if we confine ourselves to actual sense-data, this claim can evidently not be upheld. For to revert to our example, this match-box is not continuously perceived either by me or by anybody else. And yet at times when no one is perceiving it, that is, when there are no sense-data that are directly relevant to its existence, the match-box may still exist. In other words, it is not self-contradictory though it may in certain cases be false, to say both that a given physical object exists in a certain place, and throughout a certain period of time, and that during that period of time no one was sensing any such sense-data as would constitute direct evidence for the existence of the physical object in question. Consequently, if the sense-datum language is to do the work that phenomenalists require of it, it must permit us to refer to possible sense-data. And what this means is that some at least of the statements about sense-data that are supposed to yield the equivalence of statements about physical objects will have to be hypothetical. They will have to state not that any sense-data have occurred, are occurring, or will occur, but that in certain specificable conditions certain sense-data would occur. The difficulty, as we shall see, is to specify the conditions.

Now it would seem that the best way for a phenomenalist to prove his case would be to set about giving us some examples. We should expect him to take a statement like "there is a flower-pot on the window sill," and give us its equivalent in terms of sense-data. But this is something that no phenomenalist has even yet done, or even, to my knowledge, seriously tried to do. We are told that statements about physical objects must be translatable into statements about sense-data, but we do not get any translations. The most we get are more or less vague descriptions of the sort of way such translations might run. We are given recipes for making translations; but they seem to be recipes that no one can ever put into use. One reason for this, of course, is the poverty of our sensory language. The vocabulary that we have for describing colours, shapes, and the rest is not sufficient for our purpose: so that we are constantly reduced to saying things like "the sort of sense-data that you get when you look at a match-box" or "of the sort of sense-data that you get when you hear a telephone ring," where the reference to the physical object is needed to identify the sense-data in question. But I suppose that a suitable vocabulary could be invented, if some ingenious person thought that it was worth his trouble: so that if this were all that stood in the phenomenalist's way he might be entitled to hold that his programme could be carried out, "at least in principle." But there are more serious difficulties.

One that is often brought forward is that no statement about a physical object can be conclusively verified on the ground that however much favourable evidence there may be for it, it is always conceivable that further evidence will show it to have been false all along. And from this premise it is correctly deduced that no statement about a physical object can be equivalent to any finite set of statements about sense-data. For each of the statements about sense-data will be a description of a single piece of evidence in favour of the statement about the physical object; and if the evidence is to be sufficient the number of these descriptions must be infinite. I used to accept this argument but now I am inclined to reject it. The assumption is that if, for example, I am looking at my telephone and suddenly see it change into what appears to be a flower-pot, or vanish altogether, or what you will, that proves that it never was a telephone. To put the case more precisely, suppose that a series of visual and tactual sense-data were succeeded "in the same place," which here may be taken to mean "in similar spatial relations to similar sense-data," by sense-data characteristic of the appearance of a flower-pot, or that, while the surrounding conditions appear to remain unchanged, there cease to be any sense-data characteristic of the appearance of a physical object in the "place" where the sense-data characteristic of the appearance of a telephone previously were, that proves that I must have been mistaken in taking these sense-data to be the appearances of a real telephone. But does it? The only way of deciding what it proves is to consider what one would say in such a case, that is, how one would describe such a situation. What I should, in fact, say would be that my present experience was hallucinatory: that the illusion lay not in the long series of my past "perceptions" of a telephone, but in my present "perception" of a flower-pot. But suppose that I applied the usual tests for hallucinations, and that they were negative. Suppose that the object that I seemed to be perceiving felt as well as looked like a flower-pot, and that it went on looking and feeling like a flower-pot, and that when I asked other people about it they said that they perceived a flower-pot too. In that case I should probably give up the idea that I was having a hallucination, though it may be remarked that if the evidence that previously led me to believe that I was perceiving a telephone was not conclusive, then the evidence that I was not subsequently having a hallucination with regard to the flower-pot would not be conclusive either. If no evidence is conclusive all the competing hypotheses remain open. But suppose that the evidence is such that I do, in fact rule out the hypothesis that my "perception" of the flower-pot is a sustained illusion. I *might* then say that I had been deceived all the time about the telephone. I might even start to distrust my memory, and wonder whether it had not always been the case that I perceived a flower-pot, though here the testimony of others would be a check. But what I think I *should* say is: "It *was* a telephone and all of a sudden it changed into a flower-pot." I should think this odd, certainly. I should probably write to the newspapers about it. And then if the ensuing correspondence showed me that other people had had similar experiences, I should begin to feel more comfortable. "It has to be admitted," I should say, "that physical objects do sometimes undergo these abrupt changes. I wonder what the scientific explanation is."

No doubt this example sounds excessively fanciful, but not long ago I did have a fountain pen that suddenly vanished. At one moment I was looking at it, touching it, writing with it, and the next moment it had disappeared. I could not find it any more and never have found it to this day. Of course, I do not really believe that it vanished. "Pens do not just vanish," I say, in default of stronger evidence that they do. But still less do I believe that it never was a pen. I do not say: "The run of favourable evidence has come to an end as I was always warned that it might. My belief that it really was a pen that I was perceiving implied that the run of favourable evidence would continue indefinitely. Consequently my belief was false." What I say is: "There must be some explanation. Perhaps I turned my back on it for an instant, though I do not remember doing so, and somebody crept in and took it. Or, more probably, it dropped somewhere and I have not searched for it hard enough." And from this I conclude that when I said, as I often have in the past, like other philosophers, that however strongly one's sense-data may support the hypothesis that one is perceiving a physical object of a certain sort, further experience may show one to have been mistaken, I was not serious. For when a situation arose which, on the face of it, supported this view, I did not interpret it in that way at all. I did not even seriously consider the possibility that what I had for so long been taking to be a pen never really had been a pen. Neither do I think that I am peculiar in this respect. I think that the explanation that it never really was a pen is one that, in the circumstances, nobody would consider seriously.

What bearing has this upon the phenomenalist's claim? As I said before, no single sense-experience, taken by itself, ever proves that a physical object exists. From the bare fact that I am sensing *these* visual sense-data it does not follow that this is a match-box. Nevertheless the occurrence of these visual sense-data, taken in conjunction with what I remember, fully justifies the statement that this is a match-box, and would justify it, I should now maintain, even if the "match-box" were to vanish the next instant. By itself the occurrence of just these sense-data would not be sufficient, but in conjunction with previous experience it is. This previous experience may consist of previous perceptions of the physical object in question, that is, previous sensings of the appropriate sense-data, but it need not. In certain circumstances I might be fully justified in believing in the existence of a physical object that I had never before perceived: and in such cases the strength of the evidence would lie in the general character of my previous experience. For my belief that *this* is a physical object, and a physical object of a certain sort, is not based solely on the occurrence of sense-data which are manifestations of *this*: it is derived also from a more general belief that I live in a world of physical objects of which things that look like this are specimens: and this belief is supported by a mass of past experiences. So much so that if this assumption were to break down altogether, if, from this moment on, sense-data were to arrange themselves, as Price once suggested they might, in an eurhythmic rather than a thing-like order, I should not say: "I was wrong all the time: there never were any physical objects." I should say: "The world has changed: there used to be physical objects, but now there are none any more."

Does it follow then that at any rate some statements about a physical object can be translated into statements about sense-data, namely into those statements which describe the sense-data, past and present, the occurrence of which fully justifies us, on the occasions when we are so justified, in asserting that the physical object exists? Not necessarily. For in that case the truth of the statements referring to sense-data would be both a necessary and a sufficient condition of the truth of the statement about the physical object. And while I have argued that in certain cases it may be sufficient, I have not shown, nor do I think that it can be shown, that it is also necessary. No doubt the truth of some statement or other about sense-data is always a necessary condition of the truth of any statement which implies the existence of a physical object: but I do not think that it is ever possible to discover a finite set of statements about sense-data of which it can truly be said in a particular case that precisely these are necessary. In other words, though you may be able to discover sets of sufficient conditions, you cannot list them exhaustively. You cannot say, for example, exactly how much experience, nor exactly what type of experience, a child must have had in order to be fully justified, on the evidence available to him, in saying: "This is a ball." In a concrete case you can safely allow that he has sufficient evidence. But you cannot rightly say that it is necessary, because there will always be an indefinite number of other sensory experiences that would have done just as well. Thus, it makes no difference whether his general belief in the existence of physical objects is derived from the sense-data he has obtained when playing with rattles or when playing with teddy-bears: it makes no difference whether he punches the ball or strokes it, whether the angle from which he sees it makes it appear round to him or oval, whether the light is such that it seems to him to be red or orange. The sense-data that are sufficient, in conjunction with his previous experience, to establish the existence of the ball must all fall within a certain range: a sense-datum characteristic of the appearance of an alarm-clock would not fit the case: but the number of possible sense-data that fall within that range is indefinite, while the previous sensory experiences that may go to make the present evidence sufficient not only are indefinite in number, but themselves fall within a range that is extremely wide. And this is one reason why it is impossible to translate a statement about a physical object into any finite set of statements about sense-data. It is not, as has sometimes been suggested, that the physical object is eternally on probation, so that to try to establish its existence by sense-perception is like trying to fill a bottomless well. The reason is that all statements about physical objects are indefinite. The well can be filled, but there are an infinite number of ways of filling it. Consequently, the comparatively definite statements that one makes about sense-data, to the effect that such and such sense-data are being or have been obtained, or that in such and such conditions such and such sense-data would be obtained, cannot be exact translations of the indefinite statements that one makes about physical objects. And by this I mean not, of course, that a statement about a physical object is necessarily indefinite at its own level, but that it is necessarily indefinite at the level of sense-data.

III. If this be admitted, what becomes of the phenomenalist's case? What is there left for him to claim? It has been suggested that he should claim no more than that the direct evidence for the existence of a physical object is always the occurrence of some sense-datum. But if this were all there would be nothing to discuss. For, as I have already shown, the term "sense-datum" may be defined in such a way that if anyone is perceiving a physical object it *follows* that he is sensing a sense-datum: and not only that but that all that his senses reveal to him is the presence of sense-data. This does not mean that his sensory experiences must be of the sort that we are all familiar with: they might be very queer indeed: but however queer they were they would still be experiences of sense-data. Now it is not to be disputed that the direct evidence for the existence of physical objects is sensory evidence: for any evidence that was not sensory would not be called direct. And clearly if you decide to call obtaining such evidence "sensing sense-data" it will follow that you can obtain such evidence only by sensing sense-data. The only question then is whether you agree with the proposal to use the *word* "sense-datum." But surely those who have taken, or accepted, the title of phenomenalists have thought that they were doing more than extending their patronage to a word.

Yes, but what more? What is the point of introducing the sense-datum vocabulary? The idea is that it helps you to learn something about the nature of physical objects, not indeed in the way that doing science does, but that you come to understand better what is meant by propositions about physical objects, what these propositions amount to, what their "cash value" is, by restating them in terms of sense-data. That is the fact that you *can* restate them in this way, *if* you can, tells you something important about them. Furthermore, it is claimed that if you talk in terms of sense-data you are somehow getting deeper than if you are content to talk, as we all do in everyday life, in terms of physical objects. The naïve realist is not in error. Naïve realism is not a false theory of perception: it is a refusal to play this sort of game. And if a man will not play he cannot lose. But one is inclined to say that the naïve realist is missing something by refusing to play: that he is not getting to the root of the matter. And the justification for this is that there is a sense in which the sense-datum language is logically prior to the physical-object language. For it is impossible that a physical object should be perceived without its being true that some sense-datum is being sensed: but it is not impossible that any number of sense-data should be sensed without its ever being true that any physical object is perceived. For the relations between sense-data in virtue of which we are justified in claiming that we perceive physical objects are contingent: they might conceivably not have obtained.

But now it turns out that for the reasons I have given, statements about physical objects cannot be translated into statements about sense-data. Consequently, the phenomenalist is obliged to give up his original position. But he need modify it only slightly. He cannot show precisely what you are saying about sense-data when you make a given statement about a physical object, because you are not saying anything precise about sense-data. Nevertheless, he will maintain, what you are saying, though vague, still refers ultimately to sense-data and does not refer to anything other than sense-data. Consequently, he can hope to give a suitably vague translation. It should be possible to indicate at least what sort of thing we are saying about sense-data when we make a statement like "there is a match-box on the table." And if the phenomenalist can do this he may be allowed to have proved his case.

The *a priori* argument for supposing that this must be possible is that if we are not referring to sense-data, and exclusively to sense-data, when we talk about physical objects, it is difficult to see what we can be referring to. "Physical objects," is the unkind answer and, of course, it is a correct answer, correct but unhelpful. For if we use the sense-datum language—and we have not found any good reason why we should not use it; it has not been shown that it necessarily involves any assumptions that are either logically or empirically mistaken—then it looks as if we are using it as a substitute for the physical-object language. The world does not contain sense-data *and* physical objects, in the sense in which it contains chairs *and* tables, or in the sense in which it contains colours *and* sounds. One is inclined to say, therefore, that phenomenalism must be true, on the ground that the only alternative to it, once we have agreed to use the sense-datum terminology, is the iron-curtain theory of perception: that physical objects are there sure enough but we can never get at them, because all we can observe is sense-data: and surely this theory at least can be shown to be untenable.

IV. All the same, there are difficulties in the way of the phenomenalists. One, which I shall now try to meet, concerns the question of causation. Regarded by Professor Stout[2] as a fatal objection to phenomenalism, it led Professor Price to postulate, as the owners of causal properties, a set of unobservable entities to which he gives the name of "physical occupants,"[3] a piece of mythology which I understand that he has since repudiated—and it has recently been restated with force and clarity by Mr. W. F. R. Hardie.[4] The difficulty is this:

Our perceptions are fragmentary. We do not perceive all the physical objects that there are all the time: and yet we believe, and often have good reason to believe, that some of them exist when no one is perceiving them. And not only this, but we often have good reason to believe that they are causally efficacious when no one is perceiving them. An example that Price gives is that of a concealed magnet which causes the observed deflection of a compass needle. Now it may be held that what are described as causal relations between physical objects, or physical events, are analysable in terms of regularities among sense-data. But the trouble is that in a great many cases in which we postulate causal relationships, the required sensory regularities are not observed. Assuming that I perceive the deflection of Price's compass needle, then I am sensing certain visual sense-data, and the occurrence of these sense-data may, it is said, be described as an event. But the existence of the magnet throughout the relevant period of time is not an event in the same sense. For *ex hypothesi* no sense-data "belonging to" the magnet are occurring. You may analyse the statement that the magnet exists into a hypothetical statement to the effect that if certain conditions were fulfilled, sense-data characteristic of the appearance of the magnet would be obtained. But since the conditions in question are not in fact fulfilled, the statement that the magnet exists does not, when analysed in sensory terms, describe any actual event. It does not, when so analysed, say that anything exists, but only, to quote Mr. Hardie, that given certain conditions something would exist which actually does not. But this is to fall into the absurdity, as Stout calls it, of supposing that "actual occurrences depend upon mere possibilities." For surely it is self-evident that actual events have actual causes. A mere possibility cannot be a cause.

Let me try to state this objection more clearly. The argument may be set out in the following way. It makes sense to say that physical objects exist and are causally efficacious at times when no one is perceiving them. There may, therefore, be unobserved physical events and they may stand in causal relations to other unobserved events, or to observed events. Now, if the phenomenalists are right, an unobserved physical event is reducible to a set of possible sensory events. But on an "agency" view of causation this is incompatible with its being the cause, since a mere set of possibilities cannot *do* anything. And the same is true even on a "regularity" view of causation: for a possible sensory occurrence is not an event in the sense in which an actual sensory occurrence is an event, and the regularities must be assumed to hold between events of the same type. It is impossible, therefore, for the phenomenalists to explain how unobserved physical events can be causes. Consequently phenomenalism is false.

As Mr. Hardie has pointed out to me, the argument may be made independent of the empirical premise that our perceptions are fragmentary, or, in other words, that some physical events are unobserved. For whether or not a physical event is observed, the observation of it is not logically necessary to its occurrence. That is to say, the statement that it occurs does not entail the statement that it is observed to occur. Consequently, the phenomenalist's analysis of a statement which describes the occurrence of a physical event need refer only to possible sense-data, though actual sense-data may have to be brought in if the statement at the physical level itself involves a reference to a percipient. Furthermore, the causal properties of physical objects adhere to them whether they are observed or not. If, therefore, the phenomenalist is to allow that any physical events are causes he must maintain that a set of possibilities can be a cause. And this, in the eyes of those who raise this objection, is a manifest absurdity.

This argument has convinced many people, but I think that it is fallacious, and that the fallacy lies partly in a confusion over the use of the word "cause," and partly in an ambiguity in the use of the word "event." I am perfectly willing to admit that an actual event, if it has a cause at all, must have an actual cause, though even here there is a play on the word "actual," since in many cases what is called the cause will be a past event, and so, in a sense, no longer "actual." Still I will grant that, if an event has a cause, that cause must itself be an event which is "actual" in the sense that it either is actually occurring or has at some time actually occurred. But in this proposition the word "event" is being used as a term at the physical level. I do not mean by this that an event, in this sense of the word, must be physical: it may also be mental: but it is at the physical level inasmuch as it occupies a position in physical time, as opposed to sensory time, and inasmuch as it occupies a position in physical space, as opposed to sensory space, if it is spatially located at all. In this sense both the deflection of the needle, to recur to Price's example, and the state of the magnet are actual events, whether they are observed or not. The magnet actually exercises the causal properties in virtue of which the needle is deflected: that is to say, the deflection of the needle can be explained by reference to the properties of the magnet. But this is in no way incompatible with the phenomenalist's view that a proposition asserting the existence of the magnet and describing its causal properties is equivalent to a set of purely hypothetical properties about sense-data. Again, the actual event which is my observing the deflection of the compass needle also has actual causes, including certain processes in my nervous system, which are not themselves observed. Or, in other words, the truth of the proposition that I am observing a compass needle is connected by a well-established theory with the truth of certain other propositions, themselves not directly verified on this occasion, which refer among other things to processes in my nervous system. These propositions are all at the physical level. They are categorical, and, consequently, they describe actual events, in the appropriate sense of "event." But once more this is perfectly compatible with their being analysable into hypothetical propositions about sense-data. Only—and this is the important point—the sense-datum propositions, even those that are categorical, do not describe events in the same sense of the word "event." The "events" that they describe are not in physical time or in physical space. And it is only at the physical level that causal relations hold between actual events. It is indeed only at the physical level that events can properly be said to have causes at all.

This being so, the trouble arises when, instead of asking what is the cause of my observing the compass needle, which is a legitimate question, or even what is the cause of my sensing sense-data "belonging to" the compass needle, which is still a legitimate question, so long as "my sensing the sense-data" is taken as the description of a process which takes place in physical time, we ask what is the cause of the sense-data themselves. For this is a nonsensical question. It is nonsensical because the sense-data are not events in the sense in which the deflection of the needle is an event, so that the

term "cause", which is understood as a relation between events
at the physical level, does not apply to them. Unfortunately
phenomenalists, among whom I must here include myself,
have usually failed to see this and so have fallen into the trap
of meeting the question "What is the cause of these sense-
data?" with the answer "Other sense-data." And in this way
they have gratuitously laid themselves open to the sort of
objection that Stout and Hardie raise.

To make it clear that such objections are invalid, we may
restate the phenomenalist's answer as follows: There are
well-established theories, or hypotheses, which connect different propositions at the physical level. There is, for example,
a well-established theory of electro-magnetics through which
a proposition describing the deflection of a compass needle
can be connected with a proposition describing the state of
a magnet; that is the proposition referring to the needle will,
given certain conditions, be deducible from the proposition
about the magnet in conjunction with the propositions of the
theory. When this is so, then, if the hypotheses in question
are of certain specifiable types, we say that the event described
by one of these propositions is a cause of the event described
by the other. This is not by any means the only sense in
which we use the word "cause," but it is the sense that is
relevant to the present argument. Both events are actual, in
the sense that the propositions which describe them are
categorical, but these propositions, which are categorical at
the physical level, are reducible to hypothetical propositions
about sense-data. This may be expressed by saying that the
physical events in question are analysable into sets of possible
sensory occurrences; but these sensory occurrences are not
events, in the same sense of "event"; neither can they have,
or be, causes in the same sense of "cause." It is therefore misleading to say that sense-data depend upon one another: for
this suggests that they can possess causal properties in the
same way as physical objects, which is not the case. They can
however, be correlated with one another, and it is only because they can be so correlated that we have any reason to
believe in the existence of causal connections between phy-

sical events. Indeed to say that there is a causal connection between physical events is, in the last analysis, to make a very complicated statement about correlations between sense-data. The sense-data which are correlated may be actual, but they need not be. For the basis of the correlation is always a hypothetical proposition to the effect that a sense-datum of a certain sort occurs if in certain conditions a sense-datum of a certain other sort occurs, and it is not necessary for the truth of such a proposition either that the protasis or that the apodosis should be actually fulfilled. Thus a proposition of the form "if, if p then q, then, if r then s" may very well be true even though p, q, r, and s are all false. Consequently in the case of sense-data, there is no absurdity in making actual occurrences "depend upon" mere possibilities: for there is no absurdity in saying that a categorical proposition would not be true unless some hypothetical proposition were true. This hypothetical proposition states that such and such an event would occur if certain conditions were fulfilled, and there is no absurdity in holding that it may still be true even if the requisite conditions happen not to be fulfilled. But this is all that the "dependence" of actual upon possible sense-data comes to. What makes it seem an absurdity is the misleading terminology of "causes" and "events."

[In the two sections omitted here Ayer replies to some lesser objections to Phenomenalism].

VII. I suggest then that the phenomenalist's analysis of a simple proposition about a physical object, say a proposition to the effect that there exists a physical object of a certain sort in a certain place throughout a certain period of time, should take the following form. A protasis, which will itself include a number of subsidiary hypotheticals, describing such sense-experiences as would be sufficient to identify the place and time in question, or in other words, to put the physical object in its proper setting: followed by an apodosis which would describe such sense-experiences as would be sufficient to verify the presence of the physical object in question: and this apodosis will also have to contain a number of subsidiary hypotheticals to rule out the possibility of an illusion. If this were done, the truth of the whole hypothetical might, I think, pass as a sufficient condition of the truth of the proposition which it was intended to analyse. It would not, however, be a necessary condition, because of the relative indefiniteness of the proposition at the physical level. But as has already been shown, to formulate a sufficient condition in purely sensory terms is the most that the phenomenalist can reasonably hope for: and I cannot claim to have done more than give a very rough sketch of the way in which this might be achieved.

The fact is that so long as he confines himself to giving a *general* account of the way in which physical objects are "constructed" out of sense-data, or a *general* account of the way in which physical space and time are "constructed" out of sensory spaces and times, the phenomenalist does not appear to meet any insuperable obstacles. But directly he tries to reduce any particular statement about a physical object, even the simplest, to a statement, or set of statements, about sense-data, he runs into difficulties which, however he may make light of them in theory, in practice overwhelm him. The reason for this may lie only in the extreme complexity of his undertaking. But I think that there may be a more serious reason. I think that it might be argued that he was setting himself a task that could not, by its very nature, be satisfactorily fulfilled. For the language in which we refer to physical objects has its own logic. Now the sensory language to which the phenomenalist seeks to reduce the other must also have its logic, and this logic must be either the same as that of the physical language or different. If it is made the same—if, for example, the phenomenalist allows himself to speak of "sensibilia" having a continued and distinct existence in space and time—then we are inclined to say that he has not carried out his programme, because these sensibilia are only physical objects, or attenuated physical objects, in disguise. But if the logic of the sensory language is different, then we are inclined to say that the statements which are expressed in it are not perfect translations of the statements at the physical level, just because their logic is different. So what is the phenomenalist to do?

If this line of argument is correct, then the solution of the "problem of perception" may be to treat our beliefs about physical objects as constituting a theory, the function of which is to explain the course of our sensory experiences. The statements which are expressed in terms of the theory may not then be capable of being reproduced exactly as statements about sense-data; that is, it may not be possible wholly to rewrite them as statements about sense-data. Nevertheless, they will function only as means of grouping sense-data: and it will be a contingent fact that sense-data are so organized that the theory is valid. It may then be required of the philosopher to make clear in what this organization consists: that is, to show in a general way what relations must obtain between sense-data for the demands of the theory to be met. Thus, to echo Kant, he may be represented as trying to answer the question How is the physical-object language possible? And to this question the phenomenalist has, I think, the makings of a satisfactory answer.

NOTES

[1] Ayer has just been criticizing some current attempts to define sense-data.

[2] G. F. Stout, "Phenomenalism." *Proceedings of the Aristotelian Society,* 1938–9.

[3] H. H. Price, *Perception,* Chs. IX and X.

[4] W. F. R. Hardie, "The Paradox of Phenomenalism," *Proceedings of the Aristotelian Society,* 1945–6.

BIBLIOGRAPHICAL NOTES

GENERAL WORKS

Introductory and General Discussions

Perception is discussed by most introductory works on philosophy, e.g. Bertrand Russell, *Problems of Philosophy* (London, 1912) and *Outline of Philosophy* (London, 1927, published in the United States as *Philosophy*); Charles Harold Whiteley, *Introduction to Metaphysics* (London, 1955); John Hospers, *Introduction to Philosophical Analysis* (New York, 1953, London, 1956); Arthur Pap, *Elements of Analytic Philosophy* (New York, 1949). A clear and useful outline, with emphasis on the associated epistemological problems, is Alfred Jules Ayer, *The Problem of Knowledge* (London, 1956). A more detailed introductory treatment is given by Rodney Julian Hirst, *The Problems of Perception* (London, 1959), Chapters I–VI; the later and more difficult chapters of that book develop a more advanced treatment of perceptual consciousness and the scientific evidence. By the same author are the articles on Perception and allied subjects in the forthcoming *Encyclopedia of Philosophy*. Works from which selections are taken here may be used as general introductions, notably those of Ayer (Selection 9), Berkeley, Lovejoy, Montague, Moore (Selection 6), Price, and Russell (Selection 8). C. D. Broad's books mentioned below under Sense-datum Theory may also be regarded as general works at a more advanced level.

Historical Treatments

David Walter Hamlyn's *Sensation and Perception* (London and New York, 1961) is a handy survey of the main philosophical writers on perception in the past; histories of philosophy generally may also be consulted, and one which is full of useful information on recent writers is John Passmore, *A Hundred Years of Philosophy* (London, 1957). Thomas English Hill, *Contemporary Theories of Knowledge* (New York, 1961), gives a good account of the main modern positions on perception and associated questions, while detailed summaries of several books and articles are given by William Henry Werkmeister, *A History of Philosophical Ideas in America* (New York, 1949). On the psychological side

303

there are Edwin Garrigues Boring, *Sensation and Perception in the History of Experimental Psychology* (New York, 1942) and *A History of Experimental Psychology* (2nd ed., New York, 1950). All these books have bibliographies and/or references.

SCIENTIFIC AND PSYCHOLOGICAL WORKS

Human Senses and Perception by George McCreath Wyburn, Ralph William Pickford, and R. J. Hirst (Edinburgh and Toronto, 1964) attempts to present in one volume a clear outline at an introductory level of the physiology, psychology, and philosophy of perception. An interesting modern treatment of the Representative Theory by a neurologist interested in philosophy is John Raymond Smythies, *Analysis of Perception* (London, 1956). But generally works on the physics and physiology of perception are too detailed and specialized for the philosophical reader, besides being very difficult to relate to philosophical problems. Perhaps the best procedure is to read the discussions of perception in modern psychological textbooks (which usually contain some account of the scientific evidence relevant to psychology) and then follow up their bibliographical references. This method also of course deals with the important psychological questions as well. Suitable textbooks are Ernest Ropiequet Hilgard, *Introduction to Psychology* (New York, 2nd ed., 1957); David Krech and Richard Standley Crutchfield, *Elements of Psychology* (New York, 1958) or Robert Sessions Woodworth and D. G. Marquis, *Psychology* (New York, 1947, London, 1949). Another elementary psychological account is Magdalen Dorothea Vernon's, *The Psychology of Perception* (London, 1962), while a more advanced psychological source is *Readings in Perception* by David Cromwell Beardsley and M. Wertheimer (London and New York, 1958). Two significant but unconventional psychological books which raise philosophical questions of interest to the advanced student are James Jerome Gibson, *The Perception of the Visual World* (Boston, 1950) and Friedrich August von Hayek, *The Sensory Order* (Chicago, 1952, London, 1953). For a brief but stimulating philosophical treatment of psychological theories see D. W. Hamlyn, *The Psychology of Perception* (London, 1956). And for general discussions of perceptual consciousness which take into account psychological findings see: the books by R. J. Hirst and G. M. Wyburn, Pickford and Hirst mentioned above; Brand

Blanshard, *The Nature of Thought,* Vol. I (London, 1939); and Roderick Firth's article "Sense-data and the Percept Theory" in *Mind,* Vol. LVIII, No. 232, 1949, pp. 434–65, and Vol. LIX, No. 233, 1950, pp. 35–56. Also relevant are the books by Gibson, Hamlyn (1956), and Beardsley and Wertheimer already mentioned, and K. Koffka, *Principles of Gestalt Psychology* (London, 1935) (Selection 5).

THE SENSE-DATUM THEORY

Statements (*Varying Views*)

One pioneer was G. E. Moore in his *Some Main Problems of Philosophy* (Selection 6) and his more difficult *Philosophical Studies* (London, 1922). Another was Bertrand Russell in his lucid elementary *Problems of Philosophy* (London, 1912), his more significant *Mysticism and Logic* (London, 1918,—articles of 1914) and *Our Knowledge of the External World* (Selection 8), but he tended to subordinate the topic of sense-data to his special perspective theory. Clear and systematic is Henry Habberley Price, *Perception* (Selection 7), which develops a full sense-datum theory. A. J. Ayer's works already mentioned also give clear discussions. Another well-known but more difficult account is Charlie Dunbar Broad's *The Mind and Its Place in Nature* (London, 1925); earlier and fuller statements of his views, with more attention to causal problems, are in *Scientific Thought* (London, 1923) and *Perception, Physics and Reality* (Cambridge, England, 1914).

Critics

Besides G. Ryle (Selection 11 and *Dilemmas,* Cambridge, England, 1954), J. L. Austin (Selection 10), and R. J. Hirst (*The Problems of Perception*), note: Roderick M. Chisholm who has some succinct criticisms in his relatively technical *Perceiving* (Ithaca, N.Y., 1957); Harold Arthur Prichard, *Knowledge and Perception* (ed. Sir David Ross, London, 1950), who attacks Russell and the view that sensing is a form of knowing; Martin Lean, *Sense Perception and Matter* (London, 1953) who attacks Broad's version; and H. H. Price's "The Nature and Status of Sense-data in Broad's Epistemology" in *The Philosophy of C. D. Broad,* ed. Paul Arthur Schilpp (New York, 1959). On Moore, advancèd students should see Alan Richard White, *G. E. Moore* (London, 1960) and *The Philosophy of G. E. Moore*, ed. P. A. Schilpp (Evanston and Chicago, 1942), particularly the contributions by C. J. Ducasse, "Moore's Refutation of Idealism," O. K. Bouwsma, "Moore's Theory of Sense-data," and Paul Marhenke, "Moore's Analysis of Sense Perception," and Moore's replies to them.

Among many critical articles, notable are Roderick Firth, "Sense-data and the Percept Theory" (*Mind*, 1949–50 as above) attacking the sense-datum analysis of perceptual consciousness; Winston H. F. Barnes, "The Myth of Sense-data," *Proceedings of the Aristotelian Society*, Vol. XLV, 1944–5, and Anthony M. Quinton, "The Problem of Perception," *Mind*, Vol. LXIV, No. 253, 1955, pp. 28–51 (criticizing the concept of sense-data and the arguments for them); also a more advanced discussion of earlier versions in the symposia, "The Status of Sense-data" in *Proceedings of the Aristotelian Society*, Vol. XIV, 1913–14, and "The Nature of Sensible Appearances" in *Proceedings of the Aristotelian Society*, Supp. Vol. VI, 1926.

Sense-datum Language

A linguistic interpretation of sense-data is developed by George A. Paul, "Is there a Problem about Sense-data?" in *Proceedings of the Aristotelian Society*, Supp. Vol. XV, 1936, and A. J. Ayer, "The Terminology of Sense-data," *Mind*, Vol. LIV, No. 216, 1945, pp. 289–312, reprinted in his *Philosophical Essays* (London, 1954); there is useful discussion of it in the symposium "Seeming" in *Proceedings of the Aristotelian Society*, Supp. Vol. XXVI, 1952.

Sense-contents

Another significant variant is the Adverbial Analysis of sensing. The most important advocate of this approach is Curt John Ducasse, *Nature, Mind and Death* (La Salle, Illinois, 1951), largely identical with *op. cit.* in *The Philosophy of G. E. Moore*; brief statements by A. J. Ayer, *Language, Truth and Logic* (2nd ed. London, 1947), and *Philosophical Essays* (London, 1954); fuller discussion, with emphasis on the differences among the senses, by C. D. Broad in *Proceedings of the British Academy*, Vol. 28, 1942, pp. 127ff., and his *Scientific Thought* (London, 1923).

REALISM

Direct Realism

(1) New Realism. This was the name given to the first reaction against Idealism in this century. The main source is Edwin Bissell Holt and others, *The New Realism* (New York, 1912); but much was owed to William James, see the papers (dating back to 1904) collected in his *Essays in Radical Empiricism* (London and New York, 1912). For a useful collection of articles of this early period see Roderick M. Chisholm, *Realism and the Background to Phenomenology* (Glencoe, Illinois, 1960; London, 1962). Among other important and often closely reasoned articles are: Ralph Barton Perry, "The Egocentric Predicament," *Journal of Philosophy*, Vol. VII, No. 1, 1910, pp. 5–14; Bertrand Russell, "On the Nature of Truth," *Proceedings of the Aristotelian Society*, Vol. VII, 1906–07, pp. 28–49; George Edward Moore, "Refutation of Idealism" in his *Philosophical Studies* (London, 1922)—cp. Walter Terence Stace's counterattack, "The Refutation of Realism" in *Mind,* Vol. XLIII, No. 170, 1934, pp. 145–155. For a general summing up in favour of Realism see Donald Cary Williams, "The A priori Argument for Subjectivism," *The Monist,* XLIII, 1933, pp. 173–202, "The Inductive Argument for Subjectivism," *op. cit.,* XLIV, 1934, pp. 80–107, and "The Inductive Argument for Realism," *ibid.* pp. 186–209.

(2) Common-Sense Realism. Besides Austin—(Selection 10) and Ryle (Selection 11), other important sources for this are: Anthony M. Quinton, "The Problem of Perception," *Mind,* Vol. LXIV, No. 253, 1955, pp. 28–51; Gilbert Ryle's "Sensations," in H. D. Lewis (Ed.) *Contemporary British Philosophy,* Vol. III (London, 1956)—also articles by Winston H. F. Barnes and Stuart Hampshire in the same volume. In his *Dilemmas* (Cambridge, England, 1954) Ryle tries to deal also with the causal argument in a non-technical manner; David Malet Armstrong, *Perception and the Physical World* (London, 1961), defends Direct Realism but in doing so is driven towards behaviourism.

(3) Perspective Realism, and allied views such as Objective Relativism and the Theory of Appearing. Besides Selection 16 see also McGilvary's *Towards a Perspective Realism* (La Salle, Illinois, 1956). Older versions are by Samuel Alexander, "On Sensations and Images," *Proceedings of the Aristotelian Society,* Vol. X, 1909–10, pp. 1–35, and Alfred North Whitehead, *The*

308   BIBLIOGRAPHICAL NOTES

Concept of Nature (Cambridge, England, 1920); also, despite its title, George Dawes Hicks, *Critical Realism* (London, 1938) gives a Theory of Appearing. Such theories are lucidly discussed by Roderick M. Chisholm, "The Theory of Appearing" in Max Black (ed.), *Philosophical Analysis* (Ithaca, N.Y., 1950). C. D. Broad, *The Mind and its Place in Nature* (London, 1925) and H. H. Price, *Perception* (London, 1932) criticize them carefully from a sense-datum standpoint, though Price's article "Illusions" in Hywel David Lewis (ed.) *Contemporary British Philosophy,* Vol. III (London, 1956), defends a limited Perspective Realism.

Dualist Realism

(1) Representative Realism (or Causal Theory). Besides the works from which Selections 2, 14, 15 and 17 are taken see also C. D. Broad, *Perception, Physics and Reality* and *Scientific Thought,* J. R. Smythies, *Analysis of Perception,* and R. J. Hirst, *The Problems of Perception* mentioned above. Bertrand Russell's *Human Knowledge* (London, 1948) is the latest statement of his views and is in general more readable than his *Analysis of Matter* (Selection 17), which is in places very difficult. Roderick M. Chisholm, *Perceiving* (Ithaca, N.Y., 1957) gives the causal analysis of perception along with a general consideration of epistemological questions.

On primary and secondary qualities see the works by C. D. Broad, W. P. Montague, R. M. Chisholm (1957) and R. J. Hirst already mentioned. Scientific defenders of the distinction are Arthur S. Eddington, *The Nature of the Physical World* (London, 1928) and Russell Brain, *Mind, Perception and Science* (Oxford, 1951); forceful criticism of such scientific theories is given by L. Susan Stebbing, *Philosophy and the Physicists* (London, 1937), *cf.* G. Ryle, *Dilemmas.* Important articles on the distinction are James J. C. Smart, "Colours" in *Philosophy,* Vol. XXXVI, No. 137, 1961, pp. 128–42, and, for a more general treatment, William C. Kneale, "Sensation and the Physical World" in *Philosophical Quarterly,* Vol. I, No. 2, 1951, pp. 109–126.

(2) Critical Realism (see Selections 18–19). The main source is Durant Drake and others, *Essays in Critical Realism* (New York and London, 1920), which reveals the differences as well as agreements. Roy Wood Sellars' most comprehensive work is *The Philosophy of Physical Realism* (New York, 1932), and his latest word on the subject is an article "Direct, Referential Realism" in

Dialogue, Vol. 2, 1963, pp. 135–143. R. J. Hirst, *The Problems of Perception,* reaches a somewhat similar position. A primarily pragmatist view which has affinities to and criticism of Critical Realism is Clarence Irving Lewis, *Mind and the World Order* (New York, 1929).

RADICAL THEORIES

Statements

Besides the works from which Selections 20–23 are taken, note the attempts to modernize or improve on Hume, e.g. H. H. Price, *Hume's Theory of the External World* (London, 1940) and A. J. Ayer, *The Foundations of Empirical Knowledge* (London, 1940). Older theories of a Phenomenalist type, besides J. S. Mill's are: Bertrand Russell's *Our Knowledge of the External World* (London, 1914, revised 1922) and *Mysticism and Logic* (London, 1918— relevant articles date from 1914)—criticized by C. D. Broad, "Phenomenalism," *Proceedings of the Aristotelian Society,* Vol. XV, 1914–15, pp. 227–51; Karl Pearson, *The Grammar of Science* (London, 3rd ed., 1911), and Ernst Mach, *Contributions to the Analysis of Sensations* (Chicago, 1897, and London, 1900).

For statements of modern Linguistic Phenomenalism see A. J. Ayer's works from which Selections 9 and 23 are taken and his *Problem of Knowledge* (which involves some recantation); note also D. G. C. Macnabb, "Phenomenalism," *Proceedings of the Aristotelian Society,* Vol. XLI, 1940–41, pp. 67–90. Compare the sophisticated version by Clarence Irving Lewis in his *Analysis of Knowledge and Valuation* (La Salle, Illinois, 1947)—comments on the latter in Roderick M. Chisholm, "The Problem of Empiricism," *Journal of Philosophy,* Vol. XLV, No. 19, 1948, pp. 512–17, with a reply by Lewis, pp. 517–24, and Roderick Firth, "Radical Empiricism and Perceptual Relativity," *Philosophical Review,* Vol. LIX, 1950, pp. 164–83 and 319–31.

General Criticisms and Discussions

Introductory surveys are given by John Hospers, *Introduction to Philosophical Analysis* (New York, 1953, London, 1956) and C. H. Whiteley, *Introduction to Metaphysics* (London, 1955), and there is a general discussion in the symposium, "The Causal

Argument for Physical Objects," *Proceedings of the Aristotelian Society*, Supp. Vol. XIX, 1945.

More advanced and definitely critical are: R. J. Hirst, *The Problems of Perception* (London, 1959); Alfred Cyril Ewing, *Idealism, a Critical Survey* (London, 1934); D. M. Armstrong, *Perception and the Physical World* (London, 1961); James J. C. Smart, *Philosophy and Scientific Realism* (London, 1963); Richard Bevan Braithwaite, "Propositions about Material Objects," *Proceedings of the Aristotelian Society*, Vol. XXXVIII, 1937–38, pp. 269–90; Isaiah Berlin, "Empirical Propositions and Hypothetical Statements," *Mind*, Vol. LIX, No. 235, 1950, pp. 289–312; W. F. R. Hardie, "The Paradox of Phenomenalism," *Proceedings of the Aristotelian Society*, Vol. XLVI, 1945–46, pp. 127–54; Paul Marhenke, "Phenomenalism," in Max Black (ed.), *Philosophical Analysis* (Ithaca, N.Y., 1950).